FROM JACKS TO JOYSTICKS

FROM JACKS TO JOYSTICKS

An Aviation Life: Engineer to Commercial Pilot

Mick J Patrick

AIR WORLD

AIR WORLD

FROM JACKS TO JOYSTICKS
An Aviation Life: Engineer to Commercial Pilot

This edition published in 2018 by Air World Books,
an imprint of Pen & Sword Books Ltd,
47 Church Street, Barnsley, S. Yorkshire, S70 2AS

ISBN: 978-1-52671-285-1

CIP data records for this title are available from the British Library

Pen & Sword Books Limited incorporates the imprints of Atlas, Archaeology, Aviation, Discovery, Family History, Fiction, History, Maritime, Military, Military Classics, Politics, Select, Transport, True Crime, Air World, Frontline Publishing, Leo Cooper, Remember When, Seaforth Publishing, The Praetorian Press, Wharncliffe Local History, Wharncliffe Transport, Wharncliffe True Crime and White Owl.

For more information on our books, please visit
www.pen-and-sword.co.uk
email enquiries@pen-and-sword.co.uk
or write to us at the above address.

Printed and bound by TJ International
Typeset in 10.5/13.5 Palatino

Contents

Acknowledgements

Thanks are due to those good friends who have given me the guidance and encouragement to write this autobiography. Airline Captain Nigel Clark, who put me up to this a long time ago, when we talked in the cruise, while flying an air ambulance, about my experiences in aviation. Jason Pierce, who is about as close as you can get to being an aviator without actually holding a pilot licence, who reminded me that it is not just all about aircraft. Mark Hillier, an author and aviator himself, and an invaluable mentor. Paul Hamblin, who edited my manuscript and turned the work into something beyond my abilities. Also Dave Cassan, who set out the manuscript and produced the jacket art work. I have to mention the airline pilots from whom I learnt so much, while I was in the flight engineers seat. Also, I would like to thank all those people whom, in a life of aviation, gave me the chance to fulfil an interesting career of so many aspects. Lastly to my partner Leah, who put up with my absence in the study while I beavered away on the manuscript.

I gratefully acknowledge the following for permission to reproduce their images,

Veterans of the Air Despatch Association.
Aviation Photo Company.
Air Team Images.
The Ministry of Defence.
Mac Hasenbein.

Every effort has been made to establish the copyright of all material used. Errors or omissions will be addressed in any subsequent editions.

Mick J. Patrick

Dedicated to my friend David Smith,
also of the 94th Entry of RAF Apprentices, who encouraged me with
this book, but did not live to see it published.

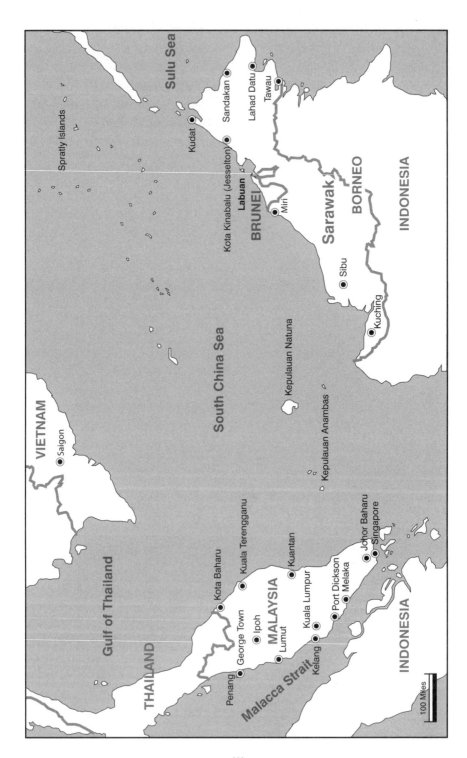

Introduction

There was no grand plan. No burning ambition to become a pilot. What actually happened was that as soon as I got comfortable in one aspect of aviation, opportunities arose to do something new so I grasped them as they came along. Educationally close to the breadline and afflicted by a kind of stammer in childhood, I could not have assumed lofty career ambitions with any degree of confidence. But as time went on, I clawed my way out of a sense of settling for what I could get, to demanding much more of myself. This story – or more correctly, journey – is one that has taken me around most of the world. It has moved me out of the hangar and into the cockpit.

I come from a family of individuals where if you want something, you are expected to get it yourself. Despite little or no advice on what to do in life, it was obvious that I needed to qualify in a good 'trade', as what was in those days called a 'profession' was not on my radar.

The RAF took me on, as it had done for both my parents before me. My Halton Apprenticeship as a Trenchard Brat began in 1960 and I struggled through to graduation in `62. The posting to RAF St. Mawgan gave me a grounding in air force life and was followed by RAF Seletar in Singapore for the Indonesian confrontation. This front line service was a life I enjoyed to the full, volunteering for anything that came along and spending quite a bit of time up in Borneo. Returning to the UK was an anti-climax and after another couple of years I left early.

Another seven years of ground engineering followed, during which I gained a civil licence working on large four engine turbo-props and jets. In 1976, after a casual and totally unplanned interview, I became a Flight Engineer (F/E) for Transmeridian Air Cargo. That career continued, working for Cyprus Airways, British Caledonian and British

Airways, for the next 21 years. I became a training engineer and examiner for three of those airlines. During this period, there were a couple of occasions when we almost came to grief and it cost me a few nights sleep. Some of my colleagues were not so lucky: we lost some in a fatal accident in Hong Kong whilst in Cyprus our aircraft crashed with the undercarriage not locked down. Happily no-one was injured on the latter occasion. Following that accident I was assigned to work with the Accident Investigator, a task complicated by an RAF aircraft crashing near our wreck a few days later.

In the early days, the aircraft I flew on did not have the level of reliability which we now take for granted. I had several engine shut-downs, fire warnings and lightning strikes. My routes took me to Africa and through the Gulf to Hong Kong. In the freighting days, if there was a load to be hauled we did it. If the aircraft went unserviceable, it was to the F/E that the company turned to and many times we found ourselves, shirts off, covered in oil and grease.

Later, when I moved on from cargo to passenger flights in more prestigious airlines there were new routes to fly and a new social life to explore. Now I had the luxury of engineering support on a defined route structure. As I grew in age, weight and confidence, my speech impediment slowly went away. With the passage of time, I was able to project myself into responsibilities and communications that I never thought possible. Sitting behind two pilots in a three man cockpit I was privileged to see some fine airmanship and occasionally some that did not belong in that category. Slowly, I came to realise that possibly there was a place for me in the front seat of a cockpit with the other guys. It did not seem so impossible and, just maybe, I could cut the mustard as well as they could. When I took my first flying lesson in Dallas, Texas, I was hooked. The obsession began.

Over a period of ten years, I gained my Commercial Pilot licences on both sides of the Atlantic. Using my F/E job, by now with British Airways, to get me to the USA, I could rent aircraft cheaply. Time at home was used to prepare for the next exam and the preparation for my next flight. I flew from Atlanta, Dallas, Houston, Los Angeles and Phoenix. Once the licences were obtained, I took other crew members out to local tourist spots like the Grand Canyon. Thanks to their contributions, I could afford to build up hours. In Texas, I did a float rating. Landing in rough water, we came close to crashing when I almost tore a float off the aircraft.

The pilots I flew with in the airline helped by coming out and operating as safety pilots for me, keeping an eye out of the window while I practised flight on instruments. I have to thank those guys for that and for their encouragement. I did my UK commercial pilot licence at the age of 48 and passed my instrument rating at 51. Back at home, over a period of time I had four shares of light aircraft, eventually buying my own aircraft, a 1946 Cessna 140. I later sold that to buy a Grumman AA5. On retirement from BA and with an incredible dose of luck, I went straight into an air ambulance job flying Beech King Air 200`s. The brat had finally got into the front of the cockpit and was quickly moved into the left seat. My learning curve was very steep and I slowly built up a comprehensive knowledge of Europe's airports. I enjoyed another seven years of varied flying, operating out of uncontrolled airports into the mighty Heathrow and other challenges. My time as an F/E had provided me with experience that other pilots did not have. It was almost as if my F/E career had been the apprenticeship for captaincy. Decision making came all the easier because at some time in the preceding 14,000 hours in the F/E seat, I had occasionally been in difficult situations and thanks to the lessons I had learned from those pilots in front of me, I could operate more wisely and safely.

Working with two medics, usually a doctor and a nurse on the crew, brought a new side to aviation and to my personal life as well. My flight calculations could be affected by how many more heavy bottles of oxygen we needed or, if the patient had to be carried with a sea level cabin pressure, how I was going to plan fuel stops to get us to our destination. Not all the patients made it home with us. The medics would do what they could, but through no fault of their own, it was sometimes not meant to be.

Through this period there was a need to perform Crew Resource Management, Aviation Security and Dangerous Goods training for the company. As I had been an instructor in the airlines, I offered and was accepted to conduct those subjects in ground training. Not content with that, the company needed an auditor, so my hand went up again. Taking a Quality Management and Auditor course, I added Flight Operations and Maintenance auditing to my CV. Unwittingly, I had now created another career move which later, provided me with work after I stopped commercial flying. As the end of my flying career hove into sight, I requalified as a simulator instructor and armed with all these strings to my bow, began business as a self-employed instructor and auditor. The simulator work introduced me to the crews of the KC10`s of the Royal Netherlands Air Force, who at the end of the contract showed us at first-hand how they refuelled their F16 fighters.

Shortly afterwards another opportunity arose to audit for a company on behalf of the International Air Transport Association. Just when I thought I had flown to most parts of the globe, this job was to take me to places that I otherwise might never have seen. The airlines we audited varied from the great and good to the small and downright dodgy.

Lack of confidence had held me back until I was in my early thirties, but emboldened by success, I went completely over the top, doing more than I ever thought likely.

It has been a hell of a ride. Sadly, beginners starting out in aviation today are encumbered by the cost of qualifications. It seems that the self-improver route is slowly being strangled out of existence yet those of that category were some of the most enthusiastic and gifted pilots with whom I ever had the pleasure of sharing the flight deck. Hopefully there will still be a route into the cockpit, whatever your starting point. Even if the objective seems too difficult, have a crack at it anyway.

Either way the journey will be life enhancing. Enjoy the ride and happy landings.

Mick J. Patrick

CHAPTER ONE

Air Force Family

The Boeing 707 rolled into a new heading and levelled off. The engines spooled up to maintain airspeed with a muted roar. There was not much turbulence but every so often the wings dipped ponderously in response to the gusts coming out of the line of thunderstorms on our starboard side. It was mid-afternoon at Houston, Texas and a long squall line of storms blocked our approach. The air was full of static and the radio frequencies were full of the sound of sizzling frying pans punctuated by a splat of lightning discharge. I heard a rise in the frying pan volume and a sudden close splat of electrical energy somewhere down the aircraft.

There was none of the usual aircrew banter on the radio with the Houston Terminal Radar Controller that is so typical of that side of the pond. Americans love to jazz up the exchanges with Air Traffic Control. But there was none of that today. The atmosphere in the cockpit was tense. We had weather radar and it was painting all the colours it could, including magenta, denoting the centre of the storm cells. There was a lot of magenta.

We were on Terminal Radar Approach Control (TRACON) steers. The US controllers are expert at guiding aircraft through bad weather but today it was never going to be a smooth ride. Despite the time of day the air was dark and malevolent.

Suddenly another sizzling reached a crescendo and we got hit just below the right side of the cockpit with what sounded like a sledge hammer hitting an empty metal dustbin. The clouds lit up briefly and temporarily blinded us from the view ahead.

Simon in the right seat never flinched. No one said anything to each other. I swore softly to myself and checked around the cockpit to make sure we had not lost any systems. The instrument panel compasses all agreed with the basic standby compass. So far so good.

It was time to make the big turn to the airport to pick up the Instrument Landing System for the landing runway. TRACON give us a new heading to fly and the 707 dipped the right wing to make the turn. We plunged into dense cloud. Rain was streaming over the windscreens. We had wipers but they are ineffective in those conditions. In any case we would have them selected on during final approach. The clouds lit up bright white and with virtually no announcement on the ether, the lightning hit us hard on the nose, exploding the fibreglass laminated nose radome and burning out the radar scanner inside. Our waveguide from the scanner to the radar screen in the cockpit dutifully transmitted a message of thousands of volts to the screen which flashed a brilliant white then went black.

We were blind, but our progress to the airport was being steered by TRACON. A further turn and another short descent on the Instrument Landing System (ILS) gave us a cloud break at about 700 feet above Houston airport. There in front of us was the rain soaked and windswept runway under a leaden sky. I turned the windscreen wipers on at the captain's request. Nearly there.

My life was not meant to turn out like that. I thought that I was going to be a farmer. However, it didn't happen so I drifted into aviation for no other reason than that my family had a lot to do with the Royal Air Force. It would be nice to say that I always had designs on being a pilot but that would not be true. If there was any common thread from engineer to commercial pilot it is simply because I took any opportunity that presented itself and one thing led to another.

The fact was that as a kid I had no idea where I was going in life. Academically I was just above the poverty line – but something told me to get a good start in life. However, I just did not have any idea what that entailed and no-one else seemed to know either. When I asked my father for guidance he just told me to do whatever I wanted and went back to the *Daily Telegraph*. My mother wasn't much help either.

Dad had joined the RAF in 1926 after the Royal Navy had ignored his application. He said it was in a fit of pique that he turned to the Air Force. His service took him to Egypt where he met and married a woman who was never referred to in my childhood. He lost her to a brain tumour, apparently. They were childless. I think that hurt so much he did not want to bring it up except to explain it to my mother when they met. I don`t blame him. Some things are best left.

Dad went on to serve in the RAF as an administrator, leaving the service in 1953 retiring in the rank of flight lieutenant. He was Mentioned in Dispatches twice during World War II. Never one to talk about it – like so many others – he would only speak about it to those who shared the experience. I can only assume he was mentioned for initiative and hard work. He was that sort of bloke. From what I can glean the first citation was for hard work in England in the first years of the war and the second was something to do with Belgium and the Battle of the Bulge where Allied intelligence failed to discover a German armoured thrust which drove the Allies back in disarray until the line held once more. We used to joke that he saved the typewriters, but apparently the withdrawal he conducted with his unit was made in good order with the German armour only just down the road. I have his citations and medals and I am rather proud of him.

Mum left school at the age of 14 and entered service. By that, I mean like *Upstairs, Downstairs*. She became a ladies companion which I suppose gave her a leg up to one above 'cook and bottle washer'.

Not much else seemed to have happened to her that I know about but she met and married a Mauritian chap and settled down to have two children with him – they would be my elder half brother and sister. Then misfortune struck her as well, as her husband died of a heart attack whilst her children were only about six or seven years old. This heart defect was passed on in the genes and both my elder brother and sister were not to live long lives either.

Mum joined the Women's Auxiliary Air Force, along with her sister, and like my father before her, found a sanctuary and a family. No plotting room for her, she did the menial stuff which runs a wartime RAF station but took to it like a duck to water. I know she spent some time on a bomber station because in a rare moment of reflection, she did say to me how hard it was when the bomber crews did not come back.

By the time my mother and father met he was a warrant officer and my mother was a flight sergeant in charge of WAAFs at RAF Northolt.

Mum related a story to me how she had gone off the station to do a stock check on stores held in a shop in the high street in Northolt. It was custom and practice to place stores in various places to offset losses if the station got attacked, which of course many were. She told us how she was walking down the street towards the shop and heard a roaring sound behind her coming up fast. There was no time to turn round as a Heinkel bomber passed over her very low right down the road and she had a clear view of the gunner in the lower turret who was shooting the place up. Apparently she threw herself on to the floor of a shop and it was all over in a flash.

On another task, she was given a briefcase full of top secret documents. A car was provided and she was driven to Bletchley Park in Milton Keynes and delivered the contents to an orderly room at the entrance, where a receipt was given in exchange for the briefcase. At the time, of course, the whole thing was shrouded in mystery but a long time after the war, when secrecy was gradually reduced, she learned that the papers had been delivered to the code breakers and analysts of the wartime intelligence centre credited with shortening the war by four years.

I came along in 1942 and of course Mum had to retire from the WAAF in which she had done so well. She would tell me in jest, years later, that I had ruined her career. At least I think she was joking. I blame my father.

As my father was by then serving at RAF Castle Donington (now known as East Midlands Airport), my birth, in November 1942, took place in a small maternity hospital nearby called Lockington Hall. This grandly titled, though rather small, manor house had been owned by the family of Lord Curzon, one time Viceroy of India and Foreign Secretary and had been offered to the nation for wartime use. In fact, the premises provided the address for a great many birth certificates long after the war ended. It is now the offices of a local company and there is a thriving website connecting all the participating 'Lockington Babes' together.

Not all the babes had such clear family connections. Many of the ladies who attended there came from the East End of London and elsewhere. Some of those families were kept apart for many years because of the turmoil of war. Sometimes the returning demobbed servicemen would come back to a larger family than they had reckoned on.

My earliest childhood recollections are of what was then called "billeting" and for us it was in the pub known as the Barge Inn on the Avon and Kennet Canal near Devizes. The Barge Inn had upstairs accommodation and my mother and I were parked there while Dad spent time at RAF Boscombe Down and then went off to France after D-Day in 1944. He was attached to Supreme Headquarters Allied

Expeditionary Air Force (SHAEF), later moving through Belgium and eventually Germany as part of the occupation forces.

I have hazy memories of farm workers in the public bar sitting on benches with twine wrapped round their trousers just below the knee. Apparently, this was to prevent rats in the farm from running up their trouser legs while they were moving hay. They would have a pint of bitter in hand and I got a sip out of each one. I know they thought it was fun and so did I but if mum caught me doing it, there was trouble. I have enjoyed a drink or two for the rest of my life.

Another vivid memory was my near demise in the waters of the canal outside, thereby closely emulating my mother's brother Len, who drowned in his childhood in just such a canal in Birmingham. There was a hand cranked footbridge across the canal a short distance away and I used to sit on the edge of it while the man operating it wound it back to connect to the other bank. When it linked to the other side it would come to an abrupt halt and lock in place. For me it was a bit too abrupt and I shot into the water from the sitting position. I remember the greenish colour of the water and hearing bubbling noises. The chap got to me just as I was going under for the third time and I shot back out of the water as he caught me by the scruff of the collar and pulled me clear. After a bit of spluttering, apparently I was OK.

People wanted to know what I had seen and felt and I told them that I had heard the fishes talking to me. At least that was how I interpreted the bubbles I was making under the water. Mother must have been beside herself - what with that and me eating the bait worms when we went fishing.

1944 saw us in a basement flat in Regent's Park next to the main railway line. It is not far from the London Zoo and the man upstairs was the head keeper for the seal house. There we lived in a "Borrowers" sort of existence looking up to the pavement outside and seeing people's feet as they walked by. We had a tin bath for bathing and an outside toilet next to the coal shed in the space between us and the pavement above known as the "area".

This was after the invasion of Europe had taken place and Mr Hitler was lobbing V2 rockets at London in the misguided hope of bringing us to our knees. On the railway line at the end of the road there was an anti-aircraft gun pulled by a train which ran up and down the line conveniently in the flight direction the rockets took.

Listening from underneath the dining table, the noise of the gun was rather exciting as it banged away at the targets.

VE Day came on 8 May 1945 and I have a picture of me, now at the age of two and a half, sitting in the back garden surrounded by Union Jack flags. So we were not to be occupied by the Nazis after all and I would not be required to be a member of the Hitler Youth.

The war had ended but mass migrations were going on in Europe and we were making a huge effort to get back on our feet. Little improved for some time and bomb sites in London remained uncleared, not rebuilt for many years. I recall housewives wearing headscarves over their curlers buying eels at a fish stall in Kentish Town. Eels would come out of the bucket writhing in the hands of the fishmonger who would cut them into short lengths for his customers. I was fascinated by this and how each short piece of eel kept twitching as he wrapped it up in newspaper.

I also used to wonder if the customers ever took the curlers out – and if so, why?

Eventually Father had arrived in Germany through the aforementioned travels as part of what was then called the British Air Forces of Occupation, British Army of the Rhine. His sector and responsibilities lay in Bückeburg, near Hannover. Now that Mother had tracked him down to an address of some permanence she pressed for the opportunity to join him and it came to pass that we joined him as a service family billeted in a substantial house with another officer's wife and children. Father had by this time been commissioned and held the rank of flight lieutenant. I assume that he had been doing fine without us and enjoyed his part in the war but now Mother had the domestic reins back in her hands, Father's life was now probably more regulated.

I had a BAFO identity card issued to me (Height 3 ft. 2 inches) in 1948 and a school report from the British School in Bückeburg read 'F', 'Good' and 'V'. Good in class, so I must have been doing OK.

There are only a few memories of that house and life in general. One concerned the owner of the house. Although having been ejected from his property, he was allowed to maintain the garden and, in particular, to grow some food in it for himself. One day, in a mood of reconciliation my mother made some toffee apples and sent me out to the man in the garden with a tray of these toffee apples to offer him and make peace. I recall quite clearly his reaction at the offer made as he shouted, "Nein!" Taking the toffee apples back indoors I informed Mother of the failure of our attempt at *detente*.

Another memory is being caught playing 'doctors and nurses' rather too enthusiastically with the little girls of the other family in the house. Things were a bit tense after that.

Life drifted peacefully along and my parents must have been glad to see each other because in 1946 my mother delivered a baby girl, presenting my father with a daughter and me with a younger sister.

By the summer of 1948 we were back in London, initially in the basement flat again in Regent's Park. Father was posted to various air force stations and we remained in the capital. I remember some appalling fog, which some Americans still seem to believe we live in, when I could not cross the road and keep both pavements in sight. In the middle you were just in limbo and had to steer the same course in order to stumble eventually upon the other side. I was issued with a National Registration Identity Card. I've no idea why, I suppose it was all part of the new post-war Britain.

Mother's determination to secure us better housing paid off and we were allocated a top floor flat in Kentish Town. It was opposite a factory building with huge windows, which gave light to the production of Lilia sanitary towels. Sitting in our flat we could watch the workers at the conveyor belts boxing up the products if we had nothing better to do.

I was enrolled at a very Victorian primary school which I found very depressing. Initially in 1950 my school reports were not too bad and my reading in class got a "Very Good" with a "Reads very well" comment. By 1952 I was only "Very Fair".

Between those two dates I had developed quite a bad stammer which held me back from achieving scholastic greatness, while socially it was a bit of a drawback. That affliction stayed with me well into my thirties and prevented me from advancing as I might have done. As for the cause of the malady, I can only conclude that I remember being chased up the stairs by a Staffordshire bull terrier. I think it was only enjoying the chase and meant me no harm, but my reaction was of outright terror. I ran to our flat door, which was closed. By this time I was hysterical and was screaming my head off for my mother to let me in. She did so and chased the animal away.

On one occasion during my rather sad time at this school we had to read out loud in class. I started well – if I could just hold my nerve for long enough I'd be able to get through it until it was someone else's turn. Unfortunately I looked up and saw the teacher looking at me and that was enough to stem the orderly flow of words. My throat locked up solid on the word 'and'. There was no credit given for the several apparently faultlessly read paragraphs that had preceded this impasse and I was now stuck fast, unable to utter another word. The method by which I was now to learn to read and remember the word "and" was for my teacher to beat me on the bare leg with a ruler.

Following that episode I played truant for two weeks and used to walk miles to watch trains shunting at Chalk Farm railway station or to wander round Hampstead Heath. All of this was a bit dodgy for a lad of 9 years old but no-one found out until at length, out of boredom, I would go home too soon and make excuses about how we had got out early. Of course when Mother checked with the school they said I had not been there for two weeks. I was rumbled and things were a bit tense again.

My newly acquired stammer caused a bit of a communication problem. Where words were difficult to eject, anything starting with an 'F' seemed to come out OK, so it was all "'effin this" and "'effin that". Is that the origins of Tourette's? I don't know, but I still seem to have a bit of it. When I refer to it as a stammer that's not really what my affliction was: the effect was like something having a strangle hold on my throat and no words could come out. What usually preceded it was the build-up of stress before some event where I was to say something in public with all the attention on me. I would therefore go to extreme lengths to avoid encounters of that kind and continued to do so for many years, even into my thirties. People seem to find a stammer joke hugely funny. I still wince and feel uncomfortable.

By this time my elder brother and sister had been returned to us from their wartime accommodation in the country out of harm's way. As we were a bit tight for accommodation and did not much cherish the view into the sanitary towel factory, my ever-resourceful mother persuaded the council to move us into another flat in Kentish Town. Eventually, she wangled us into a nice semi-detached in a newly built London County Council estate between Woking and West Byfleet in Surrey. We were in the country and things were definitely looking up.

My mother always referred to us a family of individuals. We each seemed to go through our experiences of life separately. All of us were to leave home as soon as an opportunity presented itself.

The countryside suited me fine and I became very much at ease with nature and my surroundings.

Unfortunately, my academic achievements were not up to much and I failed miserably at my 11+ exams. I was enrolled at a Secondary Modern School where I bumped along to gain a meagre 3 O Levels. Things did not get off to a good start when, climbing up a pylon with some other bad boys after school one evening, I got spotted by none other than the headmaster. Retribution came swiftly in the form of the cane applied to the rear end.

My free time was spent happily roaming the woods and commons with friends. We often used to go to Horsell Common, next to Fairoaks aerodrome where I saw Tiger Moth aircraft puttering round the circuit. Also there were several concrete anti-aircraft gun emplacements which were of interest. Wandering through the heather on the common I came across a 3 inch mortar bomb, obviously left behind from wartime training. It was very rusty and failed to go off when I threw it so was obviously a bit of a dud. I proved that by banging the nose of it against a tree and it still failed to explode. Not dismayed, we built a camp fire and cut the thing open and put the soggy black explosive on the fire. It just spluttered a bit so we lost interest and went home.

Somehow, we got our hands on some live .303 bullets. Having no weapon to put them in, I reasoned that putting one in my friend's vice in their garden shed and whacking the percussion cap with a hammer and nail should do the trick. It did actually, making a hole in the side of the shed and traversing all the gardens down the street. We thought we had better pack it in before we got caught.

As many other boys were to do for pocket money, at the age of thirteen I had paper rounds. The weekly one from Monday to Saturday brought in 7 shillings a week and the Sunday morning round earned me another 4 shillings. At the time I was getting 2/6d a week from my parents. This was swiftly withdrawn as I was now adjudged to be of independent means.

In addition to the paper rounds I took a Saturday morning job at a butcher's shop. It was part of my duties to clean out the fridge but, before that, to ride the delivery bike which had a huge wicker basket attached to the front. Being large it could carry many pounds of wrapped joints for delivery to the "posh" houses round West Byfleet. I would cycle off on my round wearing a butcher's apron round my waist. I must have looked like Granville in the TV comedy *Open All Hours*.

The weight was a bit of a problem because no matter how well I propped this monster of a vehicle up against a tree or hedge while I delivered a Sunday joint, I would come back to find the thing had fallen over with joints of meat unrolled out of the newspaper lying in the flower beds. On my paper rounds I would deliver *Farmers Weekly* into many homes, but not till I had read them first. My enthusiasm for this and for rural life sowed the seed for me to go into agriculture after leaving school. At least, that was the plan.

One of my first purchases with my new found wealth was an ex-army paratrooper's bicycle advertised in *Exchange and Mart* magazine for £3. 7s, 6d. It was a folding bike with two wing nuts holding the two halves of the frame together, simple bars for pedals and no mudguards. The idea had been to paradrop these with the paratroops and the mounted ensemble would then surprise the enemy with the speed and audacity of their cycle-borne assault. Mine had clearly never been in battle and was brand new. It did stand out against the other bikes my friends got for Christmas, though. Everyone thought it was very funny to loosen off the wing nuts when I was not looking to see if I would fall off. I saw one again recently in the Airborne Forces Museum at Pegasus Bridge in France.

A Dragon Rapide trundled up to the booth and shut down the left engine. The by-now seasoned passengers got out and rushed off to share their experience with the earthbound mortals. It was my turn now.

The assistant strapped the other passengers and me into the seats and climbed out, closing the door. The interior smelt of leather, paint and a whiff of oil. A quick thumbs up to the pilot and the left engine cranked over and burst back into life. Our pilot sat above us in the pointed cockpit up front. He was too important, or busy, to take any notice of his self-loading cargo. The Rapide started off across the grass once more, heading for the take-off point. There was no runway – it was just a field next to a fairground and this was real grass roots aviation. Lined up into wind the engines roared up to take-off power and off we went, wallowing along until the tail came up. Take-off followed shortly afterwards, not as I expected – with a rise of the nose and lots of energy – but rather with a genteel form of levitation as the aerial carriage assumed its place in flying mode. Up it went, a climbing left turn, a turn down wind, a view of the crowd, a look at the pilot who did not seem to be doing much and in no time at all we were gently descending back to the field. Landing came almost imperceptively with a gentle rumble of the wheels and the engines burbled at idle. The ride was over. Seven shillings lighter, I stepped off the aircraft. Nothing to it, what was all the fuss about?

Actually, I was only three shillings lighter because I had persuaded my father to part with the other four. That took some doing because he was a man not easily parted from his money.

The Rapide went on bashing the circuit. My pilot would never recall the short trip but I was not to forget it. Father wanted to know if I had enjoyed my first flight. Being Air Force and having flown quite a bit, he naturally wanted to know if the experience had awakened some desire in me to get my sticky flippers on an aeroplane. The answer was no, it had not, but it did leave me with a feeling of oneness with flight. Of course at that time, I was still in love with the idea of farming.

Meanwhile, it was becoming obvious that I would need some help with my stammer. It showed no tendency to go away and eventually the school and my mother led me to a speech therapist. The woman who was to rid me of my affliction reminded me subconsciously of the teacher who years before beat me with the ruler for not reading in class to her satisfaction. Naturally this did not help me relax. I was taught deep breathing exercises and told to read editorials out loud from the *Daily Telegraph*. None of this helped much so after a few weeks I stopped going. I still read the *Daily Telegraph* though.

Life eventually came to a decision point not unknown to all school leavers and I still had no clear idea how I was to earn a living. There was a part of the school programme dedicated to careers advice. I had an interview with a woman who asked what I had done so far. Paper rounds did not generate much interest but there was more when I mentioned the Saturday morning butcher's job. Did I want to be an apprentice Sainsbury's butcher? No I did not. Was I interested in Vickers Armstrong's aircraft factory at Weybridge? No, not really, it sounded like a cloth cap life running a lathe. So I said I wanted to go to farming college. After some explaining how I came to want to do that, there was some relief shown by the careers advice person who could now bring the interview to a close. It was duly noted that they would register me for the next intake and that I would be hearing from the college later. So it was settled, or so I thought.

CHAPTER TWO

Apprentice Airman

I turned over in bed and buried my face in the pillow so that my sobs would be silent and the other 15 boys in the barrack room would not hear. The Royal Air Force had accepted me.

My naive ideas about being in the RAF had not extended to how I was going to cope with the almost total lack of privacy and constantly being ordered about. In the first week my feet seemed never to touch the ground and I was so busy adjusting to everything, there was no time to reflect on what was happening to me. When the wave of self-pity broke over me, the realisation that this new life was going to stretch into infinity was just too much to handle, so I had my little cry.

Just before joining I had been to the barbers as I knew that long hair would be a bad thing. On the second day of my service I had been sent for another one. Three days later I was dispatched to the station barber once more. I felt dehumanised and utterly forlorn. I also felt intensely lonely. Surrounded by others, I had not had time to form friendships. But I was not going to quit.

Before all this happened, I waited patiently to hear from the farming college, who I was sure would not fail me. Actually they did not, but the careers advice people did. It seemed they had forgotten to forward my application – but, they said, no problem, there was another intake to the college in six months' time.

As everyone knows, six months when you are 16 years old is a lifetime away. Suddenly, I could wait no longer. I had to do something. Father, Mother and my aunt had all been in the RAF and now, so was my elder brother. It seemed natural to go the same way. So, in a fit of pique, rather like my father's failure to join the Royal Navy, I volunteered for the RAF.

My medical and selection interview were at RAF Cardington, once famous as an airship hangar. Prior to this, I had sat the RAF entrance exam and managed to scrape through.

Now I was sitting on the other side of a table being interviewed by two grey haired squadron leaders bedecked with wartime service ribbons. All interviews were painful because of my ever present stammer, which gave no sign of going away.

It was not going terribly well but when it got to what practical work I had done, my enthusiasm overcame the stammer. I went from salvaging old bikes from ditches and the Basingstoke Canal and subsequent rebuilds, to serviceable cycles from cannibalised bike parts, to when I owned a BSA scooter and had rebuilt the gearbox when a cog escaped out the side of it. That got their attention.

There was conferring. At length the gentlemen explained to me that because my Maths score was so low, they could only offer me what was then known as a Boy Entrant training scheme. I had done my homework and I knew that this was not an Apprenticeship and consequently not the best start in life.

As for what happened next, it was as if there was a voice above and behind me. This voice told the gentlemen that if I could not enter the Royal Air Force as an apprentice, then I did not want to join them at all. I was appalled by what I had blurted out but there was no undoing what I had said, so I sat uncomfortably awaiting sentence.

There was more conferring. Eventually, the gentlemen came to a decision and I was told that, in that case, I had got my wish to be an apprentice but I was to pull my socks up in Maths. I said of course I would do so and thanked them effusively. Not that it made much difference to my Maths, as it turned out.

So I was in. A few months later, on 20 January 1960 I arrived at RAF Halton, near Aylesbury, which was to be my home for the next three years. I found myself one of a big group of about 190 aircraft apprentices in the 94th entry.

We were arranged in two flights and for the first year occupied two barrack blocks in 3 Wing which held the 3 most junior entries. Later, the entries moved up to either 1 or 2 Wing on the other side of the central parade ground. They were every bit the senior entries and would let you know it.

We were accommodated in long rooms with about 15 other young lads. Each of us had an iron bed, a small and large locker and a deactivated Lee Enfield .303 drill rifle to look after.

An apprentice got paid about £6 a week, always on Thursdays. It was called the day the golden eagle shits, a reference to the eagle shoulder flash on our uniforms. The Queen`s shilling was not actually pressed into my hand; it was included in that first pay parade.

Halton was established by the founder of the Royal Air Force, Lord Trenchard, in 1922. Thereafter all Halton apprentices were known as "Trenchards Brats". The site was donated to the nation for military use by the Rothschild family. In recent years this prime piece of real estate nestling in the Chiltern Hills was to be sold off by the Ministry of Defence. That was until the lawyers found that it was still effectively owned by the Rothschild's and, if disposed of, it was to be restored to its original land condition. Removing all the buildings to return it to nature would be prohibitively expensive, so at this time, it still remains a training school for the RAF.

Our entry was one of the last big ones to enter Halton. The Cold War was in full swing and RAF stations around the world were soaking up manpower. There was a need for trained aircraft fitters everywhere. We included a few guys from the Ceylonese, Rhodesian and Venezuelan Air Forces.

The apprentices from these other Air Forces did well. They had been hand-picked and obviously were being groomed for leadership. The two Venezuelans were both called Paz. For ease of recognition they were known as Big Paz and Little Paz.

Each weekend they had permission for a 36 hour pass and could, apparently, go to their Embassy in London and draw the extra money bestowed upon them by their country for certain expenses. Rumour had it that they set themselves up in splendour every weekend and had no shortage of female company.

To win an apprenticeship you had to sign up for 12 years which would begin at the age of 18. Lads could join from the age of 15 ½ to 17. I had just turned 17 but some were not yet 16 years of age. If you did not back out immediately, you were locked in until the age of 30. On reflection, I always feel that was pretty unfair but at the time one did not know any different. We had the first 3 weeks to change our mind and could go back home with no penalty. One lad in my room did just that and took the option to go home. I have always admired him for that decision. As far as I knew he was the only one out of the whole entry to do so.

14

I soldiered on. From basic training in overalls, we moved on to our uniforms which were a rough serge tunic for everyday wear and a fine looking dress uniform for parades and going out. The shirts we were issued with were the detached collar variety, where the collar was held onto the shirt at the front and back with collar studs. These infernal things left a round red mark on your neck. The only benefit was that you could change the collar daily but make the shirt last as long as possible.

Our Drill Instructors were keen to see that we did not have to walk anywhere. Rather, they formed us up in threes and marched us to save us from the tedium of wandering around unaided.

For the first year we were only allowed out of camp in our 'Best Blue' and in the last two years only in a suit or blazer and flannels of regulation style. Drainpipe trousers and 'winkle picker' shoes were not allowed. Some enterprising apprentices had bags of forbidden clothing stashed away in the woods and motor bikes hidden away in local garages. I was not that bold and kept to the rules.

Mess food was pretty boring but we were hungry and growing. Old stock of dehydrated egg and potato was used up on us. Each mealtime some poor duty officer had the task of doing the mess rounds and observing all was well. One day a rather foolish one asked our table if the food was OK. At that moment I had just separated three or four cooked slugs from my cabbage onto to the edge of the plate. Feeling a bit stroppy, I said that no, it was not all right, because I had found some slugs in my cabbage. The duty officer looked a bit bewildered, then recovered himself and told me to go and get some more. He then beat a hasty retreat.

I recall being put on a charge only once and that was for not getting a haircut.

Our sergeant saw that I had disobeyed the order and the punishment from the flight commander was 14 days "jankers". This entailed being on a parade at the guardroom before marching to work, repeated after lunch and after evening meal and then involving polishing the floor in the offices for two hours every night. Each parade was in a different kit to the next duty so there was a lot of tearing about and changing into another uniform. I barely had time to eat but I did sleep well.

We were entitled to one 36 hour pass each month. I found that I could hitch hike in uniform quite successfully back to Surrey to go home and could time it pretty well to the nearest half hour of travelling. The public was very good in those days to servicemen and wearing uniform in public was quite normal.

The school and workshops at Halton were at the bottom of the hill across the Wendover–Tring road which bisected the camp. Our routine day was to march behind the Wing Pipe Band to the schools and back up for lunch, then back down again for the afternoon sessions. This was repeated every day except the afternoon of sports day. Then on Saturday morning there was a big parade and every fourth Sunday a church parade. All this took a lot of marching about to the tunes of the pipes and drums. In the first year, the pipe band was pretty dreadful and we would guffaw when some piper hit a bad note or failed to start or stop his serpent at the appropriate moment. By the second and third years the bands were very good and a pleasure to listen to. I have not met one ex-apprentice who does not love the sound of pipe bands. Even now I listen intently to the tunes we all knew so well and if it is played any differently I can immediately notice that the arrangement has been altered. I suppose we marched to the pipes and drums about 50 times a week.

Sports took up quite a lot of time; for some reason or other we had to be as fit as racing snakes. On reflection, I think some of that could have been cut out and the apprenticeship shortened – indeed, it was to be cut down to two years later on.

I got into cross country running and was fairly good but that was probably because most of my entry did not care to run unless it was downhill – when running against other teams, I found they were mostly better than me. When I was later diagnosed with asthma I reflected on my lack of success in competition and I now assume that the asthma was in its infancy in me back then. Fortunately it did not emerge in later examinations to pass aircrew medicals.

Most of us liked drill and so did I. The oneness and crispness of synchronised movement was very satisfying. In my flight, we offered to form a public drill squad and give up our days off to perform. The powers that be refused. Probably a wise decision: it would be hard to get us testosterone laden lads all back to camp after a taste of freedom and the sight of girls. Rather like herding cats, I suppose.

The workshops part was better than theory in school. We messed about with old grounded Hunters and Piston Provost Aircraft and did stuff like mending bullet holes in fuel tanks, metal structures and canopies. We learned the black arts of tinsmithing, coppersmithing and welding which were never going to be put to anything useful later on. If the training programme was interrupted, they would put us in the schools cinema hall as a backup and play us the old black and white, grainy instructional film of *Theory of Flight*. I lost count of the number of times we had to sit through it. In the end, Bernoulli and Newton would fight it out while we left them to it and put our heads on our haversacks and snoozed.

On one occasion towards the end of the three years we went to the airfield, which had some old aircraft, to do engine runs and the like so that we could get some hands-on experience. There was a Javelin fighter to do runs with, but first it had to be pushed out of the hangar and positioned for ground running. As the concrete parking area was sloping down to the grass edge we soon found to our delight that it was rolling backwards at quite a pace. The instructor panicked and shouted: "Brakes on!" to the chap in the cockpit and the thing reared up on its tail and smashed the exhaust pipes on the concrete. There was lots of sniggering going on which did not go down at all well.

Each entry would also go on a summer camp when we did three days of slogging round Dartmoor. In preparation for this we would have route marches around the Chiltern Hills behind Halton wearing overalls, our clothing for the march across Dartmoor itself.

Eventually, suitably toughened up and blisters healed, we were transported overnight in old railway carriages drawn by a steam train. We seemed to spend a lot of time in sidings waiting for other higher priority rail traffic to precede us. The carriages smelt of soot and the heating hissed and clanked. The following morning we arrived at our destination and were transported bleary-eyed to our tented camp at RAF Collaton Cross, a decommissioned barrage balloon centre between Yealmpton and Newton Ferrers in Devon, which was handy for Dartmoor.

From our tented home we were taken by three ton trucks to our starting point in Dartmoor and divided into small teams, navigating ourselves across country to each designated campsite for the night. Here we were given hot food, shown holes in the ground and told to make ourselves comfortable. This would be nothing to Army guys but we were only Royal Air Force so it was a bit of a surprise. Anyway, we made the best of it.

Exercise over, after a rest and clean-up at Tent City we were given a night out in Newton Ferrers. The transport on this occasion was an old double decker bus which made it down to the village but ground to a halt trying to get back up the hill to the camp.

It was a comical sight to see this ancient bus belching black smoke being pushed back up the hill by dozens of half-cut lads. In those days a few pints of bitter would have us fairly inebriated, since we did not get a lot of freedom or money to get much practice in. Fortunately, a pint of beer was only 1 shilling and 6 pence, as I recall.

As ever, my learning skills were only just adequate. We progressed on through the three years and I was lucky to graduate without a recourse to a lower entry or in passing out with a lower rank. The smart ones amongst us got accelerated promotion to corporal, while the few at the bottom passed out as senior aircraftsmen. The cream of an entry would go on to officer training at Cranwell. I managed to leave with the normal rank of junior technician, which was similar to a lance corporal but with the single stripe worn inverted.

Our Graduation Parade in December 1962 was an experience of intense pride, as any ex-apprentice would admit. Not only had we got through it but we were now men, rather than the boys who had arrived in 1960. The pipes and drums played magnificently and our own entry apprentice NCOs commanded the parade. Bayonets were fixed on our .303s and the entry looked immaculate. We had learned to loosen the magazine on the rifles so that when we came to present arms, our slap on the rifles during the "present" movement would give a resounding metallic crash which echoed round the parade ground as 186 magazines slammed home in unison. My parents attended the parade and afterwards I sought them out. Mother said that she could not tell me from the other lads and I replied that was the idea. Father said little but he did seem to be quite moved by it all.

I cannot in all honesty say that I enjoyed every minute of Halton, finding the lack of privacy difficult to cope with. Others did enjoy it more than me as I have discovered when meeting people at our reunions. In later life, I only saw a handful of people from my entry in the air force or Civvy Street, which seems odd. Later on I found that not everyone had stayed in aviation, in fact more had left than seen it through as a career. However, without Halton I would not have had the success in the aviation business which I later enjoyed and I remain convinced that having Halton on my CV guaranteed many jobs I later held.

Recently I gave a talk about this book to a group of ex brats at Tangmere Aircraft Museum. At the end of my ramblings I asked them if they had enjoyed Halton. The average response was – yes, some of it. That seems about right.

CHAPTER THREE

Cornish Air Force

The Avro Shackleton MK2 droned across Spain at 10,000 feet on course for Gibraltar. I had been assigned a detachment with two Shackleton maritime patrol aircraft of No. 42 Squadron. Four Rolls Royce Griffon engines boomed along through clear skies and many thousands of loose rivets rattled along with them in close formation. Lying in the tail cone watching Spanish villages passing below through the perspex observer's position, I amused myself looking for bullrings. Many hours later, the wheels squealed onto the runway at RAF North Front. This was the life. Man's service at last.

On leaving Halton I had applied for, and was fortunate to get, a posting to RAF St. Mawgan in Cornwall. Newquay was the nearest town and the runway ended at the cliffs of Watergate Bay. My family had holidayed in South Devon many times, staying in the beautiful little port of Salcombe. My choice of posting was to bring me back again to the area I had missed so much.

My job took me not to front line squadron work, but to the station's Major Servicing Flight, which served all three squadrons of Shackleton aircraft based at Mawgan.

The aircraft were too big to fit into the hangars so a method had been devised to manoeuvre them in sideways. This meant towing the aircraft so that the main gears rose onto big trolleys with wheels. Following that, the next job on the MK.3 "Shacks" was to disconnect the nose gear torque links and using two sheets of aluminium placed on the ground one on top of the other, rotate the nose wheels through 90 degrees and steer the whole thing sideways into the hangar. On the MK.2 with the tail wheel it was easier – we just turned the wheel round with a tow bar.

Despite having completed an apprenticeship I was dismayed to find that I was given jobs like cleaning out drip trays, lubricating control runs and replacing loose rivets. The detachment to Gibraltar was a blessing because being in the hangar Monday to Friday was getting tedious. At least the accommodation at St. Mawgan had improved, the rooms housed only four men and the blocks were more modern. Years afterwards when I was flying an air ambulance with an ex-navy guy, he was astounded to hear that RAF men did not have a room each.

I found that evenings and weekends in camp were pretty boring so I took a job in a bakery in Newquay which filled up all my spare time – finishing work by 1700 hours in the hangar, a quick bite to eat in the mess on the way back to my barrack block to change and I was often down town by 1800 hours. My job was then to help with the baking often till 2300 hours and at the weekends I got the job of driving round the pubs and beach cafes delivering the bread rolls and Cornish pasties I had helped to make. The delivery van was the Bedford Dormobile, the one with the sliding doors. I have to say that I was a bit reckless with it, frightening a lot of holiday makers in the process, but happily returning it to the bakery with little more than a few light scratches.

At that time I had bought a 1948 soft top Hillman Minx with my hard earned cash. It was a super little car. Unfortunately, coming back from a beach party one night slightly the worse for wear, I misjudged the width of a stone bridge and wiped both nearside wings off it. Later when that was patched up, the engine threw a connecting rod bearing and it was never the same again. As it was beyond my ability to afford the parts it passed to another guy when I left St. Mawgan.

A detachment to Gibraltar was interesting. The resident Shackleton squadron had been stood down for two weeks leave and we replaced them with our two MK.2 aircraft from 42 Squadron, which also served as a navigation exercise for the crews as we positioned out and back from the UK. North Front's runway is bisected by a road from the Spanish border and is closed by order of the control tower when aircraft are landing and taking off.

Years later flying in from the UK for a patient in my air ambulance, I landed and then turned back to taxi to the apron when a Spanish contractor's lorry shot across in front of me on the supposedly closed road. By the time I had dealt with the refuelling and gone up to the tower to pay the landing fee, the driver was on the mat in front of the tower chief who was giving him some grief. The driver spoke hardly any English and it turned out there was a misunderstanding about how he should cross after our aircraft had landed. Clearly he thought as soon as I had passed he was clear to go, not anticipating that I would backtrack in the other direction. I asked what they would do now, suggesting that a bit of re-education would help but they were having none of it. His pass was revoked and he was out of a job. I felt sorry for him. There was no danger to anyone on that occasion.

Back to our detachment. Soon after our arrival the Spanish Air Force lost a Douglas DC 3 out over the Mediterranean and despite political differences we patrolled the area for the next two days searching for the missing aircraft. All that was seen was an oil stain on the sea but that could have been caused by any ship pumping out its tanks. On the first search day, one of the aircraft came back with the tail cone observer's Perspex windows completely shattered. What had happened was that while an observer was lying where I had lain myself, counting bullrings on the way down, one of the camera doors on the underside of the tail just forward of the Perspex tail cone had broken a hinge and the door arced round in the slipstream smashing into the Perspex in front of the guy's face. Fortunately, he was unhurt and was lucky to get away with it. We had no spares for the Perspex so I cut a cone shaped piece of aluminium sheet and roughly screwed and riveted it into place to cover the hole. Not a repair I was terribly proud of but needs must and it stayed on till we got back.

Social life in Gibraltar was lively, there were lots of servicemen from the navy and army out on the town and Main Street was a bit rough. A trip up the Rock was fitted in but a crossing to La Linea in Spain was off limits.

Back at St. Mawgan, life went on in a most pleasant fashion, maintaining the Shacks by day and doing a bit of bar or bakery work in my spare time. For a week or so I was sent to lend a hand to finish a major check on an Avro Anson. Both the engines were removed so the firewalls of each wing were open to view. I noticed that the cables to the engine controls were rigged differently on each firewall, which was a mistake. I reported this to the sergeant in charge of the overhaul, who in turn reported it to the officer in charge and took all the credit for the observation. Creep.

After about another year there, in the autumn of 1964, I felt that I should apply for an overseas posting before somewhere dreadful like Aden or Gan was thrust upon me.

I had always had a hankering for the Far East. In my mid-teens I had really got into Chinese and Japanese culture and even decorated my bedroom at home in Chinese wallpaper and paper lanterns. Unusually for a teenager I also used to go up to London and eat in a Chinese restaurant in the Strand.

Clearly I was becoming something of an odd-ball. My elder brother had been at RAF Kai Tak in Hong Kong and it sounded good. However, Singapore sounded better and there was a bit of a war going on nearby in a place called Borneo which seemed better still.

So, I applied for Singapore and got it. The only drawback was that I was destined to go to a Westland Whirlwind helicopter squadron so before the posting I was directed to the 22 Squadron detachment at St. Mawgan to learn how the aircraft worked. I have to say that I did not learn much and my plum choice of posting was going to be marred by working on helicopters, which would not exactly help me see the world. Later, I got round that problem, but at the time I assumed I was stuck with it.

CHAPTER FOUR

Far East Confrontation

The British Eagle Bristol Britannia bored along in and out of the weather doing its best to be a whispering giant. We had already made a landing for fuel and change of crew at Akrotiri in Cyprus. By this time the self-loading cargo from UK was getting a bit tired and smelly. There were to be a couple of further stops over a period of 24 hours before at last we arrived at Paya Lebar airport in Singapore. The hostesses smiled sweetly as we deplaned. They were on a trip of a lifetime and you could see that they were going to have a good night stop. As I emerged from the still cool aeroplane the heat and humidity of Singapore struck me in the face. Straightaway I began to sweat. This was going to be normal for the next two and a half years.

The complement of passengers was processed and detailed off to waiting transports. This was a trooping flight and we were from all branches of the services. Some would be going up country to Borneo while others, like myself, were destined for the Navy, Army or Air Force units in Singapore. As for me, I had arrived to join the Far East Air Force and in Singapore we had bases at Changi for transports, Tengah for fighters and Seletar for a couple more tactical transport squadrons, as well as a Maintenance Unit and of course the helicopters I was sent out to service.

New arrivals were called 'Moonies' because we were not tanned. Also, our new khaki drill shorts and shirts set us apart from the rest. It was a status to get rid of as soon as possible.

Arriving at Seletar I passed through the guardroom and was directed to the station manning office for assignment. I had posting papers

23

indicating where I was supposed to be employed but did not proffer them. The sergeant in charge of the office did not ask to see them either. Instead he looked at the chinagraph board on the wall which represented his boring little world and asked me where I wanted to go. My chance had come to avoid the helicopters and I was not going to look a gift horse in the mouth. His laissez-fair attitude changed my life. After a bit of discussion about which Squadron had what and where vacancies lay, I plumped for 209 Squadron, which was operating Scottish Aviation Single and Twin Pioneer aircraft on the West Camp side of Seletar. Things looked promising – but that was before I had managed to find a billet.

My first task was to find a bed. There were two barrack blocks in the operational side of the camp, built on the usual three floors and central ablution area. These blocks were constructed with a wide shaded veranda all round and the rooms normally held five men each. This was the normal complement for accommodation, but the campaign against the Indonesians in Borneo was in full swing and there was serious overcrowding.

After tramping through the air force block and finding all the beds taken, I was obliged to turn to the other block which was inhabited by the RAF Airfield Construction Squadron and the Army Royal Corps of Transport, who were involved with the supply dropping missions. Things were even worse here. The iron beds were stacked up on each other as two-tier bunks which created twice the occupancy. However, there was no choice and having found a spare bunk I moved my kit in. It was mid-afternoon and I was bushed. Presently, a lot of very muscular, suntanned and heavily tattooed blokes came striding in. They were not best pleased to see a Moonie moving in with them and I was invited to get lost. This was going to take some diplomacy.

Eventually, these pretty formidable airfield construction blokes warmed to my situation after I had explained to them that the air force block was full and I had no-where else to go. When I told them where I was going to be working they thought I was OK; after all, I actually worked on aircraft. Their forte was clearing jungle strips to make landing grounds and drop zones for the guys up country. They had been all over the place clearing jungle for the bases on the Indonesian border and up country in Malaya.

I shared their accommodation with them for some months before space became available for me to move into my own squadron rooms. In that time we became good drinking buddies and I enjoyed their protection. Actually, it was very much like that, because if any trouble came up while we were out for a few beers – and it often did – they took care of me and I never felt at risk.

Soon after that, the Construction Squadron was remustered into the Royal Engineers and they were withdrawn to the UK, having done sterling service in the campaign known as the Borneo Confrontation.

Mosquitos were not really a problem at Seletar because the monsoon ditches were sprayed regularly with pesticide by local labourers. They carried a brass backpack with a pump handle and walked about spraying by hand. Nowadays, we would not allow that to happen because of the toxicity of the chemical spray. In the barrack blocks little lizards, geckos, ran across the ceilings hoping for an insect to eat. They were only ever a problem when they insisted on mating upside down and fell off on top of us in the night. One chap caught a praying mantis and put a makeshift collar round its neck with a length of cotton and tied it to his bedhead. There it took any mosquitos that dared to cruise by its master's head.

We refuelled with lots of Tiger beer after work. The NAAFI was opposite the army block and the clientele were a mixed bunch of RAF and various units of the army.

Army blokes were always more tanked up and volatile than we were so there was not a great deal of mixing. One night we sat around on the balcony in our insect-infested wicker chairs and we were joined by a bloke from the army block who was pissed as a fart. So pissed in fact, he did not know who he had sat down with and contributed to the evening by mumbling swear words to himself. Eventually he staggered off to his block and we thought no more about him. About half an hour later the station ambulance roared up to the block he had just gone into followed closely by a Land Rover with RAF police and the orderly officer. The story that unfolded was that our unwanted drinking companion had got involved in a row with a roommate and the other guy knifed him, apparently causing the chap to die of blood loss and shock.

In researching possible illustrations for this book, I got in touch with an ex-serviceman from the Air Despatch Association who, it transpired, had been the custody sergeant at the court martial for the accused. He told me that the soldier had been quite a steady chap but the aggravation from the drunk had pushed him over the edge. Found guilty of murder, he was awarded a stiff sentence and was in a state of shock and disbelief that the charge had not been reduced to manslaughter. Subsequently, the sentence was reduced and the last thing the custody sergeant had heard, the chap had emigrated to Australia to begin a new life. I hope he has done well.

I settled into daily life in 209 Squadron, maintaining the Single and Twin Pins, as they were known. Both aircraft were powered by the Alvis Leonides radial engine and were capable of very short field operations ideal for the theatre we were operating in.

At Seletar, on a day with reasonable breeze down the runway, Single Pin pilots would show off the slow stalling speed by approaching the midpoint of the runway opposite the tower, deploying the flaps and slats, allowing the aircraft to drift backwards with the headwind to the start of the runway and then executing a short landing.

The main daily task was the dawn beach patrol up the coastline of Malaya to spot for signs in the shoreline of night boat landings by Indonesian insurgents. Several times I had the job of removing telephone cable from the wing struts and the propeller hub.

We had a Single Pin on a semi-permanent detachment to Vientiane in Laos. It performed duties for the British Embassy there but was obviously involved in other things that sounded interesting. The Vientiane detachment had an engine fitter with it and being an airframe tradesman I thought it would be a great opportunity if I could wangle myself a place onto the detachment with him. Unfortunately, the aircraft had been very reliable and the only issues that came up were dealt with by the chap already there, so my offer was refused.

The flight of Hawker Hunter ground attack aircraft ran in from the sea and attacked the hill top in Johor Bahru with rockets. Overnight a small force of Indonesians had come ashore and taken a commanding position on the hill. Now they were being hammered by the Hunters. At the base of the hill the jungle paths were occupied by men of the Malay Regiment and the Gurkhas. The Indonesians really did not have a chance.

Word had got out that a strike was in progress and a few of us climbed up the side of the hangar making use of the service ladders on the outside of the building. From the rooftop we were able to see the action on the other side of the Johor Straits. I could just discern explosions on the hilltop. The rumour was that the enemy had been inserted to hold the area before a much larger Indonesian force landed. This was the only landing in that location and the party had been sacrificed just to be a thorn in our side.

There were other landings on the west coast of Malaya with groups of Indonesians arriving in boats from Sumatra. Our Pioneer aircraft would do an early morning patrol up the beaches to spot signs of landings. They were never a real threat to us and usually got mopped up quite quickly. Apparently, they thought the locals would rise up against us and they could therefore lead a rebellion.

One day I spotted a notice in the crew room for volunteers to form a train guard to the Royal Australian Air Force base at Butterworth on the west coast of Malaya. It entailed travelling in the last van of a goods train, to guard the next three wagons containing bombs and rockets being delivered from the Singapore marshalling yards through Kuala Lumpur and Ipoh, then to hand the responsibility over to the Australians. Of course, I put my name in straightaway.

A few days later two reluctant senior aircraftmen and myself were issued with a .303 rifle and five rounds each and then transported to the marshalling yards. In addition to the rifles we had packed meals for the next 36 hours. No radio or other means of communication was given to us and no instructions on how, or even if, we were to use force to protect the consignment.

Eventually the train clanked out of Singapore and we made our very slow progress up Malaya interspersed with more shunting to and fro in the marshalling yards at Kuala Lumpur and Ipoh. The journey was totally uneventful and we travelled in the last car which had hard wooden seats and a sort of cow-catcher veranda on the back that would have looked right for some American President touring the United States in the nineteenth century.

Going through very hilly jungle the train would chuff its way up the hill and when enough wagons had been dragged over the summit, it would accelerate under the now positive mass and run down the hill at something approaching a respectable speed. I found it good fun to walk along the track by the end of the train going uphill, then jump back on as it picked up speed again. It was just as well that I never missed the steps back on as I would have had some explaining to do. The two 'erks' with me barely looked out of the window as we plodded north through the Malayan countryside. They either slept or read books. I can never understand that about people. Life is not a dress rehearsal.

At last we got to Butterworth and I handed the responsibility for the ordnance to the Aussies who took us to their transit block to await transport back to Singapore.

As it turned out that we had a clear day off, we went over to Penang, the island off Butterworth, for a bit of tourism and a few beers. The next day we reported to the air movements section and were assigned a flight back. Our transport this time turned out to be a Royal Air Force Handley Page Hastings to Changi. It was the biggest tail wheel aircraft I had ever seen having four Bristol Hercules engines and standing at a high nose angle which seemed to make it tower over everything else. Being mounted on single main wheels, the aircraft was fitted with pneumatic brakes and the whole machine taxied around using bursts of engine power to turn while the brakes made it sound like a lorry, hissing and groaning. This was a character aircraft. It also had a leaking fuel tank which one could smell strongly in the fuselage. We were forbidden to smoke.

At Seletar we had some young Royal Malay Air Force aircraft fitters. Two were Chinese and one was Malay. The Malay chap was called Daz and he was able and useful. So too was the Chinese called Boo, but not so the other, called Lee. The latter did not really have his heart and soul in this business and would often be absent without leave. Rumour had it that he was off chasing the dragon and playing Mahjong downtown. Oddly, he never seemed to get punished for this wayward behaviour.

One day we had a Twin Pin on the line which needed an engine run. An engine fitter went out to do it and without any notice he was joined by a new squadron navigator who wanted to see how the start-up was done. The right engine started with the customary belch of smoke. Hearing the engine cough into life, I looked up from what I was doing to see Daz throw himself and the fire extinguisher he had with him back out of the way as the aircraft was now taxying forward at a steady pace.

At the edge of the Pierced Steel Planking on which we used to park aircraft was a concrete taxiway. On the other side of this taxiway was a deep monsoon ditch next to the hangar. As luck would have it, the left wheel contacted the concrete taxiway first and it swung the whole aircraft through 90 degrees and it set off down the taxiway in a dead straight line. After the aircraft had gone about 80 yards it came to a stop. The engine was shut down and the two guys walked back. It transpired that there were no chocks in place and the park brake was not set. Both people in the cockpit thought the other had control and had decided to move it somewhere else. How close can you get to an accident? That monsoon ditch was just waiting for them.

Shortly before I got to Singapore, in the summer of 1964, there had been race riots between the Chinese and Malays. Families living off base had been pulled into the camps. One result of the riots was that Singapore was forced to be independent from the newly forming State of Malaysia.

The Twin Pins had a "Voice" role where two very heavy speakers were fitted underneath the sponsons. In the cabin, a position was set up so that a speaker could address the rioters and tell them to pack it up. I don`t know if it had any effect on the rioters but at Christmas we sent the "Voice" aircraft up and it played Christmas carols all over the station and off-camp in Serangoon Gardens where many of the married personnel lived with their families.

Seletar had a station duty guard manned by just about anyone who could be mustered. Station guard was only about a dozen men, each armed with a .303 with five rounds and commanded by a sergeant. The purpose of the guard was to be available in any emergency and sleep overnight in the guardroom until the station came to full strength in the morning.

I only got lumbered for this once because, luckily, I was away a lot later, involved in detachments.

There was a bit of tension around with the locals, or maybe some intelligence on possible Indonesian attacks again. Whatever the reason, the outcome was that we were loaded into a three tonner and dropped off one by one at a watch tower at the perimeter fence. Each tower had a ladder to climb up and a fixed searchlight shining on the fence, the other side of which was overgrown. There was no telephone and we had no radios. The instructions were simply that if we saw anyone trying to get over the fence we were to fire a shot and the rest of the guard would come out from the guardroom. What or whom we were to fire a shot at was not clear. Quite how the blokes sitting in the guardroom would hear us two miles away was not clear either. Talk about Fred Karno`s Army.

I did my stint in the tower listening to strange jungle noises on the other side of the fence and peering into the darkness where the fixed light did not illuminate. Eventually the three-tonner came grinding back up the road and I was relieved.

I had the impression that if I had shot someone my boots would not have touched the ground and I`d be back in UK in no time. That didn't suit me at all. I liked Singapore.

Later on, the rumour mill delivered the tale of another duty guard sergeant who had put the guard out to sentry positions and then gone back to the guardroom to put one of his five rounds through the top of his head. Apparently, he had been compromised by his wife while attending to the needs of their Chinese housekeeper. Bit drastic.

Rumour had it that the powers that be reacted to this tragedy by issuing subsequent station guards with the .303s, but no ammunition.

Sometime later I was detailed for another station defence duty. This time I was shown how to cock and fire a 20mm Oerlikon anti-aircraft cannon. However, I was not given any firing practice and not advised how to use the range sight rings. Apparently previous live firing trials had been delivered across the Straits into Johor Bahru and it had annoyed the natives, so live practice was forbidden. I guess the shells had to come down somewhere.

The morning came for my turn at the dawn stand-to on the guns, so two erks and myself piled into a three tonner in darkness and were driven to the mangrove swamps on the north-east tip of the station. Our gun was mounted on a base and ringed by sand bags. There we were met by a sergeant who made sure we cocked the gun, which entailed levering the thing sharply down on its pivot to pre-tension the barrel spring and for the second man to fit the big round magazine canister ready to let fly at the enemy.

At this point, who or what would be the enemy was unclear but I surmised that we would be defending ourselves against a dawn air attack. The third man was to man the field telephone in a tent thoughtfully provided next to the gun. If it rang he was to pick it up and receive our orders.

Having discharged his duty the mystery sergeant, who may have been RAF Regiment, disappeared in the three-tonner and left us to it. As I outranked the other two and fancied a bit of the action, I strapped myself into the gun and we waited. And waited and waited. The mossies' bit hard at us as the sun came up and we watched it rising in case anything hostile came out of it. I studied the sight range rings trying to estimate how far to lead the gun on a moving target to achieve a hit. I fancy that I could have hit a barn door at ten paces but little else.

We had been in position for quite a while. Then the phone rang. Apprehensively, the erk in the tent picked it up. "Gun crew," he said nervously. Gunner Patrick and the magazine loader scanned the sky for the target, ready to fight. The voice on the other end of the line said, "Stand down and go to breakfast."

Bugger.

The Blackburn Beverley roared round the side of the valley at a bank angle of 45 degrees. As soon as the wings levelled, the Air Dispatch Regiment guys, each wearing a harness attached from his waist to the aircraft structure, positioned another one ton pallet into position and locked it in the roller tracks. At the end of the run, the aircraft swung round once more, now having prescribed a figure-of-eight turn and settled onto the approach heading. The guys waited like coiled springs. Green light on: locks released, a mighty shove and the load tips over the sill. Parachute strops pull taut as they extend down from the roof cable and the parachute blossoms out. A few seconds more on this heading sees the load smack into the ground on the forward base airstrip below. Four Bristol Centaurus engines roar in unison again and once more we bank hard round at the end of the valley.

I was now on No. 34 Squadron based at Seletar but serving on detachments at RAF Labuan. I transferred from 209 Squadron in 1965 and remained with 34 Squadron until I returned to the UK in 1967.

It transpired that one of the married 34 Squadron guys was on a lot of detachments up country and his bride was kicking off about it. The request came through our 209 Squadron office, was anyone interested in a swop? This was exactly what I wanted, time up country. In fact, I did those detachments more than many other people. The normal routine was 14 days at Labuan, then about a month back at Seletar before the next one. The married guys did not want to know and rather than a replacement aircraft coming up from Singapore with another man to relieve me, a buff envelope addressed to me with $100 inside would appear instead.

In Singapore I was part of the line crew maintaining the aircraft outside in the sun. Everyone worked in shorts and sandals which was necessary in the heat and humidity. The aircraft could be fitted with hard or soft tyres. The soft tyres had a lower pressure and gave a larger ground footprint for landing on dirt strips. Changing all eight main wheels for different runway conditions took a couple of hours of back-breaking work. To jack up the four wheeled bogies required two huge bottle jacks with a heavy beam between them which passed under the bogie to lift it clear of the ground. More than once the squadron office would change the tasking for the aircraft and we would have to change them all back again. That caused a lot of griping and I recall, at least once, someone refusing to do it. Why we couldn't operate with soft tyres all the time was never explained.

Adding to that task was the re-roling of the aircraft from freighting, para-dropping or passenger roles.

One of the worst jobs to befall me was to bleed a replaced hydraulic pump on the accessory gearbox at the back of the Centaurus engine. The engine guys would start it up and if all was well, I would work my way out down the wing, crawl all the way to the back of the engine where there was just room to squat behind the engine and bleed the pump. It was as hot as hell and being behind this noisy monster roaring away right in front of me in torchlight was not for the faint hearted. Once I had got a bit of air out of the pump and detected the change in noise as it loaded up pressure, I could clamber my way back to the access panel behind the flight deck where I would emerge bathed in sweat.

There were usually two Beverleys on the Labuan detachment and we would park them side by side with the tail booms just over the edge of the apron. As the wings were well above ground level, other aircraft would tuck under the wings, so it was not unusual to see English Electric Canberras or Gloster Javelins parked between and underneath the Bevs.

When an aircraft came back onto the ramp it had to be marshalled backwards using reverse pitch so it would fit into the space between the other smaller visitors. I grabbed the bats and did that whenever I could. As the Centaurus engines roared in reverse, it would send a cloud of stinging sand at me. When it got to where I wanted it, the signal changed from backwards to forwards, then full stop. We never gave it the stop signal while reversing in case it pitched up on its arse with the braking action.

Labuan is an island off the coast of Borneo close to Brunei. Victoria was the main town and in those days there was not much else. Occasionally there would be some time off and we would take a Land Rover up to a beach known as Surrender Point, so-called because it's where the Japanese surrendered to the Australians. On one of those rare days off, we had been up the coastline to a remote beach to swim and take it easy. A dirt track took us to the location which wound its way along the coast crossing several wooden bridges spanning the streams running into the sea.

On our way back, sitting in the back of the Land Rover, I spotted what looked like the head of a huge snake in the stream we were passing over. Asking the guy who was driving us to stop so I could take a look I climbed out over the tailgate and stepped into long grass to get nearer the spot where I had seen the head in the water. As I took my first step into the grass something big thrashed underfoot and the grass seemed to explode. A lizard about four feet long fairly flew into the stream with a huge splash and I fairly flew back over the tailgate of the Land Rover. I had stepped on what I found to be a Malayan water monitor lizard, reputed to grow to about six feet long. What I had seen in the water must have been another one of the same.

The wildlife extended to the occasional snake and although they generally kept away from us we would sometimes see one while driving around. Early one morning and riding up to the airfield from our domestic area we saw and drove right over a black snake about six feet long which though hit by our front and back wheels, just kept on sliding across the road to disappear into the ditch. One of our guys, worse for wear one night, fell off the road edge in the dark and got bitten by something on his way down into the bottom of the monsoon ditch. Within a few minutes he was getting even more delirious than his alcoholic state warranted and was swelling up under one arm where he had been bitten. Fortunately, the sick quarters kept some snake bite anti-venom serum and he was back to work after a day or two.

Very occasionally, we erks were allowed to use the beach at the officers' club at Shell House on the edge of the camp. A few cans of beer each made a nice day out. I recall one day there was a Royal New Zealand Navy destroyer tied up at the end of the jetty. Swimming out to it, the water was crystal clear and I could see right down to the ship's propeller. I managed to dive down and pass under it and come up the other side. Actually I pushed a bit too far and only just managed to surface on the other side without losing my breath. The beer had made me overconfident and I rather frightened myself.

Also, there was a Commonwealth War Graves cemetery not far from the camp and I went there two or three times. It is filled with men who died all over that part of the Far East, mostly Australians, but also some British Army and Royal Air Force personnel. It is a beautiful and peaceful place.

We also had a busy base at Kuching which was very close to the Indonesian border in Sarawak and a smaller base at Tawau which is in Sabah, North Borneo. The Indo's were in the eastern side of Borneo in Kalimantan and wanted to come into our bit. Along the border we had numerous Forward Operating Bases which were very remote. Therefore our supply drops, also undertaken by Armstrong Whitworth Argosies from Kuching and anything else capable of contributing, were necessary to the survival of the forward bases. Supply drops took place twice a day when we could but by mid-afternoon the thunder storms would sometimes build up on the mainland, making a second sortie impossible.

It was hot on the ground at Labuan and we had no air conditioning. Out of interest and also to get cool, I would often go with the drop sortie. On one of the drops, a Beverley aircraft suffered an engine failure whilst in a valley. The Air Dispatch guys released all the remaining six one-ton pallets out of the back of the aircraft instantly. Each Drop Zone had an escape route following a river back to the coast and that's where they went. Deservedly, the Dispatch Regiment guys won a commendation for that action which enabled the aircraft to get back out safely on three engines. Earlier, the Centaurus engine had been a bit of a nightmare for throwing cylinders and catching fire. Apparently, it had something to do with defective cylinder studs shearing off and a modification or 'mod' was brought out to fix it. Consequently, at least in my time in Borneo, we never had a failure though there was the occasional problem.

Fitted behind the flight deck was an engine analyser which checked the ignition systems of the engines. It could detect a single malfunctioning plug and the Flight Engineers could tell us which plug on each engine needed attention. This was a huge improvement on changing the whole set.

Also serving the bases were one or two Royal New Zealand Air Force Bristol Freighters, usually sharing our apron at Labuan. They seemed to have more than their fair share of problems and more than once suffered an engine failure, necessitating ditching the load in the South China Sea to lighten ship so they could return on the remaining engine.

It turned out that there were SAS troops from UK, Australia and New Zealand in Borneo, eager to get a slice of the action. Of course, no one at our level knew the big picture, existing in a bubble of 'need to know' with no media outlets for us to find out what else was happening. Years afterwards I was able to piece together the whole story of the forces we used to prevent the Indo's from invading. General Walker ran the whole thing and he had experience from the Malayan Emergency of the 1950's.

On the other side there was apparently about a quarter of a million armed forces and militia under arms. Walker had about 16,000 of us. Many of our foremost regiments including the Gurkhas and some naval contingents also served over the years of the Confrontation.

In addition to our blocking tactic there was a lot of political activity. Indonesian President Sukarno, who started it all by trying to prevent the formation of Malaysia on his border, was overthrown in a coup in 1965. By the time I made it to Borneo most of the work had been done and the situation was reasonably stable. Post Sukarno led to a lowering of tension and a growing acceptance by the Indonesians that it was a lost cause.

From 1964 to 1966 we had a classified military operation in effect, codenamed "Claret". This allowed for limited engagements and follow-up operations on the other side of the border. Kept under wraps and not briefed to the press, our guys on the ground turned the blocking tactic into an offensive which helped to break the political will of the Indo`s to keep up the struggle.

In Labuan, our accommodation was in a tin hut with open sides known as a 'basha'. Each one held about ten men sleeping under mosquito nets and cooled by overhead fans. When it was time to sleep you would pull the netting round the bed and tuck it in tight. The next thing was to kill all the mossies inside it. The fans could not provide much breeze inside the nets but it was better than nothing. Despite killing all I could see the net usually had three or four mossies in it next morning, too fat with my blood to escape back out again. If the lights were on at night huge flying bugs would come in and smash themselves to bits on the fan blades.

Before attempting sleep it was our custom to go to the NAAFI, which was no more than a large tent, and drink slightly cooled cans of Tiger beer. We amused ourselves throwing the empty cans at the rats' feet as they ran up the tent underneath the flysheet while the duck boards floated around us if there had been a thunderstorm.

Working every day on the squadron aircraft, about ten hours at a stretch, was normal and with what time was left, we ate drank and slept through the rest of it. I loved it.

Out on the ramp one day, I was feeling rough as a robber's dog and slumped down in the shade with my back against a main wheel. I had contracted a bout of glandular fever and a romping temperature. My pals brought the Land Rover out and drove me down to the sick quarters. The ward was air conditioned and not being used to it, I was frozen so I wrapped up in blankets and crashed out. The Medical Officer made the diagnosis and told the medical orderly to give me a penicillin shot in the buttocks every six hours. I know there is a technique for smacking the cheeks, then stabbing the hypodermic in at the appropriate moment but this guy got it wrong every time. I found it difficult to sit comfortably for a week afterwards.

Later, on another detachment at Labuan, I got a raging toothache so once more reported to the MO. There was no service dentist in Borneo at all so I got sent back to Singapore on a CHALK flight – from the initials, the shuttle flight between Changi, Labuan and Kuching.

After arrival at Changi I got a lift to Seletar and went to see the dentist. There, my tooth was declared beyond repair and with maximum force and little finesse it was extracted. These days it would have been saved but the service dentistry was rudimentary at best. My orders were to get on a Beverley and go straight back to Labuan, but fortunately it was not scheduled to depart till the next day, so I got a night's rest in my pit.

Salt depletion was supposed to be a problem so in the airmen's mess there was a huge plate of salt tablets the size of horse pills. Hardly anyone took them yet we did not seem to suffer. I reckon there must have been some salt in Tiger beer.

Our drop loads were various. Helicopter fuel was most frequent, with four 45-gallon drums to each pallet. Corrugated iron sheeting, the universal roofing for bashas, was also much in demand. Ammunition and live food, including chickens and goats, were also dropped.

When the 'Bev' was replaced by another flown up from Seletar, we would re-role it by taking the clamshell doors off the back of the main cabin with a crane and fitting all the roller drop system and fuselage deflector plates required for our primary role of forward supply.

Another less wholesome task was to empty the "honey buckets" in the aircraft. The tail boom was capable of carrying 36 passengers and had two toilets at the aft end. If the Parachute Regiment flew in the aircraft and departed out the back through the jump hatch the deposits they left with us to dispose of were pretty awful. We soon caught on to the fact that the RAF paid us an extra 2/6d a day to empty the honey buckets. After that, there was no shortage of volunteers, of which I was one.

At the end of the daily supply drop sorties, the ground crew would gather round the oil pump and a couple of barrels of engine oil and pump it up to the engine oil tanks by hand. It was tedious in that heat and why we never got a motorised pump is unclear.

Although much of the activity was on the border and especially in the Kuching area, casualties would occur anywhere in North Borneo, not always as a result of contact with the Indo`s. Bodies would be flown into Kuching or Labuan to be picked up by a shuttle to Singapore.

Occasionally I would be working out on the ramp and the first sign I saw of a body coming in would be a hastily arranged honour guard and the Duty Officer stood to at the visiting aircraft parking area. Everyone on the ramp area would come to attention until the transfer from aircraft to ambulance had taken place and the body was on its way to the morgue. Even guys on top of the aircraft wings doing turnarounds would be at attention and it was all done with great respect.

Unknown to me, some of the 94th Entry were around Borneo but of course you had no way of knowing unless you bumped into each other. One of the guys, who I am now in touch with, was given some rudimentary training as a second pilot in the Whirlwind helicopters. He had some hairy moments but it came to an end when he lost some of his hearing because of the effects of a grenade thrown at him by a Chinese dissident and also coming down with a jungle disease. He ended up back at Halton as an instructor.

Another ex- apprentice pal went on to retire after 38 years' service as an engineer officer squadron leader. I think he had been in long enough to serve under the old Queen. He was on a forward base when they thought they were coming under attack and he took up position with his rifle in a slit trench. There was some noise in the jungle and a party of Gurkhas went forward to investigate. They came back in fine spirits. They had found a water buffalo noisily wandering about in the jungle and had killed it. There was plenty of fresh meat that night.

Eventually the situation on the border was stabilised and there followed a period of drawdown. The bases were not vacated for some time yet but it was clear that there was little point in maintaining the current military posture and by late 1966 there was little to do. Our detachments became less frequent and eventually ceased. There was also a policy under the Labour government of the day to reduce the overseas bases we no longer needed. Denis Healey did a walk through the Far East and concluded that we could plan a reduction in the theatre.

Before that happened we had the task of moving men and materials about. The Beverley had a tail boom which could seat 36 people and a freight bay capable of carting helicopters or large vehicles.

We were given a job to move a party of Gurkhas from Jesselton, now known as Kota Kinabalu, to Tawau in Sabah. On arrival in Jesselton, we got the Gurkhas on board and myself and another guy who had also been assigned as a "flying spanner" for the task, stood by on the fire extinguisher while the crew started up the engines. Unfortunately, the number three starter motor had chosen this moment to shear its drive shaft so we only had three engines running. The captain decided that it might work if they ran down the runway on three engines and windmilled the other one to get it started. So the Gurkhas disembarked and we all stood around on the apron while he had a go. It did work and the Gurkhas were told to re-embark as soon as we got the aircraft back on the apron to save time. That was going fine and about half of them had boarded when I noticed that the right undercarriage was on fire and was doing quite well, being fed by some oily streaks on the main undercarriage leg and the breeze from the propellers.

Needing to reach the cockpit to tell the crew to shut down, I had to barge into the queue of boarding Gurkha passengers and stop them climbing aboard. I secured one rifleman's attention and pointed to the fire and he got the message very quickly. Now he was shouting to his mates in Gurkhali to come back out, it became even harder for me to push in past them.

Eventually I made it and shinned up the ladder to the flight deck. In the cockpit it was very much business as usual until I whipped the captain's headphone off and told him he had a brake fire. The crew shut down and evacuated so fast that I was the only one left behind. By the time I got back down to the ground everyone was off and the flight engineer had tackled the flames with an extinguisher.

About 100 yards away I could see the local Malay fire crew peering round the door of the fire station but showing no sign of attending so I sprinted up there and harried them out to the aircraft. They eventually turned up, unrolled their water hose and were about to aim it at the still glowing brake unit. Now I had to restrain them. The fire was now out and all I wanted was for them to keep an eye on it. Hosing down a red-hot brake can cause thermal shock, resulting in the whole unit fragmenting with a bang.

Now we needed a new pair of wheels and brakes as well as a starter motor. To change these items some jacks were also required. All this kit was going to be flown in to us the next day so we stood down.

Our accommodation for the night was to be the District Officer's bungalow and we bedded down as best we could. When we arrived, we were given a lot of drinks and I recall being very much the worse for wear on whisky, for which I had no capacity at all. I made a total prat of myself declaring to everyone that I wanted out of this man's air force. Actually, those days were the most enjoyable I ever experienced, so I don't know what came over me.

Next morning, I had the mother of all hangovers and my eyes were a very patriotic, red white and blue. Our equipment arrived courtesy of an RAF Vickers Valetta aircraft. The Valetta taxied up to us and without shutting down, discharged all this heavy kit straight out of the freight door at us. Heavy jacks and brake units were flung out while wheels bounded off across the apron. We struggled to handle the equipment in the slipstream behind the propellers. Having made the delivery, the freight door shut and the aircraft went on its way.

Several hours later, with the aircraft now fit for use, we boarded the troops and took them over to Tawau.

The Beverley cruised along at about 3,000 feet over the Mekong Delta on a radar steer to Than Son Nhut airbase in Saigon. Below were rice paddy fields and dotted around were small villages on slightly higher ground.

From our starboard side and below us came a flight of two propeller-driven Douglas Skyraider ground attack aircraft, painted in a light grey scheme. As they passed underneath and came back into view on our port side some spidery lines streaked out from the Skyraider wings and the paddy fields below erupted in fountains of water as the ordnance hit home. The captain contacted Saigon Radar and queried if we were in the right place as there seemed to be a ground attack going on beneath us. The controller simply replied, "Yeah no problem, you got a thousand feet separation".

Oh good.

I had got lucky again. In late 1966 I was detailed to fly on a trip to Japan from Singapore in a Beverley, which was going to be full of interest. After things had gone quieter in Borneo there was time for the squadron to consider expanding our route knowledge. This navigation exercise, to train our crews on tactical routes, was to take us from Singapore to Saigon, then via Hong Kong to Tokyo. Our return was through Okinawa and Borneo.

An engine fitter and I were the "flying spanners". The aircraft gave us no trouble whatsoever over the whole route. Our only hardship was pumping 45-gallon drums of oil over wing from the ground into the engine oil tanks and the oil reserve tank for the long flight hours. This was normal. Centaurus engine oil consumption was measured in the same fashion as fuel. It was a consumable item.

By this time, I had made an effort to catch up with promotion and had completed my tests for upgrade to corporal. Previously, I had not had time to think about it. On the other hand, maybe I was lazy and simply played too hard.

When assigned the trip my mind computed Hong Kong-Tokyo as the route and I was totally ignorant of any other option until later, when we were underway, I learned that we had a fuel stop in Vietnam. Since the RAF had no official part in the Vietnam War, (which was by 1966 was now raging,) we apparently had been given a BOAC flight number. Other people I have since spoken to had used the usual RAF callsigns.

After landing following the little episode with the Skyraiders, I thought maybe I had better do a damage check in case some Viet Cong had managed to get a shot at us before he was forced to duck his head down. I found no holes so we refuelled and re-oiled while the crew were whisked off by the USAF to file plans and get weather forecasts. We were waiting for fuel for some time, so obviously we had low priority.

There were two runways in my line of sight. One appeared to be fighters taking off while the other had transports. It seemed that there was a take-off on each runway every minute. I had never seen such an air armada and I recall thinking that if the USA does not win this war with all this kit, then no-one could.

At that time the outcome of the conflict was uncertain but the Vietnam War had been escalating in the mid-sixties and was reaching the peak of firepower. Later, the US would have about 450,000 personnel in theatre. Their efforts were restrained by political limitations and the Tet Offensive of 1968 was yet to come. Despite increases in manpower and relaxation of attack restrictions, the war, as we now know, was lost.

Historians have compared our successes in Malaya and Borneo with the US led Vietnam War. From what I can determine, I believe it is an unfair comparison. We never fought such a strong enemy, who were all the time well supported by China.

After Saigon we trundled up to RAF Kai Tak in Hong Kong for a night stop. A few of us went out for a meal and I recall eating one of the best steaks I ever had, stuffed with oysters. In this Chinese restaurant in Kowloon, there was a stage with a singer and the usual musicians, with tables grouped around the stage. During the meal there was a sudden upheaval behind us. Lots of women started screaming and I saw a huge rat emerge from the kitchen and work its way under the tables between people's feet before disappearing below the stage. The band and singer never missed a beat.

Leaving Hong Kong we progressed to Tokyo to land at the USAF airbase at Tachikawa. The main civil airport in Tokyo is named Haneda.

I was told that "Haneda" in Japanese translates to "Field of Wings". How nice.

In Tokyo we had two nights rest and a couple of us had the chance to jump on the train into town and take in some tourism, including the impressive Shinto Meiji Shrine.

One night at a very traditional restaurant near our hotel we met a couple of American DC3 drivers who flew for Air America. This clandestine 'airline' operated throughout the region for the CIA. These guys did not want to discuss where they flew at all. The conversation was off limits.

On our return to Singapore, the next stop was Okinawa and the US airbase at Kadena. There, I went out with a couple of our guys for a few beers but in a huge bar I fell in with some US Marines and became separated from the others. They could not find me so they went back to the airbase by themselves. By this time I was well in my cups and when America`s finest suggested moving on I was all for it. I thought it was to another watering hole. We piled into taxis and set off. When we came to the place they all wanted to go to, several taxis were setting down their fares and immediately setting off again with a fresh complement of marines. The place, from what I could make out by the street lights, was an open field in which there were a few large wooden engine crates, each of which had a door. Outside each door was a queue. I clocked the picture and got back into a taxi sharing a ride back to the airbase with some of the by now, satisfied customers. That was about the last thing I remember but clearly some kind person dropped me back to my billet and I was in time for the next leg back with the rest of the crew.

The return through our base in Borneo to Singapore was uneventful and the Navex was over.

The return through to our base in Singapore included a couple of days in Bangkok where we joined an army exercise and did some supply dropping in support. I later succumbed to a session in a Thai bath house where I was given several baths and a cool shower to follow and a rather chaste massage before being ejected back out into the street. I walked back to the hotel as if I had springs in my heels.

Life for so many single servicemen in the Far East was one of work and play but there was a serious shortage of eligible women. Not surprisingly, there were forays out of camp for sexual satisfaction. As you cruised along in the bar areas the girls would exhort you to come in and join them. One might say, "Johnny, come buy dink, short time jig-a-jig onry fifty dorrar". I was always impressed how they were able to figure out my middle name.

The bawdiest place in downtown Singapore was Bugis Street. The bars had tables set up on the pavement and the rats ran through the open drains under your feet. In Bugis Street 'girls' were better looking than average but looking closely you could see the Adams Apple was too prominent. Trouble was, by the time people got there after a few beers beforehand, their powers of observation were not up to much.

One of the guys on the squadron, raised in the Gorbals of Glasgow, had been attracted to one of the "Lady Boys" and before getting down to the business had gallantly indulged in a bit of foreplay. That was when he found all was not what it should be. Apparently, he demanded, and got, his money back. Not a guy to mess with. Another guy had mixed it with a local female companion before leaving to go on detachment to Labuan and had found an infestation of what we called "crabs" had travelled with him. The Medical Officer gave him instructions to shave himself and apply some solution provided to the affected area. Shortly after the medicine was administered to the now raw shaven tender parts he experienced a lasting chilli moment and sprinted round the basha, legs akimbo, desperately trying to cool his burning gonads. Entertaining stuff – and oh how we laughed.

In downtown Singapore I stumbled across Bill Bailey's bar. Bill was the man in the song "Won`t you come home Bill Bailey?" He was American and ran a bar when the Japanese took Singapore. They interned him and when released, Bill opened another bar in 1945. The bar was pretty basic, being mainly white tiled and had all the charm of a public toilet. It was empty except for Bill reading the *Straits Times*. Our arrival was greeted with, "What do you want?" in a tone implying he couldn't be bothered. A round of Tiger beers followed but Bill`s was not exactly jumping so we pushed off. Bill never went home and died there in 1966.

There were other service establishments to visit and I recall going to Changi when a group was playing there who were based at Seletar, so we went to hear them play. Later on a few of us went down to the village outside Changi to get some Chinese food. We collectively called all these little roadside cookhouses "Makan" stalls after the Malay word for food.

Not long after we sat down there was a tremendous crashing noise from up the road and a lot of locals were shouting about something. Taking a look in that direction I could see what looked like servicemen turning the Makan stalls over and the cooking fires spilling out all over the place.

Chinese taxi drivers were starting up to drive off so we jumped into one and hopped it. Later on it was alleged that the Argyll and Sutherland Highlanders had decided to wreck the place. On their way back, reportedly, they had set upon a lone RAF guy on the road inside the base. He got beaten up, robbed and thrown in the monsoon ditch. That was brave of them.

Another time, I nearly became involved in a fight at the downtown Union Jack club when violence erupted between the Army and another group. I saw a hardwood chair broken into pieces across one combatant's back. He responded by turning round and punching the lights out of his assailant. Extracting myself at all speed, I only just got out before a party of naval shore police rocked up and waded in with batons.

I was never into all that stuff.

There were sights in early 1960's Singapore that you do not see today. I remember old Chinese ladies with bound feet and in typical Chinese manner, they were called Lotus Feet. Many years before, there had been a practice to bind the feet of girl children so their feet could not grow. It was considered more beautiful to have small feet. Apparently a foot about 3 inches long and the ensuing swaying walk it caused was considered to be very attractive. It must have been very painful. These little ladies would hobble about on their heels and walking appeared to be very difficult.

Another strange sight was the funeral parlours where coffins were carved at street level. I recall seeing old people waiting to die there while lying on a concrete slab and gazing out into the street. Passing by and curious, I saw a shrivelled up old lady and momentarily our eyes met. She stared blankly at me and I saw she was alive but only just. I averted my eyes in embarrassment. Relatives would deposit their old people and they would stoically wait for the end to come. These were the Death Houses of Sago Lane. Although formally banned by that time, they were obviously still in existence.

Chinese funerals were noisy affairs with mourners dressed in white, roaring around with the coffin on the back of a lorry making a lot of noise banging gongs. It was all done at breakneck speed as if devils were chasing the dear-departed.

The Malays or the Indians were quite amicable but the Chinese were pretty anti-western. We were called *Gwai-los* by the Chinese and the description 'round eye' or 'big nose' came into it as well.

In the last six months of my time there I had the good luck to be introduced to a friend of a married colleague's housekeeper. My girlfriend was Chinese, attractive and we got on very well. She was a brave girl, for it was not seemly in those days for a Chinese to be seen with a European. The staff in restaurants could be very unkind.

Time had been passing by so quickly that I had not noticed I now had less than six months left to serve in Singapore. Before you got to the last six months you could apply to extend your tour. I tried, but had missed the deadline. I doubt if I could have succeeded because of the general rundown going on, but what a lost opportunity.

The thing to do now was to submit a 'postings preference' so I requested Lyneham, Brize Norton or Abingdon. My idea was that I would need to get some experience on civil aircraft types if I was going to have a chance of employment after my 12 years was up. I had no wish to stay in longer because the move to Civvy Street was best not delayed and I had some good postings behind me.

Well, that's when my happy time in the RAF took a nosedive. My posting was to RAF St. Athan in South Wales. I knew it was a Maintenance Unit but little else. That to me meant working nine to five Monday to Friday in a hangar and I knew that was going to be horrendous after the outdoor working life I had enjoyed in Singapore and before that at St. Mawgan. In the Far East I think I had gone a bit native. Full of concern, I did not know how I was going to cope with an MU but it turned out to be even worse than I imagined.

CHAPTER FIVE

Reluctant Return

My journey back was much the same as when I had gone out. The Britannia arrived at Heathrow in May 1967 and my mother and sister were there to meet me. On the car journey home, sheep were grazing on the grassy banks of Staines Reservoir. Weird. Two and a half years was an awful long time to be away in Singapore and I felt completely out of place back in UK.

It is easy to identify with the feeling of isolation that our current servicemen feel on return from theatres such as Afghanistan even though my experience had been nothing compared to theirs. Your whole lifestyle comes to an abrupt end and all your buddies are left behind. Adjusting to life in the UK again was difficult. It all seemed so unreal and depressing.

Later, in the post, came a General Service Medal with Borneo clasp. Having it delivered by post without a presentation of any kind seemed to devalue it somehow. Not that I wanted any staged event but there was not even a letter to accompany it and it seemed then, as it does now, rather impersonal.

In the last few years the Malaysian government struck a medal entitled the Pingat Jasa Malaysia, which roughly translates as the Malaysia Freedom Medal, and it was issued to anyone involved during the creation of Malaysia who served in the Armed Forces or Malaysian government. Initially we could not wear it but after some pressure applied to the MOD from the Borneo Veterans Association, the Queen gave permission to wear it in public. I applied for it, but unfortunately could not attend a presentation with other veterans, so it too came in the post with no covering letter. Maybe that's how it is done, but it could be better. I have just read a book about a naval helicopter pilot's time in the Falklands who flew risky missions under gunfire. He found his South Atlantic Medal in his pigeon hole. That's unacceptable.

Very recently, while in Brunei on an audit of the airline, Royal Brunei, for the International Air Transport Association (IATA), I took an extra day and went by boat across to Labuan. Some things had changed, a nice new terminal building at the airport and decent roads right round the island. What had not changed, to my amusement, was the centre of downtown which still had the same old restaurants open to the pavement and the sewers smelling much as they did in the sixties.

With the help of a young Chinese taxi driver, I covered the island in a few hours, seeing Surrender Point with its mass grave for the Japanese dead and the Commonwealth Cemetery which was still as beautiful as I had seen it 45 years before. Two young Moslem girls on a school tour wanted to have their picture taken with me amongst the graves. They must have thought I was once mates with the fallen. I take that as a compliment.

As it was lunch time my taxi driver and I had some local food at a little restaurant in a Kampong on the way back.

Visiting the the Labuan Museum, which did not exist when I had been there before, I found the period of confrontation was not mentioned at all except to say that there had been a disagreement with Indonesia and that the province held an election which voted to join Malaysia. There was no mention of the contribution of the Commonwealth Armed Forces in this period, or even their own Malay Regiments. It was as if it had never happened. I asked two curators about the absence of any reference to the confrontation and they clearly had no idea what I was talking about. An email to the museum director went unanswered.

There are different accounts of our fatalities in the confrontation, varying from an implausible 400 to a more realistic 114. A small butcher's bill by comparison to other more kinetic encounters, but it should still be respected.

Back in UK, my attempts to look up old friends at home did not work. People had moved on. I bought another Hillman Minx, this time a 1958 model. I had a long disembarkation leave, so via an introduction from my mother, I drove for the Hospital Car Service ferrying patients to hospital appointments. Mileage allowance was payable for that which kept me going in beer money till the leave ended and I took myself off to RAF St. Athan.

On arrival at St Athan I was dismayed to find that the accommodation was the same as Halton had been. I had the option of sharing a dormitory holding about 15 other guys or, as I was now a junior NCO, a single room tucked away by the side of the extension housing the barrack block ablutions. Outside the window was a wall extending away with numerous toilet downpipes attached to it. The view ended with the sight of the next barracks. Not good.

My job was night shift, Monday to Friday, replacing metal structures on Avro Vulcan bombers.

This I am afraid to say, had me considering desertion – but that probably meant a dishonourable discharge with the attendant employment problems thereafter. To add to that there was also a chance that I might spend time in Colchester military prison, where life would be worse still.

In that rather weak period of my private life I met and eventually married the person who was to be the mother of my two children. On reflection, I believe I was trying to create an environment in which I could escape the air force, with which I was now thoroughly disenchanted. It was not a sound reason for committing to family life and unsurprisingly it did not last.

After our divorce, my wife later met and married an American in the UK and eventually moved with him to Arizona. My daughter went with them and joined the US Army, doing well there. As I write she is an aide to a three-star general in Washington. My son stayed in the UK and is now a sales director in the communications industry. They both also have the family gene for hard work.

My ex-wife had a heart problem in later life and needed to have a pacemaker fitted. Driving home one day in Phoenix after telling her husband she felt unwell and was going home, she had to pull over to the side of the freeway. By the time the highway patrol came along she had died there alone.

I did manage to escape from the MU at St Athan after a few months by making a real nuisance of myself to my flight commander. My reasoning to him was that after my last two and a half years of frontline squadron service, this kind of work was not going to wring the best out of me, also vaguely hinting at finding a way to leave the air force.

Of course, I was contracted until the age of 30 so that was a pretty empty threat but I did manage to get transferred to another station although not out of Maintenance Command. So, from one end of the country to another, I moved my kit to RAF Leconfield in Yorkshire.

There, the job was maintaining English Electric Lightning fighters in storage and I found a flat in Hull. No more barrack blocks for me.

One day, which almost heralded the end of life as I knew it, I had the most intense abdominal pains and required a limited radius of action from the nearest latrine. We were moving aircraft and equipment around the hangar and I was doubled up in agony. I made it to the end of the day and drove home to my flat in Hull. What followed was apparently Hepatitis A and in the first few days I expelled anything ingested from both ends. Eventually a doctor was called, who diagnosed the illness and said although he would like to move me to the isolation hospital in Hull, he doubted that I would survive the journey. By then I was a pasty shade of yellow and quite incapable of knowing what was going on around me.

I recall coming to for a short while and my mother in the room with me. I asked how long she had been there, thinking I had dozed off for an hour or two and she replied that she had been there for two days.

Eventually, I climbed back up from the weakness and debilitation and moved out of bed into an armchair. I had been in bed for three weeks and was quite weak. I had a visit from the RAF MO at Leconfield. I recall he was a wing commander and he suggested that I come back to the station as I was now fit to travel. Having already experienced Sick Quarters on RAF stations, I had no intention of spending the coming weeks in a white tiled ward resembling a public toilet being cared for by male nurses. So, I played the card that I knew he could not outbid, explaining to the wing commander that I was a patient of a civilian doctor and that I wished to remain in his capable hands until I had made a full recovery. My trump card paid off and the wingco left me to it.

I returned to the RAF after six weeks and was given light duties for a further six. One of the effects on my now battered liver was that I could not take any alcohol; even a half pint of bitter made me feel very poorly. Over the next few years I managed to build myself up to handling a drink again and with great determination restored my boozing capacity back to its former prowess.

Back to work, the hours were nine to five and there was some hands-on maintenance including preparing aircraft for flights to keep them fully functional. This was suiting me better.

On the line I would repack brake chutes in the compartment below the hot exhaust ducts. This entailed setting the new chute connection into the receptacle above the exhaust pipes then chasing the wire cable into the grooves either side of the exhausts down to the chute compartment underneath. The exhausts were still pretty hot and chasing the wire cables in with a mallet caused a few burns. To get the chute pack into the compartment meant lying on one's back with both feet pushing the thing upwards while a mate would pull the doors closed with a T handle engaged in a slot in each door. We became pretty good at it.

We had to top up the liquid oxygen for the pilot's breathing oxygen using a cart with a LOX bottle on it. The LOX cart was a large cylindrical vessel containing the liquid and it had to be able to vent when the temperature around it rose, so there was usually a little white vapour emitting from it. The usual guff was given to us about not mixing LOX with grease or oil because it would go bang, yet we moved straight from servicing the hydraulics to replenishing the oxygen wearing the same clothes. I never heard of an accident. Maybe we were lucky.

Changing wheels was frequent. The Lightning would do about six to eight landings on the main wheels before the tyres were worn out, even less in crosswinds. While the wheels were changed someone else would refuel. The engine start system also needed topping up. The starter was a miniature jet engine using very high-octane fuel known as AVPIN. This evil stuff provided a high-pressure gas during start-up and the AVPIN starter would spin up the main engines. On the port side below the wing there was an exit for the unspent burning AVPIN fuel to flow out overboard. As it did so, there were flames falling out and it was a job I took on to pat those out with an asbestos glove.

We had some old marques of Lightning which were on long term storage and also brand-new Mk.6s straight out of the factory at Warton. These new aircraft had about six hours on the clock and were maintained in a state of readiness for issue to a front line squadron if they speared one in. Judging by the rate of issue, we assumed the squadrons speared them in quite often. Sitting in the hangar, each aircraft had three open five-gallon drums under each wing to catch the leaks. The only time it did not leak, apparently, was when it was doing Mach two point something and the wing skins grew hot enough to expand and stop leaking.

Each aircraft held for immediate issue was flown weekly to keep it all turning and burning. To see the thing climb vertically at the end of the runway and in full reheat was awe-inspiring and deafening in equal measure.

During my time there, the service had experienced engine bay fires caused by leaking fuel lines in the upper engine bay. The alloy fuel pipes routed through the fuselage and in doing so chafed against the skin apertures, causing leaks which ignited on the engine. Another fitter and I embodied a modification to provide anti-chafe blocks to the fuel lines and that work time was recorded to be the basis for planning the modifications for the rest of the fleet. Access to any part of the Lightning internals was a nightmare. Everything was stuffed in around the engines and needed the involvement of several tradesmen. Replacing engines was an operation using winches or cranes, complicated by the fact that one was above the other.

This was the kind of work that I enjoyed, but I still had it in the back of my mind that I needed to prepare for Civvy Street. On the unit there was the customary tool store run by an NCO. The man running it had been posted to Malta and I took over the inventory. It was not long before I realized that the supply system for obtaining tools could be managed to my advantage. When I left the service about a year later my engineer's tool box, which I would need to provide me with the means to conduct my trade, was well stocked. Most of the tools had the government broad arrow stamped on them but they worked OK nonetheless and my next employer would not have a problem with it.

Passing the unit notice board one day I was drawn to a new memo which stated that there was a manpower surplus in my trade and rank and that applications would be accepted for discharge. I followed it up like a shot. However, there was a drawback – the discharge was by purchase. That meant I had to give the RAF £150 to let me go when they did not want me anyway, which still rankles to this day. The injustice of that was all too plain but it was a route to Civvy Street for me at the age of 26, some three and a half years early and it had to be taken. My only problem was that I did not have that kind of cash.

I applied for and got two weeks leave and set to work to earn the money. In downtown Hull, there was a street corner where unemployed men would get picked for manual labour. So I joined the crowd of rather seedy looking men and tried to look useful. Two weeks later, after humping wet plastic bags of fertilizer off railway wagons onto lorries and potato picking in muddy fields I had amassed £100. I also had a bad back from all the bending to pick and bag the potatoes.

Adding up my hard-earned geld I found that I was £50 short. In 1968 that was a lot of money. My aunt gave me the £50 and refused to accept repayment. I am forever in her debt for giving me the opportunity to make a fresh start.

I was discharged from the Royal Air Force three months later in January 1969.

Looking back at that period, about nine years of my life, I have always said that the best thing I ever did was to join the Royal Air Force and the second-best thing I ever did was to leave it. I got the start in life that I so sorely needed through the RAF and I will always be grateful for that. However, I think the service did not get the best out of me and I did not get the best out of it, either. If you compare the man management set up in the Royal Navy by Lord Louis Mountbatten, then the RAF of the day was way behind the concept of man management and advancement offered by the divisional system of the RN. I never felt that my name was known to any of my flight commanders unless I was in trouble for something. I am told that this has all changed and man management is now something following Mountbatten's ideals. I wish it had been that way in my time.

CHAPTER SIX

Civvy Street

I entered the gates of the Hawker Siddeley aircraft factory at Brough airfield. The scene was as if Lowry had painted it and the figures had come to life. Men in cloth caps and grim expressions rode bicycles or walked through the gates to work. The more fortunate of us drove our cars.

It was then, as I was being directed by a foreman in a brown dust coat to my place of work that I found out the workforce was on a work to rule and that there was a labour dispute. My earnings without bonus would be little more than my last payday in the RAF. Things were not going well.

I had emerged from the RAF broke but free to seek employment. My long-term plan was to leave Yorkshire and head south but first, I had to earn some cash. The nearest employment was Hawker Siddeley, not far west of Hull so I attended an interview and was swiftly offered employment as a skilled airframe fitter. The next step was to join their union as it was a 'closed shop' so I took myself off to the Amalgamated Union of Engineering Workers offices.

My induction into the union was coldly conducted by a grim-faced official who would have passed for a bouncer in a rough nightclub. He took my details plus some money and I was all set.

Neither of these bodies – my new employer, nor my new-found brothers – told me that they had a work to rule in progress and that my earnings would be miniscule.

I was assigned to building the cargo hold of a Hawker Siddeley Trident aircraft. It was made in an inverted jig so that it appeared as if I was making a tube train for the London Underground.

Above: An Entry on parade at Halton 1960. (Author)

Right: The author at Halton in 1960. Any hair that went under the hat you could keep. (Author)

Above: An example of a 42 Squadron Shackleton, which the author flew in on detachment to Gibraltar, sporting 20mm nose cannons and bomb doors open. (Aviation Photo Company)

Below: A view of the ramp at RAF Labuan in the mid-sixties. Two Twin Pioneers of 209 Squadron can be seen in the foreground. In the background are two Beverleys of 34 Squadron, as well as two Javelins and a Canberra B15. (Ministry of Defence Crown Copyright 1965. Reproduced under the terms of The Open Government Licence, Ver. 2)

Above: A Single Pioneer of 209 Squadron at RAF Seletar in 1964. (Aviation Photo Company)

Below: A 209 Squadron Twin Pioneer at RAF Seletar, again in 1964. (Aviation Photo Company)

Above: A 34 Squadron Beverley in the supply drop role at RAF Seletar, 1966. Note the deflector plates fitted on fuselage. (Aviation Photo Company)

Below: Another 34 Squadron Beverley in transport role at RAF Seletar in 1966. (Aviation Photo Company)

Above: A supply drop of chickens to the army in Borneo during 1965. (Air Despatch Association)

Below: A load of helicopter fuel going out over the sill of a Beverley, Borneo, 1965. (Air Despatch Association)

Above: The helicopter fuel going out, with the parachute pack deploying, Borneo, 1965. (Air Despatch Association)

Below: The author in the tail boom of a Beverley on his way to Borneo in 1966. (Author)

This is 5B-DAN at RAF Akrotiri after the gear-up crash in 1980. Both main gears detached, the right one lies behind the wing. (Author)

Early livery TMAC CL44 with tail open and livestock boarding ramp in position at Stansted in the 1970s. (Air Team Images)

Above: A view of N447T Guppy at Stansted in the 1970s. (Air Team Images)

Below: TMAC CL44 VR-HHC, registered for traffic rights at Hong Kong, photographed at Stansted in the 1970s. (Air Team Images)

I was also introduced to my workmate who was, according to his credentials, semi-skilled. Quite how that qualification had been reached was a mystery. He had been an undertaker's assistant before this employment and he had been fired from his last job for cracking jokes while they carried a coffin. We were working to drawings which he could not read and his only experience of using tools did not extend beyond putting new roofing felt on his garden shed.

Worse still, there was absolutely no supervision and everyone just muddled along.

Days and weeks passed, scraping enough money together to enable me to cross the Humber and get a job back down south. Sorry, folks from the north, it wasn`t for me.

I applied for jobs with several aircraft engineering companies and airlines in the south. As with any other job in aviation that I have applied for, having on my CV that I was an ex Halton Brat enhanced my chances. Eventually, I had an offer from British Airways at Heathrow and one from Aviation Traders at Stansted. Fortunately, I have managed to get through my entire career without being based at Heathrow and it was not going to be my preference.

Aviation Traders was my choice of destination, so I attended the interview and was offered the job. The next pressing thing was where to live. Close to the present Stansted Airport terminal is a piece of ground that in 1969 was a caravan site. There, I forked out a deposit for a caravan and signed a hire purchase agreement for two years to pay for the rest of it. It was so close to the runway that when Douglas DC8 freighters took off in the night the whole thing shook from the engine noise.

Aviation Traders was an aircraft engineering company and served the needs of several airlines. It maintained aircraft from large piston powered types to jets.

My first job was to assist in the finishing work to the last of the ATL 98 Carvair conversions. These odd looking aircraft converted from the Douglas DC4 were produced for the channel car ferry service and were operated by several airlines. This one was for British Air Ferries and it went to work at Southend. That being the end of the Carvair conversion work, I then went over to the main facility where the bulk of the servicing was carried out.

Looking behind the aircraft tug I was riding in I was concerned to see the nose wheel of the Canadair CL44 Guppy bouncing along about six inches above the ground. I told the tug driver to slow down and

advised him what was going on but he did not seem bothered about it. Yet this was not normal and it posed a risk of the aircraft sitting on its tail.

It was pitch dark and I had been assigned to collect this aircraft from the other side of the airport and bring it into the hangar for servicing. There was a man upstairs on the aircraft brakes as well. When we got to the apron where it was intended I was to park it, we began to slow down and stop. Unfortunately, there was a downhill slope and the thing had other ideas. As we slowed down I got off the tug so that I could signal to put the aircraft brakes on. It was then that everything started to go wrong very quickly. The CL44 carried on in the downhill direction and the tug could not stop it.

As I watched, the tow bar and tug jack-knifed towards the port engines. Being a windy, pitch black night the guy upstairs could neither see what was going on nor hear me shouting "Brakes!" In the nick of time he saw the danger and slammed the brakes on. The tug was sitting just under the port propellers and wing by the time the whole thing came to a halt.

What no-one had realised was that when the aircraft had been unloaded of its cargo all the pallets were left at the rear of the cabin. This stack of pallets, weighing about two tons, was upsetting the balance so much that it was pulling the nose off the ground. I learned something that night.

I found a profound change between the RAF and civil methods of maintenance. Within the RAF we had been trained to maintain different types in a loosely generic way and to go to the manuals if we needed to know something. There were not at that time any type-specific qualifications.

In the civil system, there were fitters who were basically experienced or qualified, then there were approved engineers whose basic licence allowed them to certify work with approval granted by the employer. Lastly, there were Licensed Engineers accredited by the Civil Aviation Authority. Anyone with an approval could certify other people's work. This whole system at once appeared to me better that the one utilised by the RAF. I was now working in an environment of rigid qualifications and quality control.

When I was given a job on an aircraft, for instance replacing a component, I always preferred to continue to a point where I had completed a phase of assembly, then when I took a break, it felt nicely under control. The tea break was announced in the hangar by a bell but if I was not ready to down tools I just carried on. I missed quite a few tea breaks that way. Quite why I was like that I don't know but on reflection, I assume that's part of my character. In other words, maybe a bit of a control freak.

I soon saw that the route to better qualifications, pay and working conditions was for the taking. I got my basic licence then worked on getting a full Airframe Licence on the CL44, a four-engine turboprop made by Canadair in Montreal. It took about a year's experience to build up a worksheet showing tasks such as undercarriage and control surface changes. After that I sat an exam on the type and had a three-hour oral exam on the systems with two CAA maintenance examiners. That went well and they were kind enough to let my employer know they were very happy with my performance under examination. ATL promoted me to Inspector.

Other company authorisations followed. I obtained approvals on the Bristol Britannia, Boeing 707, Douglas DC8, Vickers Vanguard and Lockheed Constellation to add to my licence on the CL44.

I did not see much of the Constellation but when it did appear it was an Indian Air Force aircraft. The crew would be on a Navex from Delhi, which was a thin disguise for a week's shopping in London. None of the cockpit crew were normally under the rank of wing commander and the captain might be an air-vice marshal.

Their "Connie" would turn up dripping oil and with all manner of problems which we duly transcribed into defect cards, then sending a list of required parts needed to the Indian Embassy. Nothing would be heard from the embassy but after a week, the crew would come back with all their shopping, accept the aircraft back as it stood and fly off home.

In late 1972, there were some customer airlines going out of business and we lost about a third of our work. 'Last in, first out' prevailed and I was made redundant.

On my last day with ATL as an aircraft inspector, I took a job card to inspect the engine pylon mounting of a customer's B707. Inside the pylon was the robust casting that supported the attachment of the forward and aft engine mountings to the wing front spar. There my torch revealed a crack, completely through the casting. The engine was effectively attached by one mounting only. It was a wonder it had not come off. Having filled in a defect report, it was a matter of minutes later when I picked up my final pay packet and walked out of the door. My leaving present to them, I suppose.

I did earn a few months employment through an agency but eventually, after working through the agency for Transmeridian Air Cargo at Stansted, I was employed by them.

Before that, on one agency job at Manston, I had gone to an address for bed and breakfast and when I knocked on the front door, a small boy looked out of the window and shouted to his mum, "It's the Police!". We sorted out that misunderstanding but then I found they were full. However, they did give me a bed in a converted brick coal shed with a single bar electric fire powered by an extension lead from the house.

So began a long association began with TMAC. They operated the CL44 and also the aircraft I had nearly wrecked one dark night, the CL44 Guppy, which was a conversion of the original model with a huge fuselage for outsize loads.

TMAC was hard work but rewarding. The hangar we had was too small to fit more than the nose inside so in consequence a lot of jobs were carried out in the open come rain, snow or shine.

Employed as an engineer, it soon became apparent to me that there was no union, or indeed any form of representation, between the engineers and the management and there were a number of problems that no-one wanted to address. I suggested that we propose a meeting with management with two of us representing the engineers in an effort to reach some agreement.

So a foreman and I made approaches to them and attended a meeting. We had not gone very far before the management dismissed the foreman I was with as being part of the management itself and therefore, could not represent the men. That left me, so I put our proposals forward which were noted but not agreed and the meeting was closed. A day or so later, the management announced my promotion to foreman and as such could not negotiate with me for the same reason as the other guy who had accompanied me in the first place. By now I was married with two children and over a barrel. I could not tell them to stuff it and risk my job. The outcome with the other engineers was that they thought I had feathered my own nest and held me in low esteem. Despite that, they did get improvements in working conditions and I duly noted that they had done so without putting their own heads above the parapet. If I had been dismissed for rocking the boat, would they have rallied round to support me? I doubt it. I learned a bit about people and industrial relations from that episode.

TMAC`s fleet went all over the world but a lot of cargo was carried to Africa or the Middle East and we also picked up from Hong Kong. The loads were interesting: one-day-old chicks, sheep, goats, pigs, race horses, zoo animals and, while in the Gulf, even a couple of camels. Cargo varied a lot but in those days, when some countries did not have the means of production, there were a lot of hotel and catering fittings.

CL44 aircraft had an unusual feature. The whole tail would open to an angle of 105 degrees to present an unobstructed opening in order to load long items straight down the cabin. They were ex-Flying Tiger aircraft that had served the USA carrying cargo into Vietnam. Before that they had flown passengers. The windows were all scored roughly so that it was not possible to see into the cabin. Apparently, that was because on the return from Vietnam, they carried body bags. We had to replace all those obscured windows with metal blank plates because the integrity of the windows was lost and it posed a risk of pressurisation failure.

Tail loading was usually no problem because the swing tail moved the weight forward onto the nose wheel. However, there were at least two episodes of the aircraft being handled wrongly and falling on its tail.

Now I was on line maintenance. Aside from the routine servicing to turn the aircraft round and back out again, there were also defects to rectify. Many of these would-be system problems and would entail tracing the cause by diagnosis and replacing components in the systems. I found that if I compared the history of the defect with what previous maintenance had been performed, it was often possible to determine what action had preceded the defect. Sometimes it was a faulty component that had been fitted which started the repetitive defect. That gave me an enormous amount of job satisfaction as the aircraft taxied away again with the snags fixed and my signature in the paperwork. It is hard to compare, but I often think that I got as much of a buzz out of that as I did in later life as a pilot, after performing a good instrument approach in bad weather.

One CL44 had developed a strange defect. When the flaps were extended to the landing position during the approach to land, the control column oscillated back and forwards violently and only stopped once the flaps were run back up to the approach setting. Both our engineering shifts had a crack at this and we spent some time checking flap rigging and for any signs of abnormal wear in the flap mechanism.

Every time we did some work on it and released it for service, it re-occurred. I went and read through the maintenance records and, bingo, just before the problem began, there had been an elevator change. This was the control system that was oscillating and I guessed, correctly, that it was out of balance and when the flaps were set for landing, it induced airflow over the elevator causing the condition for the oscillation. It was the last day of my shift and I wanted to make sure that the elevator got changed.

The next shift was likely to disagree with my diagnosis so it was important to get as far into the job to make it irreversible. I asked the guys to work flat out and we had it off before the next shift came on, with the replacement elevator ready to go on. Faced with that, the other shift put the new elevator on and sent the aircraft out. It fixed the problem and I went to see the workshop who had overhauled the control. They were surprised but accepted that somehow it had not been balanced correctly.

Some years later, while flying a Robin 400 light aircraft, I found that while in descent and doing about 120 knots the wings wagged up and down and I could feel it in the control column. I reported it to the owner but never heard what they found. However, I associated that with another possible balance problem.

I was sent down to Bangui in the Central African Republic to change a cockpit left side main window which had broken. Well aware that the two windows, left and right, were not interchangeable, I took great care to carry the right part number. The arrangement was that I had to pick one up in a crate from Southend Airport then take it, my kit and my toolbox to Le Bourget where I was to get an Air Afrique flight to Bangui. By the time I got to Paris there was only about five hours to check-in for the flight so I sat it out in the terminal.

The flight down was marked by bad food and indifference from the cabin crew. After a bit of hassle from Bangui customs who wanted to be given some money to allow me to take the crate into the country, I got it to the aircraft. The old one was ready to remove so, 36 hours after first starting work in UK, I opened the crate and yes, that's right, it was the wrong one.

Someone else was dispatched to bring out another and after a night's rest I was told to go on to Kinshasa in Zaire to help with a propeller problem. I arrived to find not only the propeller needing attention but one of the main undercarriage shock struts had just blown its seals and would also need fixing. This was the biggest problem yet because to extract the main oleo and reseal it I would need a full set of very large jacks and to raise the aircraft 48 inches above the ground to do the undercarriage retraction checks. We got on with what we could and in the meantime, another aircraft brought a set of jacks out to us.

This drama had now involved a third of our fleet. To assemble the jacks needed the use of the crane we had used to remove the propeller. Once they were ready for use I jacked the aircraft up and completed the gear reseal job, all the while nervously looking at the weather. A thunderstorm could gust at 30 knots and that could spell disaster for 90 tons of aircraft balancing on jacks.

This saga took several days and we were accommodated in the Kinshasa International Hotel. In the hotel was a casino and the engine fitter I worked with did very well on the roulette wheel. His profits from gambling came in very handy because on my second day, returning from the airfield after dark, we were stopped at a Zairean Army road block. The soldier on my side of the car tapped the barrel of his AK47 on the window so I obliged by opening it. Their army had not been paid for a while and, as was their custom, they exhorted their pay from the population. He said something in pidgin French to me which roughly translated into "you must give me some cash". A fistful of dirty money from the casino went a long way towards helping the soldier's predicament and we were allowed to go on our way.

Another time, I had an undercarriage leg go flat but this time it was a nose oleo and it had a little pressure left in it so that there was just enough extension to wrap some rope round it to prevent it from bottoming out on landing. The crew went along with it and we limped back into base for a permanent fix.

I was sent out to Hong Kong to certify a periodic check on one of our aircraft which had got stuck there with a persistent electrical antiskid brake problem. It was on the ground for so long that even the calendar extension granted for the check had been overrun, so TMAC had no option but to contract the check to the maintenance company there. Two other licensed engineers and myself would certify the work done by the Chinese.

Flying out on a BOAC Boeing 707, the aircraft swung momentarily in the cruise and I sensed that the crew had shut down an engine. Sure enough we diverted into Bombay to replace a burst oil pipe and then continued on our way.

We had been booked into a hotel on Nathan Road in Kowloon called the Chungking Mansions. It was a real doss-house. Not knowing any better, we just got on with it but I found later that the crews were using much better hotels, so someone saved a bit of money there.

All was not well in Hong Kong. The work being done was an absolute shambles, and any question put to the Chinese engineers came back with a big smile and "yes". Paperwork had been completed and on inspection I found repeatedly that the part related to the job was still not reassembled. It was clear that they could do it if they wished but not until enough man hours had been booked on the job to give them a nice profit. The labour force was run by a very powerful Chinese manager who even the expatriate directors of the company would not argue with. So I went to see him and explained what we needed. He listened but was not offering to be helpful.

I got the message and called TMAC to say this was going to need some cash to sort it out otherwise the job was going to take a lot longer. The firm's answer was that they were not going to get involved in under the counter payments. The job drifted on and took another week. Suddenly our time was up and they had got the man-hours target they wanted. Overnight, everything was completed and the aircraft released to us.

Towards the end of my ground time with TMAC, in 1975, I did an instructor course and delivered a CAA approved programme for people aspiring to add the CL44 to their CAA engineer's licence. That was an introduction to instructing that was to form a large part of my subsequent career in aviation.

CHAPTER SEVEN

Hangar to Cockpit

Our CL44 ploughed along through the Intertropical Convergence Zone. The ITCZ runs across Africa and is an area of intense thunderstorms. Bad weather here is common. We were out of Lagos, Nigeria for Blantyre, Malawi for a return load of tea.

It was night and few of the navigation aids were functioning. Those that did were corrupted by night effect which made them inaccurate, or thunderstorms which pulled the navigation indicators to point at the nearest storm. There was a navigator on the crew but he could not get any star shots because we could not climb high enough to get out of cloud. The radar, useless as ever, failed to indicate where the storms were and we flew by eye, steering between the lightning flashes. I was now a flight engineer on the CL44 and this was adding to my flight experience. All the anti-ice systems were working overtime.

The VHF radio frequencies remained unresponsive to our callsign. Either they had closed or more likely the static had killed our reception. We had to admit we were at least temporarily unsure of our position. That is aviation code for 'lost'.

Our co-pilot tried HF radio and Johannesburg Control came booming in. At least we could tell someone where we thought we were. Not that the man in Jo`burg could do anything to help us. Eventually we stumbled out of the weather and found Blantyre.

On that trip, my experience as an F/E was fairly minimal. I had the utmost faith in the pilots and navigator. Later in life when I became a pilot myself, I realised that losing one's position was not going to be corrected except by a lot of rational, hard work but at the time, I just

thought the whole thing was just a huge adventure. I was so interested in it all, being afraid never crossed my mind.

In 1976 I had taken another career move. It was a natural progression from maintenance engineer to flight engineer and many took this route.

It was not a planned change at all, in fact the chief flight engineer sought me out and asked me if I wanted to become a flight engineer on the CL44. I said, yes I was interested, but I would have to ask my (by then) second wife what she thought. After all, it was going to involve a lot of time away. Our chief engineer was not a man to dwell on niceties and told me in no uncertain terms, "Don't effing ask her, effing tell her". Anyway, I asked her.

My training as a flight engineer followed a detailed medical by the CAA and sitting an exam for what was called the 'O' Licence, which examined the candidate on all the aircraft systems.

There was no simulator for the type so all our base training was done in real time, bashing some quiet airfield circuit and doing stalls and decompressions at high altitudes. We practised decompressions and smoke removal at 17000 feet. The pilots would go on oxygen and I would depressurise the cabin.

Once that was done I was trained to take out the over wing hatches to simulate smoke removal. I was not on oxygen or on a safety line so taking the hatch out at 170 knots, peering at the clouds scudding over the wings then refitting the hatch was a bizarre thing to be doing.

Since we had to do it all with systems running the instructor would pull circuit breakers to fail gauges and you were expected to see this pretty sharpish to prove your systems scan was good. My trainer would snap his fingers behind my head for the fun of it, just to keep me scanning. The finger clicking sounded just like a circuit breaker being pulled.

The chief flight engineer was hard to please. If I was not up to snuff he would prod me hard in the back just above the shoulder blades. If you could take that without losing your cool, you could take anything that was thrown at you. On take-off, after setting the power, he made me write down all the engine parameters and there were 16 gauges to read. As we would be airborne in about 30 seconds, it was virtually impossible. I'm sure it was for his amusement but it made me consider every indication on take-off and in hindsight it did me no harm at all.

Many people read the newspapers or listen to the news and an incident involving an aircraft is reported as "the pilot" did something or other. The press does a poor job of reporting aviation. One example would be: "the aircraft were parked on the runway". That being so, no-one would subsequently land or take off since some twit had parked his aircraft on it. Of course, when "the pilot" has saved everyone from crashing and burning, there are usually two pilots on board, so our hero should rightly have to share the accolade with the other bloke. This will often be reported incorrectly, giving all the credit to one person, not the crew as a whole.

In my day, the crew often comprised captain, first officer, flight engineer and possibly a navigator. To that complement there may also have been a load master. Short haul aircraft, being simpler, would usually have just two pilots. While most people would understand that a navigator navigates – that is, to figure out where we are and how to steer the ship where we intend to be, less may be known about the loadmaster.

If we needed to have another load on return or supervise an offload we carried a loadmaster. These guys would sometimes never get to the hotel; if they did, it might only be for a few hours. They would sleep on the rest bunk while we flew and then they would be possibly supervising loading and unloading for the whole 12 hours we took as a rest period between flights. The loadmaster compiled the load sheet and ensured the cargo was stored so that the aircraft was in balance. Our "loadies" in TMAC could be trusted. In addition, if we as F/E`s needed a hand to fix some problem they could always be relied on to lend a hand. In an operation such as ours, they were indispensable.

A flight engineer's task was to manage the systems: fuel, engines, hydraulics, electrical power, pressurisation and air conditioning. He also monitored the pilot`s flying and navigation. This last responsibility was not a formal part of a flight engineer's training, but all forward-thinking operators involved us, and any cock-up by the pilots was our fault as well for not bringing it to their attention.

Apart from running the systems, all the normal checklists were performed together with the rest of the crew when requested. When things went wrong, the F/E would read the abnormal or emergency checklist to the pilots and he became very much the manager of the procedure. In my early days on the CL44 and Boeing 707, systems often failed and the checklists came out regularly.

Later, on the Douglas DC10, things very seldom failed and it was possible to become complacent. However, when things did go wrong on the DC10, it could involve up to three or more checklists. A hydraulic failure could take you through a checklist that sorted that problem out, then a fuel dump to get weight and speed reduced to enable lift devices to be deployed with less hydraulic capacity, followed by the checklist to get the unusual flap setting out for landing and ensuring the airframe drivers had the right speeds set for landing. All that took 45 minutes on average and required some forward tactical thinking about when to perform significant checklist items. For instance, dumping fuel too early was regarded as a bad thing in case you left yourself short of the motion lotion, yet you had to get it done before the landing configuration was attempted.

While an emergency is being dealt with by execution of the checklist, the roles of each member of the crew are well defined. Typically, the captain hands over control of the aircraft and radios to the first officer. As the F/E progresses through the checklist the captain is ideally situated to be able to look over his right shoulder and monitor the F/E as he carries out the actions on his panel. All the time the others keep the F/O in the loop so he knows what is going on. When the checklist is completed and 'normal crew' procedures return, then the pilots revert to their usual roles of one flying and the other operating the radios.

An example of this crew procedure happened in 1982 when a BA Boeing 747 flew into an ash cloud near Java and ash build-up in the engines caused all four to flame out. As the pilots used the autopilot to glide down at the correct speed for a relight, the F/E went through the checklist for relighting those engines until he got them going again. Although all the engines had suffered some damage, one was too sick to continue to run so in conjunction with the pilots, he shut that one down and reconfigured the services to operate on the remaining three engines. The captain received an award for the safe handling of the aircraft, yet I know he would be the first to say that it was a crew effort. Not many people would be aware of what the F/E did.

I have been in many airline cockpits doing flight audits and it is quite common to find that the older guys had flown with a flight engineer. They invariably say that they miss having the specialist on board to handle the problems for them. The F/E would also locate the cheapest bar nearest to the hotel, so he was missed for other reasons as well.

To return to life at TMAC, the CL44 was modelled on the Bristol Britannia. It was rumoured that Canadair had obtained a Britannia and had run their tape measure over it before going back to the drawing boards. What Canadair made was something simpler albeit with a swing tail that opened up 105 degrees as well as a forward cargo door. They also made the electrics simpler and utilized a hydraulics system with a lower pressure. Instead of a Bristol Proteus engine Canadair installed the Rolls Royce Tyne. While capable of greater power the Tyne was not without its problems.

Though TMAC experimented with a pallet-loading roller mat system, the system itself took one and a half tons of payload away so it was usually dispensed with. Instead the aircraft was bulk loaded with 9G nets erected between each bay. Labour to load or offload was not expensive down route and the crew usually took minimum rest with the aircraft, departing the next day.

The unusual cargo loading from the tail ensured we had some odd loads. We had several charters to carry ship propeller shafts. These could weigh in excess of 15 tons in one lump and were mounted on steel girders to spread the load throughout the aircraft floor. I once had a trip from Sweden carrying a load of wooden telegraph poles for the Gulf. Apparently, some-one had goofed on the amount needed and they had to be flown out immediately to put things right.

There was an engine propeller synchronising system but it was useless. Any power changes meant the flight engineers adjusting the engines to set the props in harmony. Whenever the cabin was empty the harmonics of the aircraft started a vibration at the front, then running all the way down the cabin to the back end with all the cargo fittings jingling as it went.

As I had a background in maintaining the aircraft type I was made a line trainer/checker after six months and a type examiner a couple of years later. I learned a lot more about flight operations from evaluating more experienced engineers. As a line trainer, it was my job to provide training on the routes we operated on after they had completed the ground school. Usually, that took a few months. The F/E under training operated the systems in the F/E seat and I coached him from the spare, observer's seat beside him in the cockpit. When he was adjudged to be competent, the line check was carried out by another training F/E who would be an examiner. Every six months there were more checks carried out on the F/E by a line checker or an examiner. As an examiner, I had the authority to test F/Es for the addition of the type rating on their licence. The pilots had the same kind of requirements.

The company had an F/E who was always getting into trouble on his check flights and I was told to go and fail him on his next check. I did not accept that order and told the boss that if he wanted someone else to fail him, he should go ahead and find another examiner. If I was going to do it, and if the candidate did OK, then I was not going to fail him.

After some discussion, the boss told me to go and do it my way, so I met the guy and had a chat about it all. It seemed that when he was being examined, he tended to lose his composure and do something stupid. There go most of us, I thought. So I asked him to act as if completely in charge of the event, to regard it as a performance, as if he were on stage. He did as I asked and was OK, so I signed him up as a pass. I do think sometimes that when we are crumbling under the stress of things, a bit of 'acting' goes a long way. As one well known wordsmith wrote, "All the world's a stage and all men and women merely players. They have their exits and entrances. And one man in his time plays many parts."

After the aforementioned night meander along the lines of latitude to Blantyre, we checked into a hotel downtown on the main street. Following a few hours' sleep I took a wander down the street but within a block I was accosted by lepers who were begging and in pretty poor condition. I beat a hasty retreat back to the hotel.

That night we took off for the return leg with a load of tea, in the plywood tea chests we have all used for house moving. Climbing out to the north over Lake Malawi, ATC wanted us to report level at our cruise attitude for the handover to the next flight information boundary. It was hot, we were heavy and our climb rate was slow so the captain told them we were at the boundary and lied about the altitude. There was no ATC Radar and no other traffic. A little white lie, making life easier.

We gave a lift to an agricultural expert who had just spent six months in Malawi. He had taught the farmers how to rotate their crops and the use of fertilisers to quadruple their output. With the money gained from the surplus harvest not needed for their families, they were encouraged to use the extra cash to buy essentials to improve their lives. His education programme involved revisiting the villages to check on progress. This he did and found that the farmers had done as he suggested, but in realising they achieved the usual crop by farming only one quarter of the land, had not bothered with the rest of it and sat about in the village bar. Enough being enough, he upped and left.

The routes were Africa, mainly Lagos and a route through to Hong Kong. The Lagos route with the occasional one to Kano was bread and butter to a cargo airline. Other single destination charters would come up and make life interesting. In Lagos, we stayed in a company rest house not far from the airport which served as the offices on the ground floor with the crew bedrooms up a flight of stairs above the offices. We used to take our own food and drink for the night and leave the next day. At the foot of the stairs a night watchman would sleep with an evil looking Panga in his hand to deter robbers.

At Lagos, arriving after sunrise we were often directed into the hold because Lagos ATC did not recognise our landing permit number. A call on company radio would get one of our ground staff to whip up to the tower office with some readies and we were cleared to land.

One night we were plodding down Africa for Lagos, when I heard on the radio that the runway was blocked. The first officer was asleep so I quietly informed the captain who decided we would run down to within 100 miles of the airport and, if it was still closed, we would turn right and divert to Cotonou in Benin. He added how much more fun it would be if we did not tell the first officer, so we briefed ourselves on what we intended to do to get to Cotonou while our other pilot slept. The first officer was not one of our favourites.

At 100 miles, the runway still being blocked, we swung into action and amused ourselves by watching the first officer struggle to catch up with what was going on. Not very professional of us. We were granted a cool reception at Cotonou, the aircraft being boarded by armed troops who obviously took our four man crew and load of cargo to be a threat to national security. We were rewarded by rooms in one of the worst hotels I have ever encountered, which experienced a power cut one hour after we arrived.

On one trip, the captain had great misgivings about flying with a certain first officer who had, it would appear, such bouts of depression that we thought he might be tempted to end it all while he was flying his leg. The captain did not want to take the F/O's flying leg from him because it was thought that he might get upset by it. I was requested to get the fire axe near to hand and if he did anything to kill us all, to hit him on the head with it.

My seat as the engineer, was immediately behind the first officers. I eyed the fire axe. There was a blade with a spike on the back of the blade. Should I hit him with the spike or the blade? In the end, I thought the flat of the blade should disable him sufficiently.

Well, it never came to it thank goodness. Quite how a court of law would have seen it if we had clobbered him I do not know. I assume the concerns were voiced to the management but it seemed bizarre that we had even contemplated doing such a thing.

Our crew was tasked to position a CL44 from Stansted to a maintenance base but before that we had the company's permission to participate in a flying display at Blackbushe on the Surrey / Hampshire borders. The captain, Keith Sissons, was a seasoned display pilot having flown the Boeing B17 *Sally B* and an American Consolidated PBY Catalina. He gave us a briefing which outlined to us what the display pattern would comprise. For me, the main responsibility would be that when more or less power was called, I was to handle the throttles and look after the engines.

We flew down to Blackbushe and at the appointed time began our routine. This was out of the ordinary for a large four engine turboprop and Keith was hitting some huge bank angles. I was powering the engines up or down as ordered, keeping an eye inside on the airspeed and outside as the world whizzed by at low level.

On a run-in again towards the airfield was a line of pylons which caught my attention but we sailed over them with just enough clearance and banked mightily over the airfield again with lots of power on. Job done, we landed at the maintenance base and handed the aircraft to the engineers, which was probably a good move after we had wrung every last bit of performance out of it. We got a phone call from the organisers to thank us for our display. They said how exciting it was for them when we came from behind the trees and powered into the bank in front of the crowd line. I *thought* we were a bit low.

Our esteemed chief pilot was one Captain James Cook, a rangy pipe-smoking gentleman who was held in high regard by all of us.

The company was given a charter to Sydney, Australia and as Jim was an Aussie, he naturally got to take the trip. After their arrival in Sydney, at the airport on the north shore of Botany Bay, the crew checked into the hotel. Rocking up to the desk Jim announced himself as having a reservation. The clerk asked him his name to which Jim said, "James Cook, Captain James Cook" to which the clerk asked him if he was taking the piss.

Our chief flight engineer was Dave Priest, who had it in for any ex RAF officers he met as in his RAF service as he only ever made Senior Aircraftsman and he had a chip on his shoulder about it. Dave was a hard taskmaster but respected if not feared. Many of us still regard him with affection. He took no prisoners but you worked willingly for him. I later met him by accident and learned that he was living in

Portsmouth. We agreed to get in touch but I regret it was not to be. A few years later I learned he had passed away.

One night in some hot and humid handling agent's office in Africa, we sat it out, waiting for a delayed inbound aircraft. A local with good hearing, rather like Radar O`Riley in the TV series MASH, burst in and triumphantly announced to the captain: "The wind lorry is coming". The captain gravely thanked him for the news.

Cruising north and south over Africa at night seemed to be a lot of what we did. Between the North African coast and the more populated regions at the equatorial belt seemed to take forever with nothing to do or look at while we bored along in the blackness. We called it "The Great F**k All" or "The MMBA", which stood for Miles and Miles of Bloody Africa.

One night I was just gazing out into a moonlit sky when a Douglas DC8-54 slipped past at our level in the opposite direction with no lights on. I registered it in a fleeting moment and it was gone, silently flashing past out right wingtip. Just enough moonlight existed for identification, even to the extent of what model of DC8 it was. The convention was for all aircraft to broadcast position and level on the common frequency of 126.9, but we had not heard anything from him. I guess he was gun-running or something illegal and was keeping quiet.

We had climbed out of Hong Kong routing for Bangkok. It was incredibly hot and, due to our weight, our initial altitude was limited to 12,000 feet. At that level, there was thick cloud. Navigation beacons behind us faded into oblivion as we bore along to the Southwest on the best heading we had. The Navigator behind me was making frequent trips to the astro navigation sight but he had no chance to get a star shot to establish our position with certainty. He was getting a bit uptight.

Eventually we burned a bit more fuel off so I increased to climb power and the aircraft clawed its way up another couple of thousand feet. Finding ourselves still in cloud, we stuck with the calculated heading and waited for a landfall. The idea was to avoid both the Chinese island of Hainan and also North Vietnam since to blunder into that would have meant interception by the US or worse still, a North Vietnamese MIG. Our position reports were estimates since we did not have a precise fix and Saigon ATC radar did not see us yet.

Eventually we emerged from the weather and took a star shot. Simultaneously, we obtained a landfall using our barely functioning weather radar in mapping mode. All eyes were focussed on some coastal lights. The navigator exclaimed "F**k me, Da Nang" so we made a hasty left turn and beat down to the south to get to our correct waypoint before we were challenged.

Modern navigation provides extraordinary accuracy and is often based on three independent units so if one is inaccurate the other two serve to identify the dodgy one. Even by the time of our navigation problem out of Hong Kong, there were Inertial Navigation Units, closely followed by the now ubiquitous satellite Global Positioning Systems.

We were fitted with neither of these super bits of kit, hence the navigator flew with us on routes where there were few ground beacons. He needed to get his fixes by sun or stars. If that option was obscured by weather, then it was back to dead reckoning where the intended track was steered by a heading which was offset against the assumed wind drift. Winds aloft were stronger than predicted and had resulted in a gross error of the magnitude we achieved that night.

The normal route to Hong Kong was usually a load to one of the Gulf States, then empty through Bangkok to Hong Kong for a load of clothing. Return flights were usually through Bangkok again, Karachi, Istanbul and then up to Europe to drop off part loads wherever it was required before returning to Stansted. The aircraft would often turn round in Maastricht with a team of ground engineers flown out for the purpose, something I had been sent to do while still a ground engineer. After a turnaround involving cargo offload and reload while the engineers serviced the aircraft and fixed the snags, it then went back out on the route again.

In my time as a ground engineer, TMAC had a De Havilland Dove, a little twin piston engine aircraft with Gypsy Queen Engines. We had enough seats in it for a working party with tools and spare parts and were flown out to Maastricht from Stansted to do the turnaround check on the CL44 and then return in a day.

The pilot was one of our loadmasters. As there was no toilet on board, we managed to relieve ourselves by kneeling down at the doorway and peeing through the gap at the bottom.

As well as the more regular destinations there were loads for various airports in Iraq and Iran. In fact, there was no limit to where we would go if we could win the contract.

This was superb flying although it was hard work. There was no support along the way; if something fixable broke, we fixed it. If it was not fixable, it might not be declared in the aircraft log until we got back.

There were only 39 CL44`s produced and 13 of those were made for the Royal Canadian Air Force and designated the Yukon. Of the 26 civil aircraft, they started out as passenger aircraft but were swiftly relegated to cargo work due to the introduction of far superior jet aircraft like the Boeing 707. Not many survived without mishap. In my time on the CL44 we lost two. Many more were lost flying in hostile surroundings operating in less well-regulated environments. One website I looked at shows 10 of the 26 written off in accidents by the year 2000. There was also a limited production of the stretched version which was designated the 'J' model.

The CL44 "Guppy" was a conversion of the standard aircraft which provided a much larger fuselage. It suffered from a lack of performance which was no surprise, typically operating 4,000ft below the comparative ability of the conventional aircraft and about four tonnes less payload.

The "Guppy" settled into the flare above the runway at Nassau but something was not quite right. The aircraft settled hard and bounced. What followed was what in the business is called Pilot Induced Oscillation. This occurs when the pilot gives control inputs to get the nose angle adjusted when not in sympathy with the dynamics of the aircraft and, worse still, is half a second out. We got into PIOs. Another problem soon manifested itself. We found ourselves in a phugoid bounce, where if nothing is done to correct the phenomenon, the bounce gets higher and higher while airspeed gets lower and lower. Eventually Newton's force of gravity will endure over Bernoulli's theory of lift.

On the second encounter with the runway we hit hard. Very hard. Once more we rose and with no more inputs to our aircraft other than PIOs we were destined to hit much harder than the first two. Something in my engineering background told me that the next arrival was likely to smash the main landing gears up through the wings.

My cockpit discipline took off and my assertion replaced it so I shouted, "Go around for f**ks sake!" while starting to open up the power levers.

Propellers are wonderful things in that condition and the engine spools up fast, throwing great gulps of wind over the wings and

creating shedloads more lift. This caused our next potentially disastrous descent to flatten out and the pilot greased it on as if nothing had gone awry in the first place.

I classed that encounter with *terra firma* as a hard landing and carried out the check the next day, which should have been a day off for me. The pilots had their day off, though. Nothing was found bent. The CL44 could take quite a beating. As for what I learned from it, I believe it instilled in me, and in my pilot career – still some years away – the ability to recognise when the landing has gone to rats and when to power up and climb away for another try.

The CL44 Guppy boomed down the runway at Stansted and the airspeed steadily rose to 110 knots and then stayed there. Runway was being eaten up pretty quick now and we were all aware of something unusual taking place. I had the engines delivering the power calculated and nothing had gone wrong in my department.

We were past the decision speed to stop but did not have the speed to fly the aircraft. The road at the western end was getting pretty close and the light wooden boundary fence, plus the approach lights behind it, seemed destined to be our next contact. Now there was no runway left to abort the take-off. Our captain, by now simultaneously out of good ideas and runway, hauled it off and the aircraft wallowed into the air.

At that very moment, the air speed indicators kicked up another 20 knots. The obstacles passed under the main wheels by a few feet but we were climbing. A quick discussion followed about what was wrong. I offered the observation that the elevator controls had been worked on before we departed and asked if the control felt OK. It did but we were still none the wiser. The captain said that he intended to go back to land. I needed to dump some 10 tons of fuel to get us back to landing weight so prepared for that but he was having none of it and we came round the circuit and landed at maximum take-off weight. We settled onto the runway again without the slightest bounce.

Naturally we were going nowhere that day because the aircraft needed an overweight landing check. The decision was made to unload all the cargo and reweigh it: it was accurate to within a few hundred pounds, which was pretty good.

In 1978 we did not fully understand the phenomenon of wind shear. Nowadays, it is practised on simulators everywhere. Even if we were trained to understand it better, there was nothing in the sky that overcast day in December to alert us to it. No-one before or after our hazardous departure experienced what we did. Yet the only explanation left was that we had been caught in a downdraft followed by a tailwind which left us able to increase our ground speed but not our airspeed. When we lurched into the air we found the wind on the nose once more and broke the surly bonds of earth.

When people ask me if there was there ever an occasion in my flying career when I thought I was going to die, that episode always comes to mind. A fiery heap on the end of runway might have been the outcome.

We had some real odd balls in TMAC. Most of the crews were self-improvers or out of the military. No-one in their right mind would leave a good airline to be a freight animal.

Crew Resource Management was not yet born and some of our captains had a bad attitude to other people. One such guy infamous for his bad manners and bushy beard shouted back at the loadmaster to bring him a can of Coke. The loadmaster did as he was told but not before giving the can a real good shake. When the captain tugged the ring pull to open it Coke went all over him, dripping off his beard and the cockpit roof above him. Cue lots of muffled sniggering from the rest of us.

Another strange episode occurred in Hong Kong. I had to change my hotel room because it had not been serviced so I swopped it and changed the alarm call to the new room number. Waking with a start to find that I had not had a call, I ran downstairs as fast as possible to find the crew had gone to the airport already. When I caught up with them, my aircraft had its engines running and was being pushed back for departure.

Asking the ground crew to stop it and put some steps up so I could board, I told the captain that I needed to do a pre-flight inspection before I was going anywhere, but he would not accede to shutting the engines down. So I was obliged to walk round the aircraft with the propellers turning and check my panel as best I could. The rest of the crew sat in fearful silence. What a way to run a cockpit. Would he really have departed without me?

Another old chap, who was reputed to have only one lung, would smoke incessantly in flight and then when he felt a bit short of breath, take the mask off the oxygen tube and stick the tube straight into his mouth. That was bad enough, but he had a lit cigarette in the other hand. In those days the captain was God. It's good those days are over.

The company was a bit cavalier at times as well. On one trip to Tehran with a load of beds destined for a hotel, we were told that the handling agent would have our hotel rooms fixed by the time we landed, so off we went. On arrival, we opened the tail up for the agents to unload and then learned there were no rooms available because of some festival or other. Undaunted, we set off in a taxi to do the rounds of hotels in Tehran but drew a blank. The taxi driver suggested we might go to a brothel and get the women to leave us so we could sleep but that did not appeal to us very much. So, we ended up sleeping on the stacks of beds in the back of the aircraft wearing our raincoats. It was a cold night and the tail was open with no way to close it because we had no external power available. Come the morning a very miserable crew huddled in the cockpit while the cargo was unloaded. There was nothing for it but to fly somewhere else so we went to Baghdad and got some rest.

At the beginning of 1979 the Iranian revolution deposed the Shah and brought an end to the Pahlavi dynasty. The population apparently turned out in their thousands to welcome the Ayatollah Khomeini back from exile in Paris to return the country to an Islamic government. Before that, our flights to Tehran and other Iranian cities had been fairly straightforward, but as the new government formed around the Ayatollah, contracts with the West were reduced and eventually ceased.

We had been carrying a lot of goods, largely for hotel construction. Some loads were undelivered so we still had a few flights to complete.

One destination was Kish Island near Bandar Abbas, across the straits of Hormuz from Dubai. On arrival at Kish, it was clear that the Shah had operated it as a huge holiday camp for government ministers. There were hotels and villas for dignitaries. We were given a case of beer and taken to a villa on the beach. On a nearby sand bar was a wrecked dhow which still had its name plate on the stern. I grabbed a screwdriver and prised it off for a souvenir. Engraved on it was 'Shahin of Kish'. There were also golf courses on the island. I wondered if the mullahs in the new government enjoyed the facilities and what their handicap was.

We had aircraft on different registrations for various reasons. One aircraft was on the Swiss and another on the Hong Kong registers. It was a way round restrictions on operating rights. The "Guppy" was on the American register because no-one else except the Irish would accept it. Crews were given validations to their licences to make it legal.

The "Guppy" was maintained on the US Federal Aviation Authority system and needed to have a Daily Release for flight. This needed a US Airframe and Powerplant Mechanics Licence so I was dispatched to Los Angeles to undertake a course to qualify for one. It took me two weeks at Van Nuys airport. I did the crash course for the A & P Licence which was made possible by the US system of learning followed by sitting the exam after studying hundreds of possible questions published by the FAA. Thanks to my background and reasonable short-term memory, I passed the exams.

The final part was an assessment and practical test by an examiner. That was rather fun. I had arranged to meet a chap who was quite a character. Tracking him down to his little hangar at Van Nuys, he eked out a meagre living fixing light aircraft. He was impressed with my background so did not bother to ask me very much. Most of the time was spent either chatting about Africa, where he had spent some airline time, or in examining his African souvenirs and holding his dog's head for him so he could treat its ear canker.

Instead of a practical examination involving setting up magneto timing and other mysteries, he opted to give me some sample welding and riveted repairs for my opinion. As the riveted repair was a real mess and the welding had vaporised more material than it joined together it was easy to give an opinion about what was wrong. The right answer was that I would not certify that standard of work and I duly gave him my decision. I came away with an A&P. Now I was a licensed aircraft engineer on both sides of the pond and was able to operate as an F/E on the Guppy and sign the Daily Release.

The Guppy tail opened like the other CL44`s but being a much larger diameter, the tail joint inflated seal was always giving trouble. Tail seals on all the CL44`s would occasionally take a hit from a fork lift and they were normally found covered in bicycle inner tube repair patches. When the seal on the Guppy was in poor condition and leaking, it would fail to hold the cabin pressure and as we climbed the cabin would climb up with us. My repair scheme was to remove the foam from the loadmaster's seat in the cabin and cut those into long slices.

Armed with these and the crowbar I would descend through the floor hatch in the tail area and feed the foam into the gap working my way round the circumference of the fuselage until I could feel cabin pressure building up in my ears. Usually there would be a relayed message from pilots through the loadmaster that we were OK now and to come back up to the flight deck. On arrival at the destination, I would go out and snatch up my foam strips that fell out as the loadmaster opened the tail to unload the cargo as I would need those strips on the way back.

Many years later, the Guppy, N447T arrived at Bournemouth and, being virtually abandoned, gently mouldered away. After some time, a company reputed to be Australian assumed ownership and they took the engines off for servicing. At that point no-one expected the engines to be returned but to confound the critics, the engines were refitted and a major programme undertaken to restore the old girl to flying condition. At the time of writing it has been taxied and looks good. Visiting Bournemouth recently to renew my Instrument Rating, I saw what a good job someone had made so I enquired of the company taking care of it about who I might call and congratulate him on a job well done.

I was given a number and called it. The recipient of my call very defensively asked who I was and what I wanted. Not to be put off, I briefly said that I was impressed with what he had done and mentioned that I had been a flight engineer on N447T for some time. The man said that he was not looking for flight engineers and I retorted that I was not offering to be one. At that moment it appeared the conversation was over so with a quick goodbye I hung up. The next day I accidentally redialled his number.

Mr Angry said, "Who's that?" Not having intended to call him, I was at first a bit nonplussed, but realising my error and recognising the voice I said something to the effect that it was a redial in error and apologised. The answer was, "You're a pain in the arse, aren`t you?" and hung up before I could express a similar sentiment.

Good luck anyway, Pal.

On another occasion, we had arrived in Maastricht early in the morning and retired to the hotel having spent days on the Hong Kong route. Breakfast was a wind down with a few gin and tonics.

I had only had an hour or so of sleep when the captain was knocking on my door to say that lawyers were going to seize the aircraft and we had to get it back to Stansted pronto. There followed a flight best not repeated. We were as sharp as doughnuts but fortunately we picked up each other's mistakes and arrived back at Stansted without mishap.

In September 1977, CL44 GATZH climbed out of Hong Kong with a full load of cargo bound for Bangkok. As it left the runway there was

a muffled explosion and the number 4 engine blew apart. The crew could see the engine had failed, the abnormal readings were enough to show it and the aircraft needed a bunch of rudder trim to keep it straight. To add to the difficulty, then came a fire warning. The first bottle of extinguishant was fired at the engine and they timed the interval to see if the fire warning persisted. Fire still on, second bottle fired. No change.

Descending back down to 2000 feet for an emergency return to land, the fire by now was out of control and had begun to spread back to the wing. Another force more catastrophic than the first now wrenched the starboard outer wing apart.

There was a transmission from the crew. It said, "We`re going in – the engine`s come off". The aircraft fell out of control in a fireball into the harbour by Waglan Island. Four crew members were on board. Only two bodies were recovered. The locals in their sampans were soon there, plucking clothing from the cargo out of the water. The aircraft settled into the muddy bottom at about 100 feet. Most if it is still there.

GATZH was, for some time, a spare in the fleet and had become a 'Christmas Tree' providing spare parts for the other aircraft. Later, the company decided to restore it to operational status and led by a very able engineer at Stansted, it was rebuilt to flying condition. This was without doubt the best CL44 in the world, the team had made a superb job of it, but it had the worst Number 4 engine. There was a suspicion that the engine compressor had failed but as it was never recovered it was not proven.

An engine high pressure turbine is a powerful beast when it breaks apart and even modern jets have trouble when one of those lets go. Secondary damage often occurs. This one had a fuel fed fire which would not go out. It was also surmised that the air system valves were not sufficiently fire proof and had failed to contain the fire which got into the wing through the ducting and eventually ignited the fuel tanks. After that had happened there was no return.

If the engine bearings are distressed and there is a possibility of a turbine or compressor failure it would normally be evident on the scavenge oil temperature gauges. These important indicators were badly situated at the aft end of the F/E panel and hence on take-off, when you really wanted to monitor them, not in one's scan. Even before this event, I was trained to glance back at them as soon as I had set the power. After the loss of the aircraft, I made doubly sure that engineers checked them on the take-off run when I was doing any training or examining. That lesson instilled itself into my consciousness as a pilot in later years.

The company did have another similar experience but that time they put the fire out. I saw that engine and it had nodded down about two degrees as the engine mounts began to sag.

The memorial service in Stansted was attended by as many crew who were able, starting off in the pub. That's how it's done in aviation.

I had a few engine shut downs on the CL44. On one sector, we climbed up to altitude and I found the number 3 engine propeller would not come back to cruise RPM. I had the power lever all the way back to idle but the prop was still thrashing along at climb speed. I had heard stories about runaway propellers that had a propensity to continue flight by themselves and I did not want that to happen to me. I had to convince the captain that it was unsafe to continue to operate it like that. Quite how he thought he was going to land with one engine at cruise power I didn't know. We shut it down. The ground engineers worked on it and found nothing definite so released it for service. On the next leg it did the same so I shut down once more. It turned out the prop governor drive shaft had sheared and they missed it first time round.

On the way to Tripoli in 1977, we cruised happily over the Mediterranean when the captain's windscreen failed. Not quietly, but the outer pane shattering with a bang. The captain jumped out of his skin, but once we got ourselves in order we found that the other inner layer was still intact and there was no immediate danger. I reduced the cabin pressure to relieve the stress on it while we decided what to do – or rather, where to do it.

It was going to be my task have to change it when I ordered a new one sent out to us. Benghazi was on track but we had just passed Malta and I knew the RAF at Malta could supply me with the high steps which I was going to need to lift me up to the outside of the window. So Malta it was.

The next day, the loadmaster and I were busy removing the old screen. In the circuit was a B707 in Pakistan International Airways colours doing circuit training. Air Malta had just bought it and were doing conversion training with a number of crews on board. Their B707 did a run down the runway at about 500 feet and I noticed that all the gear doors were hanging vertically down.

I knew from my engineering time on the type that this meant the crew had lowered the gear in alternate, which meant there was some fault with the landing gear normal operating system. The main gears looked OK but as it passed me I could see the nose leg was swinging round in a way that suggested it had broken off from the attachments. Suddenly, there was a puff of hydraulic fluid and the whole nose leg fell off. The leg hit the ground at the intersection of the two runways and bounced about for a while. Looking up at the nose wheel well there was just a dark hole with nothing in it. Surreal. Now the aircraft needed to get down safely on the wheels it had left.

Some time passed while the crew dumped down to minimum fuel and burnt a bit more off as well. The RAF laid a foam carpet on the runway and the whole airfield came to attention waiting for the emergency landing. Retiring behind a wall on the edge of the parking area where I was working, just in case the thing got out of control, I observed the proceedings from a safe distance.

I need not have worried because it was a textbook landing and it came to a stop in a flurry of foam. Immediately, the doors opened and slides deployed. Everyone emerged without mishap. Within the hour the RAF salvage team had raised the aircraft nose onto a large trailer and towed it off. Moments later a squall of rain blew in from the Mediterranean and washed the runway clean. If I had not seen it all take place, I would not have believed it had happened. There was nothing to show any emergency had taken place. The airport re-opened for business as usual.

We had an engine failure in Muscat and being on the slip crew waiting to take it onward, my crew was tasked the job of taking it back home on three engines. With the aircraft now unloaded, we departed on three and settled into the routine. For me it was not quite routine because I had a lot of fuel cross feeding and balancing to do but that just made it more interesting. The flight took about 13 hours, being a couple of hours longer than usual but in so doing, it cost us 3 tons of fuel less than normal. Our chairman, Mike Keegan, was so pleased about the fuel saved that he suggested that we shut one down all the time. Naturally we demurred on this fine suggestion.

TMAC had a series of flights from Bombay to Dubai carrying goats. This was local food for the festival of Eid which follows the end of Ramadan. The crew with the aircraft had run out of hours and my crew were airlined out to Bombay to operate the last flight.

We had a problem with the swing tail mechanism and I did not have the spares to fix it so we had a plan to offload the goats at Dubai by opening the rear passenger door and allowing the animals down a ramp onto the back of lorries to be transported away.

So, with the plan made, the pilots had gone off to the agent's office and I remained behind to check the engine oil levels and sort the paperwork. That job done, I was walking away from the aircraft when there was an almighty crunch and the aircraft sat back on its tail.

Now that the back door sill was a mere two or three feet from the ground, the goats were jumping out one by one and gathering in the shade under the port wing munching on scraps of paper blowing past in the breeze. I knew that eventually equilibrium would be restored and the whole thing would come back down on the nose gear. The trouble was that there was now a set of steps and a power unit under the nose and if the aircraft did not hit the ground in precisely the same spot the aircraft was going to suffer damage, so I had those moved away sharpish. When about 50 goats had assembled under the wing, sure enough, the ship crashed back down onto the nose leg. Luckily no harm was done that end, but the tail area had suffered several splits in the skin and a couple of buckled frames.

It transpired that the loadmaster had explained to the locals how we wanted the goats off so they opened all the pens up all the way down the cabin and shooed the whole lot to the tail end -180 goats weigh quite a few tons and that was too much for the balance of the aircraft.

There followed lots of telexes between us and base. I described the damage and we weighed up how long a repair in Dubai might take which I guessed would be about a week. So, they asked me if it was possible to ferry it home. Nowadays that would be an absolute no-no but there was a way.

Realising that we needed to make about 18,000 feet to get back in one leg – for fuel reasons and also to avoid bumping into high ground – with no scientific reasoning whatsoever, I surmised that with only half the usual cabin pressure and not flying any higher, we could do it. Since I had an engineering licence on the type which gave my idea some credibility, everyone was in favour. If things had gone wrong, no doubt I would have carried the can.

In the event I went back at regular intervals to check the structure and all I found was that the cracks had opened up a little under the cabin pressure, but it was holding up nicely. I could see the ground underneath through the split skin but it did not seem to be getting any worse. We got back OK.

I was on a crew that had been sent to Milan to take over a series of flights through Benghazi to Sebha next to the Chad border in Libya. Colonel Gaddafi was building a military base there and we flew 'Portacabins' down there in the Guppy.

The crew gathered together in the arrivals area at Milan with our cases and the captain went over to the airport bank to change a traveller's cheque for some taxi money. Our attention was taken up with admiring the local women and we paid no attention to the boss. There was a bit of an uproar when the boss found his briefcase bearing about £22,000 in $US and unsigned Travellers Cheques no longer at his feet. We looked around quickly and covered the exits but the briefcase, quite noticeably covered in hotel stickers, was not to be seen. We called the airport Carabinieri who slowly – rather too slowly, I thought – grasped what had gone on, but did nothing.

The handling agent knew the previous crew owed a lot of money to them and that we would be coming in with that and more. Credit cards did not exist at that time. It was a well-planned job and we all knew that if we had challenged the robbery, we may have come off rather badly. I am grateful to this day that I saw nothing and did not do anything heroic. The cheques were turning up all over Europe within 24 hours. This was no amateur effort.

Unable to pay for fuel and fees, we checked into a nice little hotel on the shores of Lake Maggiore and took the weekend off. We had no other choice, the banks were closed till Monday and no money meant no flights.

At the hotel, we made a thorough nuisance of ourselves by getting merry and nicking concrete gnomes from front gardens. The gnomes were used to decorate the balconies of our rooms. Fortunately for us we checked out before our misdemeanours had been discovered.

Once the financial hiatus had been eased by a bank transfer of funds, we resumed the flights into Libya. On arrival at Sebha there was very little in the way of airport facilities and our cargo of Portacabins appeared to be the nucleus of an airport terminal. On a hill nearby overlooking the airport was a French Foreign Legion fort, then not occupied by the legion but used instead to house Idi Amin, the ex-despot of Uganda. If he had any sanity left, he must have been bored witless.

During the Rhodesian guerrilla war in the late 1970's, the opposing parties in Mozambique and Zambia were being attacked by Rhodesian forces in retaliation for that country's civil aircraft being shot down by guerrillas armed with missiles.

In October 1978 Hawker Hunters of the Rhodesian Air Force conducted air attacks on guerrilla training camps outside Lusaka, the capital city of Zambia. The force leader called up Lusaka tower and told them that he would be taking over their airspace for a short while explaining that their issue was not with Zambia, but with the people threatening Rhodesia. The Prime Minister of Zambia, Kenneth Kaunda, subsequently appealed to the British government for a missile system to protect his capital from the Rhodesians and that is where TMAC came into it.

The UK agreed with the request and reportedly approached a cargo company in the UK to transport a missile system to Lusaka but were turned down. The issue for many of us was that we were sympathetic to the Rhodesians and did not want to be seen to doing anything against them. Whilst I was away on another flight, our company was approached by the UK Foreign Office to take the system to the Zambians. The rumour mill had it that the FO sent someone to the company and explained that the system would be virtually useless to the Zambians and moreover, it had been agreed upon by Ian Smith to keep Kaunda happy.

Subsequently, in January 1980, I was the F/E on the CL44 Guppy with a Tiger Cat missile system on board bound for Lusaka. When I got to the aircraft to begin my pre-flight, the loading was still in progress. The missile system had been brought from the army store at Catterick and apart from a fresh coat of olive drab paint, it did not look in very good shape. The system comprised wheeled units including a generator, mounted on what I would call a bomb trolley, a radar set, and a missile battery unit capable of firing the missiles themselves. Scores of missiles standing upright in open boxes comprised the ordnance. The wheels on the units themselves appeared to be locked solid with corrosion and would not rotate so were being dragged towards the aircraft by our forklifts.

Out of curiosity, I opened the radar cover and looked at the contents. The whole thing had been freshly sprayed inside and out in olive drab. What intrigued me was that wire cables appeared to have been joined up with masking tape.

After some delay, we got underway with the whole system in the fuselage and all the missiles standing in their boxes down the back end of the cabin. As we rattled our way down Africa, I could not help casting a doubtful eye on the missiles and wondering that if one did go out through the roof, whether we could survive the event.

Years later when I was regularly going to Lusaka once more, then in a BCAL B707, I used to look out for the missile battery on the way in, but I never saw it again.

I recall a flight from India with a collection of animals and some cargo thrown in for good measure. Right up front, just behind the cockpit door we had a young elephant.

This little guy stood about six feet tall at the shoulder and was encased in a teak cage built something like a collection of pallets nailed up around him. He was hobbled so could not move his feet but in his boredom decided to try and pull his cage to bits. By the time the loadmaster fetched me out of the flight deck, the elephant had smashed the cage to bits and was picking up lumps of broken teak with his trunk and throwing them about the cabin. We moved the bits out of his reach but he obstinately clung on to one bit and appeared to be mightily enjoying the whole experience. It took a sandwich to get him to release it. There was not much we could do about him and he stayed put until we landed, still hobbled and believing he could not go anywhere. He was quite a character, it was a shame to say goodbye.

We carried a lot of day-old chicks and stacked into the aircraft in their boxes, there was a real chance of overheating and losing some. In fact, we were insured for a percentage of losses. One day after loading them, we had a problem on start-up and despite having fans rigged up in the fuselage and having the tail and wing hatches open, the temperature soared. It was a desperate move but the ground engineers came out and moved as many of the boxes as we could to give them some fresh air. Seeing hairy-arsed engineers trying to revive little balls of yellow fluff was quite moving.

On one trip, we were flying north out of Muscat and the Sultan of Oman requested we carry two of his best camels to Amman as a present to the King of Jordan. The two camels were hobbled and loaded into open topped boxes with a cut-out at the front for their necks. We got them loaded easily with a fork lift but on arrival at Amman, we found the locals only had a crane, their fork lift having gone tech.

They put a couple of ropes round the camels' bodies next to the front and back legs and swung them out of the boxes into open topped lorries. Having a huge neck and head, the centre of gravity of the beast was not where they had hoped and the poor animals were swung off the aircraft with heads down and bums pointing at the sky. There was a lot of roaring from the camels, who did not like the experience one bit.

We carried breeding pigs to Lagos and two suffocated, having been trampled upon by the others. The Nigerian customs refused them entry as the dead pigs may have had a disease. Clearly, they needed some cash easement to accept that the pigs were not diseased, but as no-one did that, we carried our dead back to Stansted.

Another trip we had a load of sheep and the loadmaster and I shoved one into the cockpit and shut the door on it. Our captain was not amused.

In January 1980 we did series of flights from Bournemouth to Bucharest taking sections of BAC 1-11 aircraft for assembly in Romania, which was to become the start of a production run of the type in this location.

On the first arrival we were screened by some very formidable military security who put all our stuff through X-ray. They got a bit uptight and asked our agent to interpret. The question was, did we carry guns? "Pistola, Pistola!" they kept saying.

Of course we said no, but they said that Aeroflot did so we might be carrying them as well. A bit stroppy now, we said of course not. Our first officer was told to open his suitcase. The tension grew a bit. Then he made a bit of an error and reached inside his case for something. The security men opened their holsters and in readiness, laid their hands on the stocks of their pistols.

He pulled out something in Christmas wrapping which was destined for his young son from his grandparents in Bournemouth and, not having any idea what was in it, he opened it for them to see. It was a child's toy gun made to look like a Colt 45. Of course, it was not actual size but on X-ray you could not tell the difference. For an instant everyone was stunned, then the funny side of it hit us all and everyone roared with laughter.

Every time we went through the security after that the guys pointed at us and fell about laughing. What a way to make friends.

By 1980, TMAC had been taken over by another cargo company and they asset stripped it. A smaller company carried on but the CL44's, with the exception of the Guppy, were disposed of and most of us were out of a job.

Thus, for me, ended nearly 11 years of employment based at Stansted, with all of that time involving the CL44. TMAC had been a tough environment to work in. Every day was a challenge, both for the engineers and the aircrews. It cost some their lives but for the rest of us, there is a perverse pride in what we accomplished.

The TMAC story cannot be concluded without a couple of references to our chairman, Mike Keegan. He was a man of some character. There was a story about how he had fired someone in our cargo shed for loafing about with his hands in his pockets. The bloke was a bit taken aback. He was a delivery driver waiting for his load of cargo to be unloaded and happened to be wearing the same kind of overalls we used.

The other story happened one day when I was talking to Mike on the ramp. One of our engine fitters passed by with the sole of his shoe flapping loosely. Mike pulled out a huge wedge of cash from his pocket and called the chap over to us. Carefully taking the elastic band from his wedge, he proffered the elastic to the chap with the loose sole and said, "Put this round your shoe, that'll hold it on".

CHAPTER EIGHT

Cyprus and the Gear Not Locked

People from TMAC went in different directions for work. Some took extended gardening leave. It was a bad time for employment, being at the bottom of yet another cycle of boom and bust. I looked around but there was no work to be had in the UK. There were opportunities in Saudi Arabia or Cyprus. They only serve drinks in one of those countries so it was a no-brainer.

Cyprus Airways needed a flight engineer with type rating examiner qualification for the CL44 and that was firmly on my CV. A few weeks later I joined the other expatriates already there, nominally as the chief flight engineer for one aircraft and three crews. All the guys were ex-TMAC and the aircraft was ex-Tradewinds Airways, now re-registered as 5B-DAN. The aircraft was not wanted by Cyprus Airways but the Co-operative Growers Association of Cyprus had pressurised the Cypriot government to operate a cargo aircraft to export their produce.

We did Gatwick once a week and other days down to the Gulf and back with fresh fruit and vegetables, usually returning empty. There was little interest from the airline in our operations and getting spares or support organised through the office of the Cypriot chief ground engineer was hard work.

I rented a sparsely furnished flat in Larnaca, not too far from the airport and bought a bicycle to get around on. In addition, I was maintaining a house in the UK and had little money to spare. I was married for the second time but our separation was not keenly felt and I knew I was hurtling along for another divorce. It was only a matter of time.

The aircraft was reasonably serviceable but being a CL44, still had the odd snag to spoil your day. One day, doing some crew training in the circuit at Larnaca, I noticed that the front cargo door operating jack had extended and was trying to force the door open. Since the door opened outwards – and assuming it overcame the locks – that could be a very bad thing. The jack was attached to the door operating beam by a monster pip pin. There was a huge side load on the pin and it was quite immovable. Briefing the rest of the crew that I was going to take drastic and very noisy measures against the pin, I bashed it out with the fire axe. The jack duly extended against thin air and we continued with the training detail.

Aside from operating the aircraft, there was little to do. I did learn to windsurf in my spare time but otherwise it was a rather boring existence. At least I was in a job. These days, with a mobile phone and internet I am sure an expatriate's life is less isolated.

We tended to meet to eat and drink in the same little restaurants and became connoisseurs of Metaxa brandy, Keo beers and wines. Summers could be extreme, reaching 38 degrees, so it took a lot of beer to stay cool. Conversely winter could be really cold with a bitter Siberian wind so it took a lot of brandy to stay warm.

One of our number was a keen cyclist and he would go off for hours on end before he got back all hot and sweaty to his wife. The bicycle only played a small part in his condition. He had found a diversion in the shape of an attractive Cypriot lady.

While there, I had a real dose of man flu and had to be grounded with blocked ears. The Greek doctor I went to said that I could recover faster if I gave up smoking. Now, I had been smoking for 25 years but having little in the way of sense of smell or taste, it was not too hard. Eventually, a few weeks passed and I was fit to fly again.

Having got that far in the no-smoke effort, I continued my abstinence and the weeks became months, the months turned into years. I used to have a very vivid dream that I had just had a cigarette and blown all the hard work of packing it up. In the middle of the night I would sit up in bed in despair but as the realisation dawned that it had only been a dream, relief would flood over me. That dream, or nightmare, went on for about five years but happily, I never smoked again.

5B-DAN bored along towards Larnaca and reaching "top of the drop" the engineer trickled back the power and the CL44 started down for landing.

In the circuit for landing at Larnaca the crew selected the gear down. The doors opened, the gear began to lower but that's as far as it got. They had three red lights.

There had been a total loss of hydraulic pressure but the hydraulic contents looked OK. The checklist came out and the engineer took the pilots through the alternate method to lower the gear.

The alternate gear pressure bottle was selected but nothing happened. By now the guys were getting concerned but there was one last method, a hand pump operation on the hydraulics. They had ascertained that there was plenty of fluid in the reservoir therefore, tedious as it may be, this should work. The engineer started to pump the handle on the step by his feet. He knew it did not feel right because he was not building up any resistance and even after an awful lot of pumping the gear still did not lock down. None the less he kept pumping till he had blisters on his hands but it made no difference.

Now they had to declare an emergency and consulted where best to put it down. Larnaca was not the best place, but RAF Akrotiri was. The air force laid out a foam carpet and they went for it.

The main gears, hanging loosely down, had taken the position where the oleo legs were pretty much in the vertical, but the bogies had not rotated from the vertical "tip-toe" to the level which would present all four wheels each side for landing. Furthermore, neither main gears nor nose gear had locked down.

The captain eased it skilfully onto the runway. As he did so, one main gear locked down but with the bogie in "tip-toe" the other main leg collapsed. When the nose gear contacted the runway, it was shifted back into the locked position. That state of balance did not last long. The propellers on the low wing side dug into the runway and slashed slices into the tarmac. This dragged the aircraft off the runway and it ploughed across the rough ground losing bits and an undercarriage leg as it went. Amazingly the nose leg put up with this rough treatment and the aircraft came to a halt in a cloud of dust. The crew got out without the aid of the escape chute by just exiting the front door and making a run for it. No-one was hurt but the aircraft was a write off.

We, the off-duty crews, got to hear of the accident and unable to access the air force station at Akrotiri, waited for them in our favourite bar. We knew they would come there. No-one goes home to bed after an episode like that.

The flight engineer sought me out immediately and recounted the whole thing, wanting to know if there was anything else he could have done. There wasn't. He had done everything he could, as I knew that he would do, because he was a good flight engineer.

The aircraft was naturally a write-off and all that remained to do was to claim the insurance, cut it up for scrap and find another job. For me though, there was another duty first. I was seconded to the Accident Investigation Branch from the UK, who were the designated party to act for the Cypriot CAA. Since I had a maintenance licence for the type and also was the chief flight engineer, it seemed a good idea.

When I met the accident investigator I found he was alone and furthermore was a metallurgist with little systems knowledge. His forte was plotting wreckage trails which proved later to be pretty handy.

I reasoned that the hydraulics had been rendered inoperative by an internal leak and since the problem had been experienced before with a system off-load valve I took that off to send to Farnborough. In regard to the failed air system for alternate extension, I found that the air bottle still had the full charge and had not operated. Removing the electrical plug revealed a broken and burnt wire. So that came off as well and went into a bag for examination.

The last failure to extend the gear was more puzzling. The hydraulic hand pump had been operating and had pumped the contents of the reservoir into the air system which was the correct line for alternate extension. That was all fine and dandy, but where had the oil gone? In the alternate air system line there was a calibrated bleed to dump unwanted air bottle leakage pressure overboard. This was a modification that was retrofitted to the aircraft type because a leaking air bottle had been known to blow the gear down without selection. I bet that was a surprise in the cruise.

When I took a look at where it was fitted to the skin line there was a streak of hydraulic oil, so I took this calibrated bleed off and measured the bleed hole. It was at least twice the diameter it should have been. This had allowed all the oil from the hand pump to escape overboard without having any influence on the undercarriage jacks. That little item went into a bag for Farnborough as well.

It was probably on our third day of investigation that we arrived at Akrotiri to find another crash had taken place. In the early morning, an English Electric Canberra aircraft had reached take-off speed and suffered an engine failure.

When this undesirable event took place, if the required one engine climb speed had not been attained, it was practice to pull back on the live engine and land ahead into whatever lay in front of the aircraft. Apparently, the crew ejected and we heard that one had gone out when the aircraft was at 90 degrees of bank and the last guy out when it was inverted. The aircraft carried on for some distance, passed over our sad wreck and crashed further up the airfield.

Now word came down from Farnborough that my metallurgist friend was to investigate the Canberra as well; after all, he was their man in Cyprus.

He was a bit overloaded. The Canberra engine condition was easy to establish but the wreckage trail was a bit confusing for him. This was because he could not identify which bits of mixed up broken structure came from which aircraft. I was able to show him that the appearance of British rivets was totally different from American rivets, so that made it simple.

Sensing this was soon to be the end of my engagement with Cyprus Airways, I was making strenuous efforts to seek an interview with anyone in the UK who would have me. As luck would have it, Laker Airways and British Caledonian Airways both offered an interview and I joined BCAL. But before that we had to pay a visit to the aircraft maintenance company who had the contract to maintain 5B-DAN.

The chief pilot and I duly met with a deputation of worried men in suits at their maintenance base. By that time, the faults that I had discovered had become known to them and I had requested in advance records of certain maintenance activities. These were made available to me but the modification records for the overboard bleed which had been incorporated with the flawed calibrated hole were not there.

So, I questioned that, and the response was that that record had been lost. I said, "You found all the records except this one?" They squirmed in their shiny suits and said that yes, that's how it was. That seems to me to have been a disgraceful act of aviation.

In the end, we presented the evidence to Cyprus Airways and they said to forget it, they had got the insurance money and did not care about the cause. Someone at the maintenance company got lucky. Our crew were lucky as well but what if they had been severely injured or worse? As the Cypriots were happy, it was taken no further.

CHAPTER NINE

The Stars Go Sideways

It was night time over the Sahara, or rather, early morning, about 0400 hours, en-route for Lusaka. We were all at a low ebb – myself and the first officer monitoring the cockpit in a dreamlike state, the captain asleep with his chin on his chest. Engine noise was muted by the slipstream rushing past the windows. Stars shone in the night sky.

Without warning the Boeing 707 broke into a Dutch Roll. Now the stars were rushing horizontally across the windshields. For a couple of seconds, I was transfixed by it then I got thinking, yes, I had seen this before, but in the simulator where we practised these things. That had me worried because I knew that when we did this training exercise in the simulator, some of our pilots could not fly it out of the Dutch Roll and recover to normal flight. In that case the instructor poked the freeze button and we talked about it. Then we did it again. Trouble was, the real thing did not have a freeze button.

All this took no more than three seconds. Capt. Bob raised his head and in one fluid motion reached up and snapped off the yaw damper switches with one hand, disconnected the autopilot with the other and flew the Dutch Roll out in one cycle, back to normal stability.

Thanks buddy, I owe you.

That did not recur on the rest of the sector and we landed as normal in Lusaka. I handed the defect over to the station engineer and we investigated the problem together. The full hydraulically operated rudder authority of a 707 was about 25 degrees. Coupled to the autopilot was a yaw damper that should damp out side to side movement known as yawing, in the rudder channel. If it does not damp out the oscillation, the wings begin to roll in sympathy. The two movements combine into the unstable rolling sway known as a Dutch Roll.

The full range of the yaw damper system operates to 13 degrees of rudder movement. In this instance, the yaw damper had gone to full travel and for an aeroplane at near the maximum cruise altitude, cruising at Mach .78, this is not good news.

After landing the station engineer and I looked at the Yaw Damp computer in the avionics bay below the cockpit and sure enough, it indicated a failure. On equipment like that, there is a Built-In Test facility named after the title and known as a BITE check. This we functioned again and again and it would not fail. As there was no spare yaw computer to be had the engineer cleared the defect in the Technical Log and dispatched the aircraft back to Gatwick. It never happened again.

By now of course, in December 1980, I was employed by BCAL and trained onto the B707. Our simulator, the first I had ever been in, was at Lufthansa in Frankfurt. We would usually get the lunch time slot and after the session, nip off downtown to a restaurant not far from the hotel where we tucked into Schwein Axle and a few beers.

It was an enjoyable course and the line training was well conducted. I had an advantage on the B707 as in my ground engineering days I had been granted full airframe authority so I knew the systems. Based at Gatwick I moved eventually to Sussex and have been in the county ever since. BCAL was a great company to work in. We had a few oddballs but generally things were very happy.

My success at the interview was in large part due to the company having already employed ex-TMAC flight engineers and we were held in high esteem. As my first jet, it was interesting operationally.

We had a couple of pure cargo aircraft and the others were passenger models. The company had acquired the 707`s from various sources and they had come from original owners who specified their own model requirements from new. Consequently, though we had seven in total, there were about six different variants which made it interesting trying to remember which one you were on that day.

The routes were cargo to Houston and passenger work down the west coast of Africa terminating in Banjul. We also had an almost daily service to Tripoli. Lusaka was twice a week. Some crew rest periods were in Freetown. Wherever the line crews' night stopped, there was a good social life. Marriages were made and ruined on those routes. The company image of the "Caledonian Girl" was genuine, they were extremely and often too attractive in those kilts and blouses. I recall that the blouses were a bugger to iron.

Waiting for the 707 to turn up down the route and in need of some duty frees it was always a blessing when "The Great Off-Licence in The Sky" turned over the airport beacon and came into land.

We had some interesting characters. The airline had been formed, as many are, by several mergers. One such skipper we had was an Australian called "Bluey" Wilson. Though no oil painting himself he had a knack of getting the attention of the girls by addressing them as "Spanner Face". When he had done that a few times they fell for it and wanted to know why he kept calling them spanner face. His answer was, "Whenever I look at you darling, you make my nuts tighten."

I could play squash in Lusaka, tough at 4300 feet above sea level, windsurf in Freetown, or be a beach bum in Banjul. Happy days.

One day in Lusaka a group of us had taken a mini-bus for an outing. There was a couple of us flight deck guys and also some cabin crew. On the way back into town the school children were flooding across the roads to get home. Crossing roads in African traffic is always risky. A boy ran across in front of us and our African driver clipped him with his wing mirror. We did not stop.

As awful as that sounds, it was far too dangerous. If you did so, the locals would immediately exact revenge or worse. I looked back and could see him back on his feet clutching his shoulder. The girls with us were very upset but we just could not stop. It was something I was not too proud of, but I believe it was the right decision. Another evening, leaving a restaurant at the show ground area of Lusaka our taxi was blocked in by a Land Rover with three or four locals in it. Having stopped us, they started piling out of their vehicle and approached us looking to cut up rough. I acted instinctively and shouted at them to get back in their vehicle and get the f*** out of my way. To my amazement they did exactly that and we drove away safely.

When we took a rest period at Freetown, Sierra Leone, our hotel was on the other side of the river from Lunghi Airport and was reached by a car ferry of dubious quality. I recall a crossing where one engine failed and as each was on the aft corner of this rectangular shaped boat, any single engine steering needed lots of rudder, a fair wind and the current in the right direction. As some of those conditions were not optimized, the ferry charged around in circles as it meandered across the river. With great seamanship, the master finally smashed it firmly into the landing stage on the other side to allow us to disembark.

The accommodation was the Bintumani Hotel, which had been built in 1980 for the annual bash of the Organization of African Unity. As with all concrete structures in the tropics, the façade was stained with black mildew.

One night, the hotel allowed the local villagers in to the swimming pool dining area to entertain us with drummers and dancers. I got up from the party and moved round the poolside to get closer to the action. At my new location, I found myself downwind of the dancers and the real Africa was borne to me on the night air.

Whilst we were there for a few days, the local Lebanese traders invited the whole crew to a party at the house of one of their number. Now this was normally accepted as free booze to airline crews usually does the trick, but for the hosts it was a thinly-disguised exercise in trying to shepherd the girls into the shedding ring and cut one out.

Outside in cages were various animals that the owner said he had "rescued" from the locals who had killed the animal's parents or some other semi-plausible story. He was congratulated by some for his attitude to the animal`s welfare, but it did not ring quite true. Later, I noted that the cages were nothing more than for transport, being insufficient to provide a normal healthy existence. So, this guy was in all probability an illegal animal dealer.

For a change, we had gone out to a village near Banjul to eat at a restaurant which itself was a bit of a health risk, but hey, you're only young once.

Two local taxis were arranged and we piled into each one. This car was a peach, virtually no lights, an engine that would only run if you held the throttle down and if you braked only one front wheel brake worked, so you had to snatch it over the other side to slow down in a straight line. Cool.

I talked the driver into letting me drive it back. After all, this was an experience not to be missed. Trundling down the road to the hotel, there were some lights in the distance. Taxi man starts telling me about a problem, but I'm too absorbed in this primitive motoring to take much notice. The lights turn into a police road block and I wrestle the car to a stop. This Gambian policeman is very angry about me driving a taxi without a licence and says I am under arrest. I think otherwise. He explains that I will have to appear in court tomorrow. I explain that that is quite impossible as I am the flight engineer on the BCAL flight out of Banjul tomorrow and if I am not there it will not depart. He sees the logic and we revert to an instant fine.

Now I am getting quite confident and remonstrate with him about the fine. We settle for a couple of quid for him and a couple of quid for his officer who keeps a respectful distance from the negotiation. Honour satisfied, I cough up some cash. Then he says get out and let the taxi man drive. Problem. If I let go of the throttle the engine stops and the battery is flat. I try and explain this but the negotiation breaks down and I am forced to get out. The engine dies as predicted. The taxi driver is now behind the wheel and several Gambian policemen are pushing to get us going again. A cheery wave and off we go.

After TMAC, operating an aircraft in BCAL was relatively simple. We had ground support everywhere and my input to fixing defects was minimal.

A couple of inflight problems occurred but it was fairly straightforward. In one case we had no locked down indication on the nose gear. We deduced it was only an indication problem after I had checked the down lock from the viewing window below the cockpit. As a back-up, we decided to use the alternate system on the nose gear mechanism as belt and braces. The procedure involved the use of a metal bar, known in the business as the "Johnson Bar" to actuate the secondary system. So, I fitted the bar to the mechanism and turned it to the appropriate position. But it was jammed.

We declared an emergency but fortunately landed without any mishap. It transpired an over length bolt had been fitted in the alternate mechanism which jammed it. I bent that bolt trying to assert the lock position. The week previously that aircraft had transported the Pope and his retinue. Just as well it did not happen for him. It would have made bad press for BCAL.

The other little bit of excitement was a fire warning on our number four engine as we approached Tripoli for landing. I operated both our fire extinguisher bottles on it but we still had the warning. By now, with the engine shut down and no visible signs of fire it was pretty clear it was only a false warning. When I opened up the cowlings with our Libyan engineers we soon found and replaced a chafed fire warning wire which had shorted and therefore given us the indication of a fire. New extinguisher bottles were fitted and off we went back to Gatwick.

By August 1984, I had been moved onto the DC10 and completed the conversion course. The 707 had been an enjoyable couple of years but the DC10 was even better.

CHAPTER TEN

Airprox in a DC10

We were leaving Canada to the south of Gander and about to pick up our North Atlantic Track (NAT track) from ATC which would carry us to the UK. We were out of Dallas for Gatwick. The frequency was very busy and we had been ignored by ATC on several calls and stepped on by others cutting in on our transmissions. All very frustrating for us and also for the controller. There was a lot of traffic that night.

We got an on-board advisory warning of conflicting traffic at our level. Another aircraft was 16 miles away but predicted by our Traffic Collision Avoidance System (TCAS) to be on a collision course with us. A little yellow diamond shape tracked across our indicator. The other aircraft got a warning about us at the same time, as that's how it works. Eventually the conflict would turn into a hard warning and the yellow diamond would change to red. Then both of us would get automatic guidance to avoid each other by disconnecting the autopilot and flying the command we were given. At least that is what should happen.

Now we were aware of the conflict and the captain, who was running the radios, tried to get a clearance to descend out of the way of the threat. ATC were not listening again. The target tracked closer to us. Therefore, I suggested that we go down 500 feet then return to our assigned level. This wasn't heeded by the pilots and we just sat there waiting for the inevitable conflict resolution to tell us what to do.

At length, with the other traffic only a few miles and not so many seconds away, the co-pilot whose leg this was, gently pitched the autopilot altitude setting down to start us descending. Maybe he did not want to alarm the passengers or spill the champagne in first class. There was too much lag and then the Resolution Command kicked in with "Descend, Descend!" coming through the speakers. The autopilot was still engaged, this was not standard procedure.

My last observation of the red warning showed it was a mere two miles away and we had only descended 150 feet. The target was closing with us fast from behind and to the left of us.

I leaned across to the left side cockpit window and saw the left, red navigation light and the cockpit white lights of the other aircraft flash over us with no more than 200 feet to spare. It was so immediately above us that I could only see one wing tip of the other aircraft. My crew reported an Airprox with another aircraft at our position. The controller came back with "Negative, you've got ten miles separation".

The radio was silent for a while. Then another controller came on the frequency. Someone else was feeling scared now, this time at the ATC centre.

That was a big screw-up.

The episode really bugged me and I could not sleep for a few nights. I was angry about it, too.

The captain said we should get our thoughts together so that the report we would each have to submit would be the same. When everything had settled down and the aircraft was flying the NAT track we wrote what we reckoned had happened. We were all different in some respects because our perception of events was not identical. I learned that was not unusual.

It later transpired that the other aircraft was an Air Portugal Airbus A310. An unverified report reached me that the Portuguese captain saw us on his TCAS and waited for the conflict resolution. When he got it, apparently it told him to descend as well. He could see we were descending so he stayed at his own level.

Why that dangerous resolution should occur I do not know. Maybe the system was confused by our change of level at that crucial intervention. Whatever the explanation, things were not going right that night. Again, if someone asks me if there was ever a time in my flying career that I thought I was going to die, that one comes to mind.

An air proximity is filed when there is a danger of conflict with another aircraft. There is a system of examination to classify the risk and recommend measures to mitigate future occurrences. Some are high risk, like the one just described, others are not so dangerous. The TCAS systems fitted on large aircraft give mutual warning to each aircraft, then if required, resolutions in the vertical plane to resolve the conflict. TCAS commands should always take precedence over ATC instructions.

Plymouth Approach transferred us to their Military controller. We continued to climb the King Air ambulance aircraft, passing through about 8,000 feet in uncontrolled airspace to join the airway. It was a cloudy day with occasional breaks of clear air between layers. My peripheral vision picked up a fleeting glimpse of grey shapes passing down my left side so I turned to look back over my shoulder as the three F-15 fighters curled round behind us. The guy in the right seat looked over his right shoulder and saw the bogies in formation in a left descending bank. I called Plymouth Mil and asked if he had contact with the formation we just missed. He said no but his information led him to believe that they were at 20,000 feet and not working his frequency yet. Our controller asked if I wanted to file an Airprox and I responded in the affirmative.

This episode occurred some years after the DC10 Airprox, but it too was a communication foul-up. By this time I was flying a King Air after retiring from British Airways. Some weeks later I got the response from the Airprox Review Board and they categorised it a low risk. That does not bother me so much as the way in which the conflict occurred.

The jets were heading out to the ranges south of Plymouth and to give them a tactical edge the formation leader had turned his transponder off so that could not be tracked on radar by the opposing force in the war game. He did not check in with Plymouth Mil in what is called a 'timely fashion' and used his attack radar to steer round us. Not such good flight management and in the report it said words to the effect that the formation leader was invited to an interview with the boss without coffee.

Fair enough. What annoyed me was that the fighter jock had said that the lateral miss distance was about one and a half miles. Immediately I wrote again to the Review Board and commented that my mate in the right seat had clocked the tail identification "LN" on the fins of the F15`s in camouflage paint and how keen his eyesight must be to see that at one and a half miles. Their Airships of the Review Board did not see fit to pass further comment.

My DC10 conversion course, in July 1984, was conducted on a simulator at Gatwick. A good friend of mine from the TMAC days joined me on the course and together we turned up wearing ties and jackets for the first briefing with our instructor. The man strode in, took a despairing look at us two and told us only the instructors wore ties here and to get them off. The scene was set for the next ten four-hour simulator sessions. When I was later a simulator instructor I made sure not to emulate that behaviour.

The DC10 was a fine aircraft, appreciated by crew, engineers and passengers alike (unless you were the passenger in the middle seat of five in the centre aisle). It was remarkably serviceable and could dispatch on the route with a number of minor defects. I compared that one day with a company B747. This was well before 9/11, when having visitors to an airline flight deck was normal practice. On the DC10 we would have, on average, four allowable defects to the systems and these were recorded in the Technical Log and marked on the instruments by a little yellow alert tag. One day I was positioning on a "classic" B747 in the company and went up to the cockpit for a chat with the crew. I noticed an extraordinary amount of yellow tags dotted around the cockpit. The flight engineer said they had in excess of 30 defects being carried. While that in itself was not illegal, they did say that they could not remember which things were unserviceable, there being so many.

Of course, there were some fatal accidents on the DC10 and people played this up, calling it the Death Cruiser. I do not know a large public transport that has not had them. When I used to get any sarcastic comments from crew on other aircraft I could always quote them their own problems. That usually shut them up.

A friend of mine, also a flight engineer, had the unfortunate task of dealing with a death on board a DC10. An unfortunate person passed away in the seat and was lolling over the person next to him. This was brought to the attention of the cabin crew who went up front and informed the captain. The captain sent the flight engineer.

The decision was made to move the deceased into the floor of the galley. No-one offered to help but passengers were complaining that something needed doing about it. Of course, moving the body down the aisle to the galley could hardly be missed, but now the passengers suddenly became engrossed in the film or the book they were reading. My friend manfully struggled towards the galley pulling the dear departed away by the shoulders. Just as the feet disappeared under the galley curtain, the passengers heard him say loudly, "Did anyone else have the fish?"

The routes in BCAL for the DC10 were North America, through Dubai to Hong Kong and the west coast of Africa – Lagos and Kano in Nigeria, Gaborone and Lusaka. Saudi Arabia came into it as did South America with a route via Recife and Sao Paolo to Rio de Janeiro.

With our rest days in Sao Paolo, the first officer and I got a cheap flight to Iguazu Falls which are on the border of Argentina and Brazil. The falls are huge, being the largest in the world but a dirty brown colour. We night stopped in a wonderful old colonial hotel with distinctly splendid Spanish architecture. None of the other crew had wanted to come with us and when we got back, they were sitting round the hotel pool looking bored and now wishing they had come along.

Bermuda, with a shuttle to Tampa, was very pleasant. I had seen some of our ports of call through the windscreen of the CL44 and the B707 but this route system opened up parts of the world I had not operated to before now and it was fascinating. The North American routes included New York, Atlanta, Dallas, Houston, Phoenix, Los Angeles and San Diego.

For a short while we had a route to Sanaa in the Yemen. Landing in Sanaa you turned the clock back a century or two. On one occasion, the first officer and I took a walk downtown and wandered through the crumbling buildings and dusty streets. My companion was an ex-RAF fighter jock and took a keen interest in a MIG 29 making a show of force to the locals, flying over the city at not much over 500 feet.

I bought an old 1874 Graz rifle in the souk which I stripped down into barrel and stock so it just about fitted in my case. This got declared as usual, but the customs officer at Gatwick couldn't be bothered to read our crew declaration so I brought it home unhindered.

Some locals who worked for us took us out in a group to the main souk which is a medieval place thronging with people. We had some good-looking girls on the crew and the plan was to get into the souk and for them to buy and wear the black abaya which would give them some relief from the attention that women get when not dressed appropriately in these places.

We followed our guide through a melee of locals – all men of course, no women would be seen there – in a single file with our men leading and bringing up the rear.

Ahead of me was a blonde hostess who immediately attracted attention and I clearly saw two boys of about fifteen making a beeline for her. One of them darted into the line and cupped his hand between her legs before jumping back into the crowd. There was nothing you could do, I scowled at him but any complaint to the police would, as usual, turn against the foreigner. She was clearly upset but had to put up with it. Oddly, once the girls had got the abayas on, they were left alone.

Some of the routes did change over the course of time. Lagos was apparently quite lucrative. In North America we were well received by the customers who called us "British Cal". We were established in government policy as the "Second Force Airline" under the patronage of Margaret Thatcher who was leading the government. Not long after that, Lord King, chairman of state owned British Airways, got up close and cosy with Prime Minister Thatcher and managed to persuade the government to float BA on the market. So, within a very short space of time, BCAL went from a second force to an airline under threat. Routes were reshuffled to support BA's flotation and we took Saudi Arabia in exchange for South America. I was on the return inaugural BCAL flight from Jeddah and we positioned out with BA. It was clear from comments to us that we were taking on a loss-making route. BCAL was on the slippery slope and by early 1987 BCAL was struggling to form alliances to avoid a takeover by BA. There was a short flirtation with Sabena, but eventually BA took over BCAL. It was termed a merger, but we all knew it was a government policy-driven takeover.

BA set up a number of seminars for BCAL people as a form of induction into what they barely managed to hide, namely that BA was the senior airline. A lot of people were reshuffled in the seniority list and some captains lost their commands to someone else. The pension schemes were amalgamated and that caused more problems. Personally, I did OK out of it and managed to gain another pension year.

The BA training philosophy was that crew wear uniforms in the simulator to give it greater realism. We moaned about that, taking it as an insult that it was assumed that we would not have given it our best shot wearing civvies.

Meanwhile, from my introduction to the DC10 in July 1984 to the merger in 1987, I enjoyed a happy professional life while blowing a second marriage. This was getting to be a habit and I seemed to be constantly rebuilding lost assets.

Down route social life took my mind off my matrimonial failures. There was a good deal of partying. Dubai was heaven. There was wind surfing at the BCAL sponsored sailing club on Dubai Creek where the desert wind blew me over a smooth water. Back at the hotel there were squash courts to enjoy and after that, a meal and drinks with the crew downtown.

Hong Kong had less downtime but it was enough to head for Ned Kelley's bar in Kowloon and, in the morning, catch the Star Ferry to Hong Kong Island and take the tram up the peak for lunch. The Star Ferry across the harbour is one of my all-time favourite things to do. For the equivalent of about 20 pence you got the most magical boat ride and that was on the first-class deck. If I am ever there again, I never miss it.

During one night stop in Hong Kong we had more than the usual 24 hours so there was a crew trip out to the floating restaurants at Aberdeen, on the other side of Hong Kong Island. Actually, they don`t float, being on piles set into the sea bottom. As you come on board there are tanks of fish. You can choose the one you want and later it will appear at the table ready to eat. We went for the safe financial option and ordered from the menu, which was essentially Dim Sum. The main problem was that despite it being a tourist hot spot, we only had an incomprehensible menu where it seemed Chinese had been translated into English by use of a slide rule. The orders went in and almost everything appeared at the table in steaming bamboo baskets which had little similarity to our expectations. I noticed that we had not been given any chicken dishes, which most of us had asked for, so I had a go at a re-order.

Going from table to table was an old lady who dispensed Dim Sum boxes from a steaming cart. Speaking no shared language, I made a passable impression of a chicken. The basket got plonked on the table and she wrote an additional Chinese character on our chit. Someone decided it was time to try the chicken and took the top off the basket to find chicken. Trouble was, it was only chicken feet, lying in a gloopy fat, still with claws on. No-one had the courage to try it.

On the African coast there were beaches, more wind surfers and beach bars. The hotel in Freetown, Sierra Leone had been constructed for the meeting of the Organisation of African Unity in 1980. Already, it was suffering the usual problems of low maintenance and power cuts. One night, the hotel allowed the local villagers in to the swimming pool dining area to entertain us with drummers and dancers. I got up from the party and moved round the poolside to get closer to the action. At my new location I found myself downwind of the dancers and the real Africa was borne to me on the night air.

Bermuda was a beautiful place to spend a couple of days, taking a bus round the island and having lunch at the old dock yards. It must rank as one of the most interesting places to go, having a craggy coastline around an extinct volcano and plenty of history. Wish I could see it again.

We were on approach for Phoenix Sky Harbour airport. The weather was fine and nothing about this flight would indicate we were about to have a problem.

The captain had given the first officer this leg, so the F/O was doing the flying. ATC gave us a speed reduction so the F/O asked for the leading edge slat lift devices to be selected and set a lower airspeed on the autothrotlle system. I monitored and saw the light come on indicating movement but the light did not change to the selected position so I called the problem and we selected the speed back up to the safe setting again.

My abnormal checklist came out and while the captain monitored and the F/O flew and alerted Phoenix to our problem, I took the pilots through the checklist. There was no lateral roll movement so it appeared the slat system was stuck. The checklist demanded that we select it back in and go through a procedure to use flaps only for the landing. I took the guys through those steps and prepared an abnormal landing speed card to fly our approach and landing. Now we were ready for flap extension and configuring the aircraft for landing.

At the F/O's request we selected the flaps out. Unbelievably, this totally separate indication system told us that the flaps were also not running. My knowledge, trained into me over the years on the DC10, told me that we had to select the flaps back up and if certain actions did not rectify this problem we were going to land very fast at Phoenix with no lift devices at all. I suggested that I go back into the cabin to verify where the flaps were and the captain agreed.

Down the cabin I tried not to spook the passengers while I looked out behind the wings to check the flap position. It looked good to me so we settled for the indicator being wrong and an abnormal landing flap configuration which, while not correct, would allow us to make the landing. We were now operating outside the book but landing clean at an airport altitude of 1200 feet above sea level was not such a great idea.

The captain had the option of taking control for this landing but did not want to deny the F/O the opportunity. I concluded the checklist by reading to the pilots the notation that we would land by only using a slight flare onto the runway. If we didn't, the aircraft could float along the runway and risk running off the end.

We approached at the required high speed and the F/O did exactly what was required of him so we landed at the right speed and in the right place. The landing was very firm and my chin slammed into my chest. We hauled on the reverse thrust and braked down to taxi speed.

As the passengers left the aircraft I noted an unnatural iciness about them. No-one thanked us for a nice flight. Not surprising after that landing.

I kept in touch with the station engineer and he later told me there were no faults discovered with any part of the flap or slat systems during many function checks so he cleared the aircraft to fly back to the UK. Apparently, it did not reoccur.

A week or so later I had a call from the union representative whose job it was to investigate in-flight irregularities to ask me why I had not logged a hard landing. The Flight Data Unit had recorded 2.3 times the force of gravity. We had no way of measuring that force. Having a simple "G" meter fitted somewhere could have given us a rough indication, but there was no way to tell until the weekly FDU download.

I explained my reasoning for not reporting the event by pointing out that as I was a simulator instructor who witnessed the abnormal exercises in the simulator many times, I had become conditioned to a firm landing taking place. In fact, the simulator was inclined to crash at an alarming angle if any side load was involved in these abnormal landings and we instructors hung on for dear life as it slammed about before coming to a stop. I believe the landing limit was something in the region of 1.8G but quite how we were to measure that was not clear.

The hard landing check was performed as soon as the company could get engineering onto the job and to my knowledge, nothing was found broken. I took from the episode that if in doubt, put it in the aircraft technical log and let someone else worry about it. Additionally, it gave me the assurance that the DC10 was constructed like a brick outhouse and could take quite a lot of punishment.

Oman is a country I always enjoy. Muscat, the capital, has many upmarket hotels that I could never hope to afford to use but it is still a pleasant destination. The new leader, Sultan Qaboos, who deposed his father in 1970, took over the country and from then onwards the population came to benefit from his social programme. At no time was it ever allowed to become another Dubai. This leader, trained with the British Army at Sandhurst, put in place infrastructure not previously enjoyed. Anyone with a dirty car or with litter on his road frontage was hit with a fine.

On a few days off at Muscat while working for British Airways, I rented a car and with another chap and a couple of girls from the cabin crew, set out for the Jebel Akhdar, the mountain plateau about fifty clicks inland which rises more than 9,000 feet above sea level. The object was to get into the mountains and reach the plateau for a look-see.

Taking the keys to a brand-new saloon and a local map, we went up the newly-laid tarmac coast road and took a left turn as directed. The road soon turned into a dirt track which further deteriorated into a boulder strewn version of the Khyber Pass. As I weaved along between huge cliffs, the undercarriage of the car was taking a fearful beating. I feared for the sump, which if holed would rob us of the engine oil and bring catastrophe to the expedition.

Eventually, I reached a steep incline to the Jebel and ground up in the low gears but found myself sliding backwards on loose shale. There was a village on the side of the mountain and as we slid backwards down the slope curious Omanis came out to see what was going on. Very soon a small crowd of interested onlookers gathered round and then parted to admit a young man who clearly had their respect. He introduced himself as the son of the headman and, apologising for his father's absence, invited us into the village. The chief's son settled us into the Majlis, the village meeting room, and with shoes off, we sat on the carpeted floor leaning on cushions. On the walls were old Lee Enfield rifles and some that looked a lot older.

With incredible speed dates and coffee were produced. The ladies brought small children and engaged the girls with family talk and our host chatted about life in general in the village. I had by now discovered that this very personable young man was 15 years old and went to school in Muscat. Considering the distance out of town I asked him how he got there. He told me how the Sultan sent the government helicopter for him on Sunday and brought him back on Thursday.

The elder tribesmen came by to take a look at us but did not engage in conversation. They had the craggy characterful faces of the region and wore the Khanjar knives on their waistbands. In an attempt to repay their kindness, we gave them anything we did not need, so biros were given to the children and the girls gave the women make-up items from their handbags.

After a tour of the date palms and admiring the water management that provided this oasis with its water we bade farewell and drove back down the track that led to the main road and so into town. It was altogether an unforgettable experience.

Also unforgettable was the condition of the hire car. Not only was it covered in dust and slightly scarred but the tarmac road, being hot and wet, had blasted the sides of the car with splatters of tar. I returned it as rapidly as possible and scarpered off before they could take a good look at it.

The aircraft had reached our initial cruising altitude of 31,000 feet and we were routing north out of Gatwick for North America. Passing Honiley navigation beacon at Birmingham, we encountered some poor weather. We had all seen worse but there were thunderstorms on our track. The pilots asked for, and got, a course deviation to avoid the worst of it.

With very little warning, however, we took a lightning strike on our right engine. It was heard OK, and the location of the strike was obvious. Most of the right engine indications failed on my flight engineer's panel and some went down on the forward instrument panel as well. The engine was running fine but I had no way of monitoring it.

After some discussion, we all agreed that it was right to go back to Gatwick and for the only time in my career, I dumped fuel in anger to reduce us to landing weight. Having dumped about 60 tons of jet fuel over Birmingham we turned back.

Lightning was a permanent risk. It was not totally possible to avoid it and most commercial aviators have had experience with it on at least one occasion. Normally one would track storms on radar or by use of the Mark 1 eyeball. Most of the time our flight levels would allow us to glide serenely over the top of the thunderheads but when they were too tall or we were lower down, we threaded our way through, avoiding the worst as we went.

My triple strike going into Houston was not the first. You could often hear sizzles and clicks and maybe not realise that the aircraft had taken a belt. At other times it would be very apparent.

I recall having a refuel stop at an African airport and a storm rushed in on the airfield like a huge black curtain. The bowser driver rightly disconnected from our aircraft and drove off at high speed. We were stuck on an apron miles from anywhere and when the storm hit we had nowhere to go. Tropical rain belted down. Then the lighting and thunderclaps came with no time difference as it passed overhead. Lightning was hitting the apron a short distance away and crackling across the ground all around us. This was frightening with a load of fuel in the tanks but no-one left the shelter of the aircraft.

In Texas, those good `ol boys used to call them 'thirty–thirties'. The reasoning was that the storm would be 30 miles across and moved at 30 miles per hour and that was about right.

Many years later, while doing an audit observation on an air carrier at Aberdeen, I was in the forward cabin row by the left door, having done my flight deck observation on the outbound leg. I knew the weather was poor and could sense that we were holding off to let a storm pass by. The crew decided this was the time to have a crack at the approach so we rolled out onto the ILS and started down. My seat next to a window was a great place to see what happened next.

I could hear the static sizzle building up and then almost in slow motion watched a bolt of lightning reaching out at us from the boiling clouds. It went straight for the side of the fuselage behind the captain's seat and about five feet in front of me. There was the usual loud bang as it struck but the fascinating thing for me was the red semicircle of fire ringed by black smoke. The whole thing lasted about half a second but this 6 feet fireball was pretty impressive.

After landing, I let all the other passengers go off then checked with the guys up front. They were looking pretty surprised. I said, "Thanks, that's my fifth". The captain said it was his first. For me to have only five serious strikes in about 20,000 hours' airtime I thought fairly normal.

When we got out and looked at the skin where the strike took place there was a buckle and about ten blown rivets. Behind the affected area was an electronics bay stuffed with transformers and relays. Wrong polarity, I guess.

Flying through dusty air would sometimes create St. Elmo's fire on the windscreens. At night, this was a lively display of miniature lightning shooting up the screen in fascinating patterns. It did no harm and was caused by the friction of the particle laden air. Braver souls than I said that you could move it around the windscreen with your finger with no risk to yourself. Recalling the science master's trick at school, where he would have us all hold hands while he cranked a magneto, I thought better of it.

Another flight engineer pal of mine told me about a time when he was on a B707 and the static had reached such a pitch that a fireball of static came out of the instrument panel, went through him, the cockpit door and down the centre aisle of the aircraft. It glowed white and was about the size of a football. Some screaming was heard back in the cabin.

In later life I worked with a pilot who had been struck by lightning. He was flying a Boeing 737 and had rested his arm on the metal structure around the cockpit window during a flight near a storm. The lightning reached out and hit them, travelling through the window structure and his arm, exiting out of his chest. That cost him his medical but fortunately his career continued as an instructor on the simulator.

Lightning can go from cloud to cloud without striking the ground and apparently, seen from space, is capable of traversing distances of 100 miles or more down a line of storms. Other astounding phenomena which occur above active thunderstorms are so-called sprites, a form of lightning discharge which goes up from the top of the storm to a height of around 40 miles above the earth. Other accounts maintain that the lightning can reach up from the ground to meet it coming out of the clouds.

Similarly, it is alleged that sprites can come down from the upper atmosphere to connect with clouds below. Fascinating stuff as long as you are not in the way of it. There is enough about lightning to fill a book and there are several to be read.

During my time on the DC10 I was able to get my parents on my staff travel concessions and took them away with me for a trip each. My mother came to Hong Kong with me in First Class while I worked the flight deck. The cabin crew were always great with relatives, taking great care of them. We did the Dubai stopover and I took her down to the Dubai Creek to show her the Arab dhows which ferried to and from Iran with goods. I lost sight of her and retracing my steps I found she had wandered into a little mosque. I got her out quick.

I took my dad to Dallas, which was real man stuff and we went to Fort Worth Stock Yards for steak and beers where he bought a souvenir cowboy hat. He was also upgraded onboard into First and had a great time.

During that period, which I often refer to as my 'between marriages' or even my 'blue' period, I had several girlfriends and remained staunchly unmarried.

One of those was an inveterate traveller, and if anyone was cut out to be an airline employee, she was. I only had to agree to go somewhere and she would arrange the whole thing. We had been on safari in Kenya before, but with a group in a minibus which was the usual way of doing it. She had come to hear about a car hire place in Nairobi which would rent me a little 4X4 and proposed doing our own tour. That sounded OK so I went for it.

After a night in the Norfolk Hotel in Nairobi, we picked up a little Suzuki Jeep from a Sikh garage owner. The little Suzuki had a bad reputation for rolling over on its side in cross country driving. Not ideal then. Mr Singh gave me a couple of tools to go with it and, ominously, a spare capacitor for the ignition system. Apparently the capacitor would overheat and the rough roads in the parks would cause it to fail, hence the spare.

We headed out of town for the Masai Mara and as expected, the roads turned from tarmac to potholes and then to dirt. Later in the afternoon we were bowling along a dirt road with about 25 miles to go to our lodge and looking forward to getting there. The track we drove was rutted by the wind and the ride was pretty rough. That's when the capacitor decided enough was enough.

We were on a track bounded by tall grass. I noticed the amber grass was exactly the same colour as the park lions so I put my girlfriend on the roof to keep an eye out while I changed the capacitor. While I was doing that a tour bus driver stopped to see if I was OK, so I said yes but if we didn't get into the lodge before nightfall would he mind sending someone out for us. I completed the job and we got going again, rolling into the lodge just before sunset.

The first thing I did was to find the driver in their compound and give him one of my good shirts and our thanks. Fortunately, the new part was better than the last and it did not fail again, which was just as well because that was our only spare.

While we were novices at safari driving, the local drivers were not and moreover had radio links to each other. It was fairly simple to navigate following the Mara River and hill features. When we saw dust in the distance from tourist buses all heading in the same direction it was pretty easy to follow them to see game.

Of course, my attempts at off-piste exploration should never have happened. I often wondered if the park authority would ban idiots like me from driving around to stop them getting into trouble.

I encountered a number of lone buffalo on the Mara but wisely gave way. One morning we had decided to do our own thing and cross and recross the Mara River to see what we might find. I have always been keen to spot leopards but luck is not often with me. While looking for the elusive leopard, I approached a shallow ford and stopped by a tree at the top of the bank before driving into the water, in order to take a look at what I was going to drive through. Detecting a small movement at my side of the vehicle I looked down by my door. There lay a sleepy lioness and I had almost driven over her paws.

Slowly I realised that there were other lions stretched out not too far way. We decided, unwisely, to move closer so I pulled off the track and moved through the long grass towards them. Small acacia bushes screeched along the bottom of the vehicle. I had not gone very far before the whole pride roused from its slumbers and looked up at us. I was right in the middle of them. Then we got a sight never to be forgotten. Three lion cubs put their front paws on their mother's flanks and peered at us over the grass. Problem was, she was getting a bit pissed off with me and lashing her tail. Reversing out got more screeching from the acacia and more grumpy tail lashing from the pride. My heart was in my mouth but we had been so close it was almost worth the risk.

On another occasion I almost drove us into serious trouble. We had been going slowly along a track when from the side of the road emerged a family of elephants led by an elderly matriarch and followed by others of various ages. I kept back at a respectful distance while my girlfriend snapped pictures. At the rear of the herd came another senior matron, who on seeing my little vehicle and probably unhappy with a car she had never seen before took umbrage and started towards us waving her trunk about and screaming.

Now, I had been told they will feint twice and hit on the third charge so like an idiot I took the first in my stride. She stopped her feint to see what effect it had made and seeing me in the same place commenced her second charge, again screaming her trunk off. Still taking pictures, my girlfriend told me to hold still, the matriarch will stop. The snag was, this elephant had not heard about two feints and a charge and kept right on coming.

I slammed reverse gear in, gunned the engine and stalled.

In moments of absolute panic, I started it again and reversed out of there as fast as I could with the, by now, quite athletic elephant showing what a turn of speed she could produce. Eventually she gave me a look of utter disdain and turned back to the herd. I still have a picture, canted at an angle, of a charging elephant with trunk up, ears wide and dust coming up from its feet. It gives me a shiver up the spine every time I look at it.

In 1988, we took a journey round part of the Pacific. The easy part was a staff travel ticket to Los Angeles. To spring out to the Pacific we took an American carrier to Fiji. After Fiji we visited the Cook Islands. These islands, a colonial dependency of New Zealand, were laid back and relaxing. I reported to the police station and bought a Cook Islands driving licence, then rented a car for a look round. I always thought it would be great if stopped in the UK to present that licence. Unfortunately, that never happened.

By this time, I had obtained my private pilot licence and when in Fiji, I underwent a check-out on a Cessna 172 and asked if I could go out to an island called Malolo Lailai which had a little runway with the sea at both ends. I was told by the Fiji Flying Club that without filing a flight plan with 24 hours' notice all I could do was fly round Fiji.

Since I did not have much time left I sought out the Civil Aviation Director who was a UK CAA man on secondment. He listened to my request and told me that if I got airborne telling ATC that I was flying round the coast of Fiji, they would have no idea where I was, so to go ahead and do what I wanted.

That was understood. As soon as I was out of sight we flew out to Malolo and landed. After an hour or two on the beach we trundled back to Fiji and ATC were none the wiser.

Another super holiday took in a week in Sri Lanka and a week in the Maldives afterwards. I needed the week's rest in the Maldives because we packed a lot in touring Sri Lanka. Staying in Colombo, we went to Kandy to see the Buddhist Temple of the Tooth and then went up north to Sigiriya Rock which was a very historic early settlement. It was also as far north as the taxi driver would go as the government was fighting the Tamil Tigers in the north of the country. He insisted that to be safe, we had to go back to the south before dark and being a bit late, he floored it all the way back.

The hill tea planter's hotel was a fantastic night stop but a hotel in Galle in the south of Sri Lanka was one of the worst nights I have ever endured. The hotel was about 300 years old and had no air conditioning. The bed had bugs in it and having no air conditioning I had to sit in a chair all night with the shutters open. Outside in the night, fruit bats with a three foot wing span cruised past the window and the mosquitos came in and fed on me.

The week in the Maldives meant a flight to Male and then a fast boat out to an island with white beaches and crystal clear water in the lagoon. There was a diving school there run on the American

Professional Diving model so I enrolled to do the course. Diving in those waters was fantastic with clear water, coral and lots of marine life. Unfortunately, I could not handle the pressure changes and spent the week with a lot of pain in the ears. My girlfriend also did the course, but she could not swim and was afraid of being out of her depth. To her credit she completed the course without ever learning to swim unaided. I could also hire a windsurfer and with a gentle breeze inside the smooth waters of the lagoon, it was paradise.

In the clear waters of about six feet in depth, I could see young sharks about three feet long like little muscular models of battleships. I could chase them on the windsurfer from one coral rock outcrop to the next. They would move at incredible speed until I caught up with them, then dash off to the next hiding place.

CHAPTER ELEVEN

In the Front Seat

Bob got out and said, "Do three touch and goes then come back and pick me up". He shut the door of the little Cessna 152 and left me to it. This was going to be my first solo as a pilot. Oddly, I had no worries about it. I had trained under the US FAA system at Addison Airport in Dallas, Texas and the method there was to cover every aspect of basic flight then you went solo.

So, to do some circuits was no big deal and I took off and executed some good circuits which all went like clockwork. Afterwards I taxied back to pick Bob up to fly back from the quiet little airport we had gone to. He gave me his big Texan smile. "How did it go?" All I could think of saying was that it was a lot quieter without him.

This was in the summer of 1987. Everyone remembers their first solo. In fact every flight keeps you awake for a little while afterwards as you run it through your internal debrief. Bob was a great guy to learn to fly with and we still exchange cards every Christmas. He still flies for Delta. Even so, my landings were poor to begin with and he used good judgement in passing me over to a more experienced instructor to get that bit sorted out before we carried on with the course. He used to have to tell me to look out of the window.

I had spent over 5,000 hours as a flight engineer by that time and I was an instrument panel monitor unused to looking out except in moments of idle curiosity. After all, two pilots in front of me had the view out, so my job was on the gauges. Eventually, I became a reasonably good instrument pilot and I like to think much of that stemmed from years of monitoring other people.

By now, that stammer I had been troubled with from my childhood had slowly ebbed away. When I refer to it, I always explain it by saying that I had talked myself out of it, which is pretty much how it came to pass. No longer did I lock up trying to say something.

I was gaining confidence. As through life I became surer of myself, I attempted to take on more high-profile situations involving communicating with other people. As confidence rose, so the speech impediment receded. The thought that I could have operated an aircraft radio for instance, was at one point, quite impossible. Largely because of this affliction, any sort of career plan to become a commercial pilot myself was not even on the back burner at the time. I had advanced into the cockpit as a flight engineer and as far as I knew that was going to be that.

However, as time went by I became interested in what the two guys in front of me were doing and witnessed some fine flying and cockpit management. I also saw some poor pilotage and it occurred to me that I might be able to do as well as the best if I gave it a try. So when Bob asked me on our first lesson if I wanted a licence just for private use or as a commercial pilot, I optimistically said 'commercial' and that is how we went forward with my training.

I flew east into the dawn sun. The Texas farmland lay out in front of me in neat fields and roads in a north-south-east-west grid pattern. My computed heading since leaving the pattern at Addison and waypoints had been flown accurately. Now I was arriving at my solo cross-country destination where I was to land, get my log book signed and fly smugly back again. No sweat. Looking out ahead there was no airport runway there.

My right foot kept hitting the rudder pedal, my knees were shaking and I was struck by a wave of panic.

What to do? Eventually the training kicked in. If lost, locate an identifiable feature. Turning north I flew for 10 miles or so to the main highway and identified the town beneath me.

I realised that the airfield had to be south of me where I had come from, so back I went. Within a few minutes, there it was, a black ribbon of tarmac with a few hangars. Incredibly, I had flown right over it and had not seen it.

I had navigated the aircraft faultlessly to my destination but had not looked out of the window enough. Bob was right. If I had looked out a bit more I might have spotted it first time. If I had dipped a wing and looked down I would have seen the runway directly below, but when I looked ahead, the little engine out front blocked my view and I just panicked.

Thinking it over afterwards, I also realised that in the early morning sun, all the field edges painted a north-south shadow. The runway was north-south and the black surface blended with all the other dark lines. Not only that, I was partly blinded by the low sun on the nose. Why was I stabbing the rudder pedal with my right foot? My instinct was to put the car brake on and stop it moving – one of the oft referred to motor actions. I learned something from that flight. Good preparation can overcome a lot of problems and keep the situation under control. I had not thought ahead, I should have been looking out earlier. Unconsciously, that lesson has been taken on every flight I have made since, though I did not realise it`s origin for some time. This was not the last time I would experience fear while flying, there would be a few more in store for me but I did not know that at the time.

From then on, I had little time for anything other than flying. I used the airline bid system to get to places where I could rent an aeroplane. At home between trips I prepared myself for exams and flight checks. In the cockpit, I looked after my responsibilities as a flight engineer and then boned up for my next flight. The other guys took a lot of interest in what I was doing and later when I was practising for an Instrument Rating they would fly right seat with me acting as safety pilot while I tracked beacons. Thanks, guys.

I completed the US FAA Private Pilot Licence in October 1987 and had done the extra requirements in the UK to get a UK PPL as well. Over the next few years, I progressed through the 700 flight hours as a pilot to obtain a UK Commercial Pilot Licence.

By 1992 I had my UK CPL and Instrument Rating. As I built up the flight hours towards the 1,500 total required for the UK Air Transport Pilot Licence, I added to my US licence by doing the US FAA CPL and IR as well. Before I sat my Air Transport Pilot Licence examinations, I attended a two week crammer at a training school in Bournemouth. By now I was 50 years old and it was hard work. The rest of the class were self-improvers like me and some military pilots getting qualified for flying with the airlines.

I overheard a young fast jet pilot complaining how tough the course was and how he never worked this hard at university. Up till then, I had self-doubts about being able to cope, but that one remark told me that if he felt that way, I could see it through. Later, during the

Instrument Rating course, I had occasion to witness other ex-RAF pilots struggling with instrument flying and once again it made me realise that if 30-year-olds find it tough, then there was hope for me at 50.

Like many people, my UK Instrument Rating did not earn a pass first time and I had to re-test one non-precision approach. During the first test, I knew everything was going OK. All I had to do was complete a Non-Directional Beacon approach on one engine and it would be in the bag. I had to time two and a half minutes from passing over the beacon to placing myself in the landing position.

At the appropriate time, I hit the aircraft's stopwatch and maintained a perfect track. After a while, I checked the clock and thought I saw one and a half minutes elapsed so pressed on another minute before announcing that the runway was ahead. Next thing I knew the examiner took it off me (I am behind blind flying screens) and hauled it off to the right, requesting a landing from ATC on the intersecting runway. Whipping the screen down, I saw the runway threshold disappearing under the nose. I had flown one minute too long and had failed.

Cursing the clock which had a tiny, indecipherable minute hand but a second hand as long as a broom handle, I resolved to invest in my own kneeboard mounted stopwatch. After that lesson learned and the purchase of a useful stopwatch, I never had that problem again and passed the rating on the second attempt. Everyone who has gone through that knows that an Instrument Rating renewal is never as hard as the first. Thank the Lord for that.

Those years of learning were very enjoyable. When you stop learning, life can become a little dull. My time was full of flying and new discoveries.

Later, after the merger between BCAL and BA, there was a surplus of flight engineers and the company decided to select some for pilot conversion training. The cut-off age was 38 but I was not included as I was north of that figure. Guys who were chosen went off to Perth for training and then were brought back onto the DC10 on the basis that if they knew the systems, they would know how to fly it.

That was a mistake, because clearly you need a lot of handling time before you are ready for an aircraft weighing in at 260 tonnes and getting maybe two landings a month. Most of the guys struggled with it and the situation was made even worse by the expectations heaped on them by the management and the other F/E's, who naturally wanted them to succeed.

Above: BCAL B707 at Gatwick 1984. (Author)

Below: BCAL DC10 landing at Gatwick. (Air Team Images)

Above: Morning scene at Gatwick. BCAL DC10`s being readied for departure.
(Marc Hasenbein)

Below: AA5A G-PAWS at Goodwood. (Author)

Above: Authors Cessna 140 at a farm strip. (Author)

Right: Author with his Cessna 140. (Author)

Below: Preparing the Beech 18 for flight at San Diego. (Author)

Left: Being charged by an irate elephant. I stalled the car seconds later. Masai Mara, Kenya. (Author)

Below: Up close to the lions. Masai Mara Kenya. (Author)

Above: Refuelling the floatplane before flight. Note the aircraft sits on the trailer ready to be towed down to the water. (Author)

Below: Doing the float rating in wellington boots. Jacksboro, Texas. (Author)

Above: The restored aerobatic Fuji 200. (Author)

Below: Author waiting for a patient. (Author)

Above: The office of the air ambulance. (Author)

Below: Inside the ambulance. (Author)

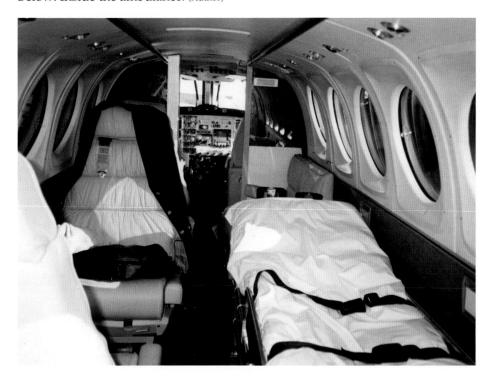

Above: F16 on wing tip of RNAF KC10 tanker. (Author)

Below: With she who would rather die in a ditching that be seen with her hair wet. (Author)

Moving from F/E to pilot is not as easy as some would have it. There is obviously a hierarchy in the cockpit and beyond that, the F/E was a specialist in his own right. His domain was running the systems and monitoring pilot actions but yet the initiative for the flight rested with the pilots, usually of course with the commander. To take on a completely different mindset in order to take responsibility for forward planning and tactical decision making required ditching a lot of the supporting role model for one of leadership. That could be a difficult transition for some. For me, possibly because I had a strong trait of single mindedness, I did not find it too difficult when it came to my turn to lead but I'm sure my leadership skills improved with the passage of time and experience. Hopefully those who flew with me did not suffer too much.

There was another tranche of training a couple of years later and the age was raised to 40. However, the clock had not stood still for me and I was out of scope again. I could not help but wonder if they were avoiding having to take me on as a pilot because I already had a licence. Another way to look at it was that they wanted to train F/E's from day one as ab-initio pilots only or employ experienced pilots with more hours than I had achieved. Either way I did not fit in with those categories and lost out.

The Tucson Bone Yard was 500 feet below. I cruised up and down the huge parking lot of decommissioned aircraft. There, right underneath, was a huge area covered in Boeing B52 bombers. Looking in other directions, there were Lockheed C130's, Fairchild C123's, McDonnell Douglas Phantoms, Douglas Skyraiders, Vought Corsairs, De Havilland Caribou and Huey Cobras. All the left-over kit from Vietnam.

The park stretched almost as far as I could see. The controller said, "No problem, do what you want, just don`t cross to the west side of the runway". A C130 rumbled off the runway beneath my left wing and turned away. Flying to the end of the Bone Yard took three or four minutes to cover the distance, then I turned 180 degrees to have another look. Only in America.

Arizona has a nice dry climate for aircraft storage and the desert is hard enough to park the old kit without worrying about the weight. Some work was going on to take some parts off for reuse, but generally the old birds just sat there baking in the sun.

We followed that epic by visiting the Pima Air and Space Museum next to the Bone Yard. There are aircraft there that embody the post war period of US military aviation. Monsters like the Boeing Stratocruiser and Lockheed Constellation dwarf all the hardware from the Vietnam War and earlier. Unfortunately, there was just not enough time to do it justice.

I visited the Confederate Air Force at Harlingen, Texas and saw their Grumman Bearcats, North American P51 Mustangs, Boeing B17 Flying Fortresses and many more. They put on a display of seriously heavy metal. There was a re-creation of Pearl Harbour, with North American Harvards dressed up Japanese Zeros. The pyrotechnics were awe-inspiring and the sound waves from the explosions hit you in the chest. In the melee of aircraft, the Grummans chased off the Zeros. That was not quite what happened at the real thing but never mind. It was all unforgettable and intensely 'US of A' patriotic good stuff.

At Harlingen, there was a museum of nose art. In wartime it has always been the case that warplanes boast nose art, usually something involving cartoon caricatures of scantily clad women riding on falling bombs. Some were more serious with a message like a picture of the Grim Reaper. The museum collection was of nose art skin panels cut from old aircraft. Much of it was from B17's and Second World War fighters. The art work was lusty and the message clear. Don`t mess with us.

At every place in the US we served I got a flight school checkout on anything they had. I would phone them two days before and book my plane and if needed, a rental car to get there.

In Dallas, there were places to take other people out with me. One of those was a country airport just over the Red River in Oklahoma. I would take a Cessna 172 with two other guys and three sets of golf clubs. There was a nine-hole course next to the runway.

One day I approached the airport and there was a Fox News helicopter flying overhead apparently filming. When we got onto the ground there was a reporter doing a piece to camera in front of a very battered Cessna 310 light twin. It transpired that this aircraft and another had collided on the approach. The twin was underneath the other one and had suffered several deep propeller gashes along the cabin roof ending at the shattered windscreen. Tragically, the other aircraft had gone over the nose of the twin and crashed straight into the ground killing those on board. Somehow the twin driver had landed, then taxied to the apron, parked it up neatly and walked away.

I would offer a spare seat on my rented aircraft first to the other guys in the cockpit, then to any of the cabin crew. I seldom flew alone. They would chip in some money and I got my hours in with their help. From Dallas, I would go north into Oklahoma or any of several good airport diners at other airports around Texas while from Houston I would do tours from Wayne Hooks airport in the north of the city to Galveston on the Bay of Mexico. Also, out of Houston I would take people to see The Alamo in San Antonio with a late lunch at the River Walk area in downtown.

One day, whilst en-route to Galveston from Houston, the area controller advised me of opposite traffic, a Boeing B29, 500 feet below. A minute later the B29, "Fifi", operated by the-then Confederate Air Force, slipped by under the left wing looking stunning in a polished aluminium finish. She was, at the time, the only example of the aircraft that dropped the atomic bomb on Japan in 1945.

Flying up to the Red River, separating Texas from Oklahoma, I got completely carried away and did something utterly stupid and dangerous. The river meandered through open country and no-one lived nearby. I had a Cessna 172 with a couple of cabin crew with me. I thought it would be great fun to fly low down the river and I went as low as I could until the girl in the back seat said she could see a wake in the water behind us. When I got that low and having frightened the passengers, I then did a rapid climb out from the river which was also not nice for them. How stupid. Don`t try that at home folks.

On another trip, I rented a Cessna 209 and filled it up with cabin crew who wanted a night out in New Orleans, Louisiana, to see the sights. Arriving early enough for a bit of tourism, we joined a tour that showed us the old mansions along the shoreline of Lake Pontchartrain and the trees hung with Spanish moss. Later we went downtown and ate in a Cajun restaurant where the locals danced to a Cajun band.

That night we all piled into a family room in a Days Inn and slept anywhere we could find, including on the floor. The next morning was our day to return to Gatwick from Houston on the DC10. Getting them back in the Cessna 209 was like herding cats. We made it back to the crew hotel with about two hours to call time. That was cutting it a little too fine.

From Los Angeles, there were destinations like Palm Springs, San Diego and Avalon on Catalina Island. At Catalina, an airport up on the hill above the town, you needed a cab to take you down to the town and on the way, we drove carefully past the wild bison that live on the island. In 1924 the bison were imported to the island for the film industry and had bred successfully – so much so that they were hunted and exported to the mainland to an Indian Reservation. They could turn nasty so the locals gave them a wide berth.

I heard about a 1950s Beech 18 available to fly in San Diego's Montgomery Field, which was right on the Mexican border. The pilot guide mentioned a hazard of unauthorised persons crossing the runway. Of course, they were all heading north trying to evade the border police.

I got in touch with the check pilot and he faxed me the pilot notes. I also arranged for me to do the whole pre-flight with him, which apparently no-one else had asked to do before. This was an old classic with Pratt and Whitney radial engines and I wanted to get my hands dirty before I flew it.

At Torrance airport in Los Angeles I rented a Beech 76 twin and, with my captain and one of the cabin crew flew, down to San Diego to fly this old bird enjoying a great day out. Some flights are never forgotten while some are only barely remembered from your log book. We did the usual stuff for a check out, even though their insurance would not let me fly without an instructor, but I always enjoyed the stalls and steep turns on a new type.

That done, we did some touch and go patterns at Montgomery. While in the pattern I heard ATC tell an inbound Southwest Airlines jet that we were in the downwind. The Southwest guy replied, "We got the growler". That made us feel pretty special. I never flew it again, but only a couple of years ago a visitor to Goodwood kindly let me have 15 minutes on the controls in his Beech 18. It's beautiful to fly.

Americans have a wonderful way with the aircraft radio, loving a bit of razzmatazz to go with it. They would modify the correct procedure for repeating back a clearance. One example I heard was a frequency change, issued by a controller to an aircraft, to alter to 125.250. We in the UK would laboriously spell each number out with a decimal point thrown in for good measure. This fun-loving pilot repeated back, "twenty-five and a quarter". Farnborough Radar might not appreciate that.

Another was getting a bit of tongue lashing from a female controller and he asked her if they had ever been married. She got pretty huffy about that. One controller issued a rapid-fire clearance to one old Marlboro' smoking cowboy who asked him to speak slower 'cos he couldn't hear that fast.

Atlanta was another chance to fly but we only had a night stop on the east side of the US so it was a quick one hour fly up to the Blue Mountains and back from Peachtree-DeKalb airport, then an hour or two in bed before the afternoon DC10 flight back to Gatwick. I tried to get something organised in New York but getting out to New Jersey to find somewhere to fly took too long.

On one holiday, I rented a Grumman American AA5A Cheetah and was impressed by its handling and helicopter like view out. This little four-seater, with only 150 horsepower up front, took us from minus 200 feet at Death Valley at a temperature of + 40 degrees centigrade to a breathless 12,500 feet flying through the Sierra Nevada Mountains from the desert to the Californian coastline. Later I bought one in UK and had many great flights around France and up to Denmark.

In New York, there to top up my required roster hours, I did all the tourist things one usually does. Empire State Building one trip, the Metropolitan Museum the next. One day I woke early, as is usual when first in America, and having listened long enough to the New York police sirens and noisy car horns, I decided to walk across Manhattan to the Intrepid Air and Space Museum on the Hudson River.

That was all very interesting and I made my way back to the hotel through some quiet back streets. It was Sunday morning and the street was empty save a rough looking guy outside a drug store. The odd thing was that the shop people in the drug store were looking at him intently through the window and he was eyeballing me. I was wearing one of those zip-up bomber jackets popular at the time. As a bit of bravado, I moved the zip down a bit and put my right hand momentarily under my left armpit. He got the implied message, thought I was packing a piece, and moved back against the wall. One never knows, but I think it saved some aggravation.

It's always important that one does not look like a victim. As an aside, I was walking along a busy street in the UK when a lowlife asked me the time. I turned to look at him and he started moving slowly away from the wall towards me. On my left another sleazy example circled around to get behind me. With my left-hand up to the first one's face I read the time and then moved my hand to point at the second one on the move. Circling sleazebag stopped and moved back. All this time I was looking into the first man's eyes.

All of a sudden I saw the ludicrous side of this half-cocked attempt at a pavement robbery on an old grey-headed passer-by. I grinned at the guy and he grinned sheepishly back. I went on my way. It is possible to take control of a hazardous situation by seizing the initiative. I suppose that was what I instinctively did.

Another time, in downtown Manhattan, Bill Clinton's motorcade had just swept into the basement car park of a hotel and his security agents had swung out into the middle of the road, blocking traffic as the motorcade went through. A taxi driver with a fare on board wound his window down and gave the agent a mouthful for holding him up, whereupon the agent strode over to the cabbie and smacked him across the face.

This cabbie gave chase and punched said agent in the back. Next thing the agent had his gun in one hand and showing a federal badge in the other ordered the cabbie back in his car. By the time the guy got back to his car, the fare had got out and run off. Not a great move by the taxi man.

I was in the Chinese quarter of Canal Street when a fire broke out in a restaurant kitchen in the first floor of a tall building. NYPD and Fire Department shut the street down in no time and they had a Chinese speaker on a bull horn ordering the Chinese people out of the building. That had no effect whatsoever, as the people above the fire just leaned out of the windows to get a better look. Fortunately, the fire was brought under control quite soon so no-one appeared to be in danger of becoming part of the menu.

When we got the Phoenix route with a shuttle to San Diego, it opened up Arizona for me. I got my checkouts at Phoenix Scottsdale airport and rented anything they had. North of Phoenix is of course the Grand Canyon, the airport being 6700 feet above sea level. On the way was Sedona in the red rock country where the airport was on a 'mesa', a table of land resembling an aircraft carrier scaled up.

Once I had scouted the route and how to fly in the special rules area of the Grand Canyon it was fairly straightforward to load up some $50 thrill seekers from the DC10 crew and take them up over the canyon. I would have them airborne by 0900 hours, point out Sedona and the extinct volcano field en-route, fly over the canyon, traverse the north rim then cross back over to land at the airport. When you launch out over the rim at 500 feet above the rim, the canyon drops down sharply from 6,700 feet to 1,500 feet above sea level to the Colorado River at the bottom.

Visually it is a white knuckle, buttock clenching experience. It was a short ride from Grand Canyon Airport to the town at the south rim for lunch and some tourist browsing, then back down to Scottsdale. I had my passengers in the hotel bar for dinner with the rest of the crew by 1830. The trips were very popular. Making a shorter trip to Sedona was also a good day out.

There was another airline crew that apparently had four up in a Cessna 172 who took off with full tanks from the Grand Canyon airport. They got off the ground but flew on straight into the pine trees. Apparentl,y no-one survived. I lost count of the number of times I flew the canyon but it must have been about 16 and I went there at other times on holiday by car.

I got married again. We took holidays in America, usually renting an aircraft. We drove up to the canyon from Phoenix and rode mules down to the Phantom Ranch on the Colorado River bank for a night stop. Everything for the Phantom Ranch at the Colorado riverside was brought down on pack mules and all the trash went out the same way.

It took the mules about five hours to pick their way carefully down but taking a different trail back up, they leaned into it and got back up to the rim in about four hours. I'm told horses are like that, going back faster than outbound in anticipation of a stable with a nose bag in it. I was no horse rider so placed my faith in the animal which was well founded. My wife however had been riding for years and had her own horse, so would not trust the mule she had. I think it was glad to see the back of her.

I also retraced my steps in Kenya to the Masai Mara but this time wisely deciding to let a driver or a charter aircraft pilot from Wilson Airport in Nairobi take us where we wanted to go.

I rented aircraft from Fort Lauderdale in Florida and flew twice out to the Bahamas. Nassau was pleasant but the little islands were very basic, quite flat and featureless. To be honest the best thing about the Bahamas was the ocean which was a beautiful emerald blue in the sunlight. Hotels on the out islands did not offer much more than a state highway motel.

Arrangements had been made to meet some friends at an out island and the weather turned for the worse, so it was not all constant blue sky flying. After delaying till the next day, I took off for a short crossing of only about 40 miles but shortly after take-off I saw a line of impenetrable thunderstorms heading on the wind towards me. The sky was turbulent yet the sea beneath the squall line was flat as a mill pond. There must be huge downdrafts to produce that effect.

Turning round, the tail wind propelled me back to my airfield of departure and I entered the circuit in an impending storm and threw the Cessna 172 on the runway. Taxiing fast back to the apron, I spun it round into wind and shut down just in time as the gust front hit me. The aeroplane sat rocking in torrential rain and as it passed through the airport manager drove out to pick up and take a crestfallen and chastened aviator back to his hotel.

Arriving back into Florida, a flight plan was mandatory and with it came a clearance through the Air Defence Identification Zone. If you busted the ADIZ without permission, you were in big trouble. Every flight inbound from the Bahamas would have to land at a customs airport, where unsmiling Drug Enforcement agents searched us and the plane thoroughly.

If you wanted to enjoy an airborne view of the Kennedy Space Centre, a tourist in a light plane could secure clearance to give it a flyby for a look-see. So, I called up the tower and they gave me permission to fly down the runway at 500 feet so that we could see the facility close up. The runway is 15,000 feet long and it took some time at 100 knots.

Having done so many flights around America, I started going to odd places simply to get the airport name in my log book. Many of the names were in rural areas, or places of Spanish origin. Here is a few: Possum Kingdom, McGehee Catfish (with a restaurant serving the catfish) Tehachapi, Mariposa Yosemite, Big Bear, Chalet Suzanne, Wichita Falls (a disappointing trickle), Just Plane Fun (nice one), Albuquerque Coronado, Agua Dulce, Palo Alto, Peachtree Dekalb, Hawks Nest, Treasure Key, Nacogdoches, San Carlos Apache, Alamogordo White Sands, and, my all-time favourite, Kickapoo Downtown.

One day, I flew from Dallas out to Breckenridge, about 100 miles west. The only reason to go was that I had not been there before, so why not. After arriving I noticed some activity going on in a hangar so I walked over and asked if I might see the work going on.

Inside was a restored Hawker Sea Fury which was ex-Iraq Air Force having a new Pratt and Whitney R3350 radial engine fitted in place of the Bristol Centaurus that it came with. The man who flew it sat watching and I struck up a conversation with him. This taciturn, gruff ex-Marine Corps pilot was Howard Pardue, well known as a heavy metal display pilot. When I owned up to having some knowledge of the Centaurus he took a little more interest in me and asked if I had driven out from the city. When I told him that I had flown out in a J3 Cub, he grudgingly said "Way to go", and that was all I got out of him.

Pardue flew Grumman Bearcats among other historic aircraft and sadly died in one during a display in 2012.

At about this time in my flight engineer career I started to suffer a repetitive nightmare that I was in the DC10 doing my job and as we taxied into the parking position, nose in to the terminal, the aircraft did not stop and crashed through the glass windows of the terminal. The dream went exactly the same way every time and I probably had it once a week.

Later, when I became a commercial pilot and had ceased to be an F/E the dream went away. A shrink would have a good time with that one but I suppose once I had learned to fly I was no longer comfortable not being in control; once my status was elevated to being Pilot in Command, the fear went away.

We were out in the middle of the lake and Steve, the owner of the floatplane, told me to just keep coming down for a water landing and if he thought it was too rough I was to climb away. I peeked a look out of the left side window and I could see that the waves were short and about two feet high. This was only a little Aeronca Chief and not suited to rough water. We had always landed in the lee shore so far, so surely Steve with his experience would not want me to try it. "Try landing," he said, so I let the aircraft settle into the water. Immediately, water flew all over us as the floats cut into the wave tops. "Go around!" he shouted and I tried to haul it off again. We hit three wave tops before lifting off again and on the third there was a loud crack. Looking down to the left, the nose of the left float was waving from side to side. Bad news. We had just broken the plane.

Climbing away at 65mph, the float gently wagged from side to side. We discussed putting it down on this lake or flying back to our base not too far away. I reasoned that if we did not exceed our current speed, the float should stay with us. Agreed. We would take it back. Steve would do the landing and as soon as it was on the water we would cut the engine and Steve, being the heavier of the two of us, would jump out onto the good float and counterbalance the tendency for the Aeronca to turn over and sink.

In the calm water of our base lake the little aircraft settled gently onto the lake surface. Immediately the nose of the loose left float dug into the water. Engine off and a large Texan went to hang out on the right wing strut. We were still more or less upright. I restarted the engine and taxied to the shore with Steve hanging out there as if we were sailing a racing yacht.

It turned out that the damage was not too bad. We had torn the front float strut bracket out of the left float and the bracing rods between the floats had stretched and one had snapped. The cabin had buckled slightly behind the left door. Steve had it back in the air a couple of weeks later at a cost of about $150. It was the only time I ever broke a plane.

In August 1996, I had seen an advert in airports around Dallas for float ratings on a lake about halfway across Texas on what was called the Dry Line. West of the line there was little rainfall, so there were few lakes. This lake, by the side of a hard runway was the nearest to Steve's base airport in West Texas that he could find to put it on, but still about 100 miles out from Dallas.

I signed up for the five hours it takes to get the rating and on my next Dallas trip rented a car and headed out to see him. The quiet little airport had a few hangars – in one was the Aeronca on a trolley and a vehicle to couple it to for taking it to the lakeside. The tow vehicle also had a fuel tank and a hand pump fitted inside to refuel the aircraft; it was all self-contained. There was also a trailer for storage and to provide overnight accommodation. As it was a dry county, I always took a six pack with me to pass away the evenings. No-one else used it and Steve would have one of his flight school students fly him up there with his float instructor.

It was winter and the water was cold. We flew wearing rubber wellington boots thereby showing that sensitive feet only have a small part to play in flying. I was warned not to step into the water without looking as there were water moccasin snakes in the shallows.

The rating was completed in the five hours and afterwards I asked more in hope than anything else, how much time would his insurance need before I could fly it solo. To my surprise, it only needed ten hours so we arranged to keep on going with the other five hours. Later they found it inconvenient to keep flying over to get the floatplane out for me to fly so Steve asked me if I thought I could do it all by myself.

I worked out a way of fuelling it up, putting it into the water then replacing it in the hangar at night without any help. When I had flown, I just rang them up and gave them the flight time to charge against my credit card. It was a great arrangement and although I only flew one and a half hours each trip to Dallas, it kept me happy doing all the stuff it needed to launch and retrieve it back into the hangar.

One afternoon, I water taxied back to the slipway and nosed the float onto the bank. I needed to tie a rope on something to enable me to go and bring the vehicle and trolley down to the water's edge. A large rock on the bank looked just right. When I bent down to tie the rope round it, the rock rattled. OK, rattlesnake, you have that rock and I'll find another.

I had asked Steve what permission was needed to fly into other lakes so I could try other landing spots. He described it to me as, firstly to fly low over the water to check for any submerged logs and if while doing that I did not notice any gun flashes, to go ahead and land. Only in Texas. As good as float flying was, I only did about 20 hours on that Champ. I needed hours for a commercial licence so I looked for other types to fly.

Steve also had a contract with an Arab airline for their students to be awarded a US CPL which involved 250 hours flight time. They had a job waiting for them when they returned to their sponsor airline. Steve had noticed that the aircraft they used to build up their cross-country time had recorded the running hours but had not burned the fuel. In other words, they flew somewhere quiet and read a book or something while the engine was running. What dummies.

I flew the Cessna 172 to the right of the Texas Interstate highway so I could keep my eye on the road. This was real IFR. (I follow roads, not Instrument Flight Rules). The rain was intense and I was scud running under 300 feet of cloud. This was dodgy, lit towers and similar obstacles were marked with a red light but I was down in the weeds. My finger trembled on the spot on the map where I reckoned I was. Taking my eyes off the road for an instant I saw an airfield marked on the map next to a lake on my right. If I could only find the lake.

Out to my right appeared a faint image of a lake shoreline, so I turned right on a southerly heading and flew over the lake. At least there was little to fly into over the water. Now I had to find the airfield on the left bank. I made a quick measurement and calculated a time to fly. Two minutes should do it. The clouds were closing in around me and I was getting seriously worried.

Back then I had no Instrument Flight Rating to rely upon. Time up, I had to turn to where the airfield should be but all I had was nothing but low cloud and lake water. Nothing else to do, I turned 90 degrees and hoped for the best. The cloud grasped me and rain beat on the windshield. I was scared witless. Rain water squirted into the cockpit around the poorly fitting windscreen and sprayed in my face.

Suddenly a huge rain soaked runway emerged right on the nose. I splashed down onto it and nearly got religion.

The airfield was deserted and it had no control tower. Parking up and tying down the aircraft, I sploshed across the airfield to the only sign of life which was a mobile home. A woman answered the door and let me shelter inside while she called the town's cab driver to take me to a motel for the night.

This was small town America and being in the Bible belt, it was also dry. I got to the motel and checked in. The clerk confirmed the bad news about no booze. However, he could fix that. In a windowless room at the back of the motel they had a member's only drinking club. I swiftly enrolled. Dumping my kit in my room I called the flight school in Dallas to tell them I would be back in the morning and headed for the drinking club. There I found three or four good ol` boys drinking Budweiser who welcomed me into their company. One of these guys was wearing rattlesnake boots and a matching waistcoat. We got talking. He made a living by skinning rattlers and making boots, shoes, waistcoats, hats and handbags out of rattler skins and did all the trapping himself. That was a fascinating evening.

The morning dawned bright and fresh and the town cab driver took me back to the aircraft. I had a serene early morning flight back to Dallas.

I was now at the point where I needed to chalk up more twin time, so I looked around to rent twins and inch closer to a flying job. The cheapest thing I ever found was a rough old dog of a Piper Apache with 150 HP engines. With one engine off, it could not maintain altitude. Truly then, as we say in aviation, the other engine would have served to take me to the scene of an accident. On the bright side, it was only $95 per hour including fuel.

All this time spent in America started me thinking about living there and I spent some time looking into how to acquire the Green Card residency permit. It was not going to be simple, requiring either a job I would be unlikely to get, since they had plenty of guys like me, or setting up a business, which I could not afford to do. Others had settled there by buying a property and getting their pension paid to them in the US. Their status would be a tourist entry visa, only valid for six months after which you would have to leave for a period of time, then come back with hopefully the same tourist condition. Trouble was that any immigration officer could decide on the spot that you were not a bona fide tourist and turn you back out again. That would have left me with a property to dispose of while being unable to get back in to oversee the process. It all sounded like a nightmare I could not risk, so it came to nothing.

It was a great pity because living on an air park in Arizona with a little aircraft hangared inside my home would have been my idea of heaven. I always met the most hospitable Americans on my travels, especially where the common bond of aviation applied. Nothing was impossible. It fits that the end of American spells "I Can".

Of course, via my job, I also spent time in other parts of the globe where I was able to undertake similar flying excursions. On one occasion, I rented a four seater in Lusaka, Zambia to fly down to Victoria Falls. The Lusaka Flying Club instructor was a white guy who was obviously without means. He had a hole in the seat of his trousers. We had to file a Flight Plan with ATC even to do some circuits for the check-out and the plan had to be filed with 24 hours' notice. Check-out done, I booked it for the next time I was back in Lusaka.

On the next trip, I had three others with me and climbed up to 9,000 feet to run down to the falls. To find the falls, I followed the main road which meandered through the bush in a fairly straight line. In addition to that rudimentary aid to navigation, Lusaka Radio had a very powerful transmitter whose frequency could be set on the Direction Finder fitted in the aircraft. It was a simple matter to backtrack the needle pointing behind me and wait for the falls to show up.

Every flight in Zambia had to be on a flight plan and was watched by the military. I had been assured the aircraft would do over 100 knots so filed a time that would work on paper. In the event I was half an hour late because the speed was way down and there was some wind on the nose.

Before landing I got clearance from the tower to fly over the falls which was duly given with the caveat that I was not to fly over the Zimbabwe side. Since we were some distance from the airfield and they had no radar to see what I was doing, I flew over the entire falls anyway at a few hundred feet.

On arrival at Victoria Falls two soldiers rocked up and escorted me at gunpoint to their officer who had me explain to him why I was late and accused me of making an unauthorised landing somewhere else. It took some time to get him to understand the problem with a slow aircraft into wind and it was all rather unpleasant. Eventually, I was released from the military and we grabbed a taxi down to the falls.

It was mid-season and quite a lot of water was thundering over the edge. You could just about see from one end to the other. Every so often there were viewing balconies in the trees on the rim where the water vapour drifted through the sunlight creating miniature rainbows you could stand in. The locals call the falls Mosi-oa-tunya which translates to "smoke that thunders". As the huge volume of Zambezi water roars over the lip of the falls, the vapour rises and the whole thing can be seen and heard from some distance.

We walked across the bridge into Zimbabwe and lunched in the Livingstone Hotel, itself a stunning piece of colonial history. The bridge, made in England and completed in 1905, was the idea of Cecil Rhodes as part of a railway line from Cairo to Cape Town which never came to pass. On the Zambian side there was a steam train graveyard where huge old railway engines rusted away. The artist David Shepherd famously painted these relics and brought them back to life.

Back at the airport, I was introduced to a back packer who could not get a flight back to Lusaka and wanted a lift. I foolishly allowed him to squeeze into the aircraft. Overladen and at an airfield altitude of 3,500 feet, we staggered off the runway and headed home. It was nightfall by the time we got back and the town lights of Lusaka stood out clearly against a backdrop of darkness. The airport lights to the north of the town came in sight and I eased the tired old aircraft back on the runway.

CHAPTER TWELVE

Aircraft Shares

While I was a flight engineer for BA, my retirement age was in 1997 at the age of 55. If I had gone early as soon as I had a CPL and found some kind of flying job, I would have had to forfeit a third of my expected pension. That kept me tied down till I was at the BA retirement age but I carried on flying anything I could get my hands on to build more hours.

While renting, mainly in the US, I bought into flying groups in the UK, mostly based at Shoreham. I was involved with four groups and found it much easier, and above all cheaper, to be a group member.

My first share ownership was in a Beech Musketeer and that was a nice little four-seater, though lacking in performance. I sold the Musketeer share and moved into a Piper Vagabond which was a two seat, very basic and the nose wheel had been fitted at the back. This was the cheapest flying you could get and I enjoyed the tail wheel challenge. I found the aircraft fishtailed in any turbulence, no doubt because it was a fairly short fuselage.

Bored again, I sold the Vagabond share for one in a Robin 100 four seater. This had all the bells and whistles. It was the all metal variant with the 200hp engine. There were 20 group members and it was not readily available. The aircraft was also not very reliable and spent rather a lot of time in the hangar. The group voted to sell the aircraft and disband.

At the time a BA pilot and I had a hankering for something aerobatic and we looked around for something suitable. What we found was a Fuji 200 with an 180hp engine. This aircraft, built in Japan, was capable of being used a four-seat tourer, or with two up could be flown aerobatically. It had not flown for some years and looked sorry for itself.

The paint was original and dull, also being well decorated in pigeon poo. The engine, as we expected, had internal corrosion from disuse and would need overhaul. In addition to all that it would need an annual inspection. We discussed a price with the owner and bought it. Fortunately, we only had to wheel it to the hangar next door to get the work done, and shedloads of cash later it was good to fly. Now we looked around for a paint job and later I ferried it up to Norfolk and back to have it stripped and repainted. This was now a very handsome aircraft and selling shares in it was no problem.

I got some aerobatic training from my co-owner, who himself had been a fast jet pilot in the RAF before joining BA so he knew what he was doing. With trepidation, I would go off by myself and do some aeros over a river, road and railway feature so I could orientate myself easily. The first thing I would do was to spin it from a safe height so that if anything did go badly wrong with my manoeuvres, I might just sort it out before hitting the deck. Fifteen minutes was about as much as my stomach would allow and I often flew back to Shoreham wings level and ever so gently, hoping I would not barf before landing. I was never going to be great at aeros but it gave me a lot of confidence if in future, attitudes accidentally became unusual.

A near neighbour of mine, Nick Berryman, was an ex-wartime pilot who had served time in an Air Sea Rescue squadron flying Supermarine Spitfires, Hawker Hurricanes and, most interestingly, the Supermarine Walrus. He had been stationed at Warmwell, in Dorset, and Harrowbeer, in Devon.

Nick wanted to go to Devon before time overtook him to explore his past once more. As he was of advancing years we flew to Plymouth Airport and were met and taken to Harrowbeer. The dispersal he had flown from was still there and in good condition. In a retirement home nearby lived his aircraft fitter from those days, still making powered model aircraft and driving everyone under the tables whenever he decided to fly one.

Nick had taken the controls for part of our flight there and back. He did not fly straight and level, and kept weaving gently all time. Seemingly, his wartime habit of not being a sitting target for an enemy fighter had not gone away. Nick is no longer with us but his book, *In the Nick of Time*, still is.

The co-owner of the Fuji aircraft moved his base from Gatwick to Manchester to take another flying job in BA and we both sold our shares in it. I also sold my BA shares at an opportune moment and with some free cash and money from the Fuji, I looked around for an aircraft to buy.

Eventually I bought my first aircraft, a Cessna 140 tail dragger made in 1946. I did not regard that as too old because after all, I had been made in 1942.

When I found one to look at it was in a hangar at Kemble and was the property of a retired RAF Air Commodore. It was covered in smashed flies. Clearly the owner was accustomed to having someone keep things in order for him. I haggled and he obstinately refused to budge. As there was not another to be bought, he made a sale.

I had some tail wheel time by then, but I took the number of a chap who could convert me onto the type. After several failed attempts to get together for a check-out, I fired the 140 up and did three circuits at Kemble by myself. Then with the landing fees paid I flew it down to my Goodwood base.

The old girl only had 85hp and it needed nursing along. Losing altitude meant a maximum power slog back up again. I think all the horses in this engine were geldings. The engine was made by Continental and being carburetted was prone to carb icing. I duly took all the advice I could get about carb ice and used carburettor heat often to prevent formation of ice which might starve the engine of air. That good habit stays with me and I use carb heat more than most pilots I fly with.

The 140 provided me with the means to get around much more of France and I took it right down as far as Perpignan on the Mediterranean and over to the Alps at Annecy. Plugging away at 6,000 feet in the heat of summer, we had to have the side doors open to let the heat of the engine escape. We took it to little grass airfields and it usually produced some interest from the locals. One little place we stayed at for a few days even went so far as to feature it in the local newspaper. It was only fitted for Visual Flight Rules and there were periods of flying which were completely outside the limits of the aircraft. It was a grand little ship and I miss it now. I used to put my first border collie in the back behind the seats and even with a 40lb dog in the luggage space you noticed the difference in longitudinal trim.

The dog was pretty cool about the whole affair and used to disembark at whatever airfield we flew to with a great display of importance.

Eventually, on an annual inspection my C140 was diagnosed with internal corrosion in the area around the door frames. Also, there was a suspicion of corrosion at the wing joints and the wings came off to allow a closer look. The bill was going to be horrendous, so with a heavy heart, I parted with it.

Shortly after that set back, I once again committed my bank balance to a regular assault from aircraft bills by buying a Grumman Cheetah, AA5A G-PAWS. Several had been imported into the UK at the same time and they all got registrations related to the cat family. Once on a trip out somewhere I was asked if I was a veterinarian because of the registration "paws".

I ran this aircraft by myself for several years, but in the end set up a group with three others to offset the costs. One of our group, a Polish aircraft engineer, took it all the way to his home town in Poland which was good use of the machine.

Later, the same guy had a bit of a spat with his wife and went off to fly as arranged. His distraught wife thought he was going to kill himself in it so called the police. By this time my pal had got airborne for a bimble round the county. The police had him tracked and shut the airfield. Back he came, thinking the circuit was a bit quiet, landed, shut down and started the fill in the flight log.

There was a knock on the window and he found two policemen standing there who took him into custody and marched him off in handcuffs to the local nick. While he was being interviewed, the police broke into his car on the airfield to check for any evidence of a misdemeanor. Well, they found nothing, but broke three side windows in the botched attempt to get in. The outcome was that no charges were brought, unsurprising since he had done nothing illegal and he successfully reclaimed the cost of the broken windows. I am amazed how sanguine he was about the whole episode. I would have been fuming.

Eventually, we decided to sell the aircraft which was a bit of a blow. I sold it to a film stunt man with the condition that he did not bend it.

Now, I rent a Maule 160, which is a version with the tailwheel fitted at the front. I wish they had not done that, because it is much better round the other way.

When I had been granted the licences I wanted, I looked around for what else to do. On the DC10, we had a pilot who as well as working for BA, was also an examiner for an air taxi company in the UK who operated Beechcraft King Air turboprops. He could do the schedule of test items with me to add the type rating on my licence. We talked it over and thought maybe we could do it more economically in the US.

As it happened I knew of a really cheap King Air at Addison Airport in Dallas which was available for very little money. It was a dog. The engines were beyond their maximum life for commercial operations and the fuel tanks were affected by algae growing in them. The algae were given a chemical treatment to kill them off and when I drew some fuel from the tank drains to check for water contamination, pints of white snot came out before the fuel ran clear.

We were faced with some really nasty weather but the aircraft was available and we did not want to lose the chance to do the rating. The whole of Texas was poor, as were the neighbouring states. In the end, every circuit I flew had to be an instrument approach and all this in a type I had not flown before. We got the upper air work done, then bashed the circuit for about five approaches. The night circuits had to wait till we were back in the UK where we hired another King Air at Biggin Hill for an hour to complete the rating.

At the time, I had no idea that the rating was going to be any use to me but later on I had cause to be very grateful to my pal for doing it with me. I was still a couple of years away from retirement at BA but kept my hand in every year by renting a King Air in Phoenix with an instructor.

For me, BA continued much as before after the merger. We at Gatwick were known as "The Country Cousins", a title I was quite happy with. There was no doubt that the power came from Heathrow. Meanwhile, our flight engineer union merged with the British Airline Pilots Association so we became a virtual work force with no voting clout.

Within BALPA, the main fleet at Heathrow – at the time the B747 – held the power by voting strength. So we paid our dues, often under the concept of union protection from management, but achieved little out of it. I had at one point asked BALPA if they would extend me an interest free loan to pay for my Instrument Rating. They told me in no uncertain terms that some of their pilot members had been recently been made redundant and that funds would be going to pay for new ratings for them. Thanks, BALPA. I hope the re-employed pilots were grateful for my contribution.

There were notices on the bulletin board inviting flight engineers to go onto the B747 or Concorde, both of which would be based at Heathrow. I had avoided Heathrow for years so I was not about to go there if I did not have to, even if I had been chosen for one of those fleets. My best career move would have been the B747 because that could have extended my working life by another few years as a flight engineer.

However, I was now running up hours towards my Air Transport Pilot Licence and I was awash with self-belief in my ability to walk out of BA into a pilot job.

I had been given a type rating examiners post on the DC10 and was on the simulator training or examining other F/E's. This made my roster about one third simulator time with the rest on the bid line system. The bid system worked by each person having a choice, based on seniority, to bid for their choice of work provided it made up a line having the required working hours for the month.

It was a great success because some people did not want long trips away and others chose destinations according their interest. I bid for the two night stops at a destination which gave me time to enjoy a day out and in the case of renting aircraft, the chance to go further afield. There was a huge benefit in working on my home time zone in the simulator. I would see other guys coming on the simulator looking tired with their body clocks somewhere about 30 degrees west. Once more, as a trainer, I learned quite a bit from observing other people operating the aircraft.

During this time BA won a contract to train Japan Airline Systems DC10 crews and I was assigned some of their simulator conversions. They were very accurate in all they did but there was definitely a cockpit hierarchy from the captain down to the rest of the crew. This I found to be culturally based and is a recognised problem in parts of the world. If the head honcho is doing something wrong, the other guys do not feel empowered to stop him and will sit there till it all goes wrong. That has got to be changed but it is no easy task.

The guys would do their own briefing in the hotel before we in turn got to brief them so they were very well prepared. Respect played a big thing in their culture and they would never show us any disrespect, even if we were not totally correct about something. I managed to take the Japanese flight engineers out for a taste of English pubs and they loved it. Also, I took them up in the aircraft in which I had a share.

We went to Headcorn in Kent and at low level past the white cliffs at Beachy Head on the way back. At the end of the course, they surprised us with presents from their airline which left us embarrassed, having nothing to present to them.

BA had given me an Instructor's course and in the 1990s we took on the concept of Crew Resource Management. Some people think that CRM only applies to multi crew cockpits but that is not true. The principles behind good cockpit management applied just as much to the single pilot. This was something new and alien to some of us but for those who understood how to lead effectively, it was affirming what they had been doing all along. In other words, to prioritise your tasks, have an open mind, and listen to others while still being able to make good leadership decisions.

When I compared this with some of the dinosaurs I flew with back in TMAC, we had come a long way.

During the introduction to CRM we spent a lot of time absorbing some interesting subjects including, controversially, interaction of personalities. To illustrate personality types to us and to enable crew members to understand our own and one another's traits, the company had us complete a questionnaire to determine what personality type we thought we were and also required us to ask three other colleagues to fill one in about ourselves. The object was to see what type of person they thought we were by comparison. The assumption was that although we might key-hole ourselves into a slot we would prefer, the accurate assessment would come from the average of the external viewpoint of our colleagues.

The result often came as a surprise. I recall finding that I was more single minded than I thought but, interestingly, not the team player I had assumed myself to be. Some people were very disturbed by the whole experience and rumour had it that a few guys quietly took advice from a psychiatrist. Nevertheless, it was a very stimulating exercise which did shape my thinking towards other people and must have affected my own leadership style in the later part of my career as a pilot.

One object of the exercise was to illustrate introvert or extrovert personalities. Unsurprisingly, anyone on the extremes of either register would not be desirable in the cockpit, so it came as no surprise to find that the participants featured somewhere in the middle, with no massive swings of personality either way. Of course, that does not mean to say that we would not have a little of each in our personality soup. The percentage came out in favour of the introvert, which constituted about two thirds of us. I thought that was strange because seeing aircraft take off or land, with all that energy and noise, one would be forgiven for thinking that the drivers inside must be running on high octane testosterone. However, I reasoned that all that stuff does not happen without much calm calculation and risk analysis, so 'introvert' sounds right on balance.

To the above must be added the cultural differences encountered where East meets West in the cockpit. Working with Asians was very different to, say, rodeo types from Texas. With the ever-widening employment opportunities for pilots, there are multiple nationalities working together in the cockpit and bringing those cultures together into an efficient team can be a challenge.

An aviator is different to a pilot. Anyone can be a pilot but to be called an aviator is a compliment. To define an aviator is always difficult, but, in my mind, it has always been someone who has exceptional situational awareness, monitors changes and has a plan to cope with any eventuality. Attached to those qualities is airmanship, which kind of sums up the foregoing skills. If you have airmanship, you can be referred to as an aviator. Some of that can be learned from books, though experience has no substitute. Flying with an aviator is a privilege.

Each debrief after training on the simulator would involve CRM principles and to assist that we had a camera and tape recorder fitted in the DC10. After the session, we would play back some parts of it for discussion. After the post flight debrief it was erased so there was no record of it.

We were not the only company to use that simulator, some came from developing countries who did not have an open mind towards this kind of thing and quite possibly worked in a high threat management environment. First of all, we would find banana skins and chocolate wrappers in the recorder. Later, someone nicked the camera so that was the end of that.

CHAPTER THIRTEEN

Ambulance Driver

Ikept the speed up at the controller's request. We had big jets behind us. I kept 180 knots as long as I could then pulled some power off to get the flaps out. This was 27L at Heathrow and I was the captain of this little twin turbo-prop. For a second or two, I wondered if all this was real. I only had about three months' time on the job and there I was, left seat on approach to Heathrow.

Landing clearance came, gear down, full flap, a passable landing and a swift exit to the right. The controller thanks me for expediting my approach and runway exit. No problem. Hope I sounded cool.

I had been lucky. Retirement came at the age of 55 in BA. Many people never worked again and festered in the pub and the nineteenth hole reliving old times. The more enterprising went on to other companies where they often found another 10 years' work. When my time was up at BA I had a UK CPL/IR, a 'frozen' ATPL, awaiting more hours to qualify, and the King Air rating to my name. My US licences were valid but they did not get me any employment.

In November 1997, I applied for a job with an air ambulance company and was fortunate enough to be offered it. The chief pilot of the day was an ex-British Aerospace Harrier test pilot from Dunsfold who had enjoyed working closely with engineers in the Harrier development period. As my CV included my engineer background he invited me in for an interview. The chief pilot was Swiss and good at making his own decisions. He took me on without reference to the owner. That might have been the start of his undoing for the owner was not used to anyone taking decisions and could be a little frosty about it.

139

Taking the Operations Manual home, I had boned up on the Standard Operating Procedures. Before I was cut loose for line training I did a check flight with the company examiner. As I had learned the SOP's from the manual, I applied them. So, I opened the throttles, checked power stable at 40% and called "Set Power". The "Uh?" response from my examiner left no doubt that little was observed in the way of documented SOPs so I had better see what everyone else does.

My first flight with the chief pilot, with me in the right seat, was novel. As the ex-test pilot opened the throttles he called "Mark", which I suppose was for me to record the time of take-off. As I did not understand that, we agreed to drop the non-standard call. We had another co-pilot called Mark. There may have been some confusion there also.

The chief pilot was a 'deemer'. That is, he was always deeming things and making on the spot decisions. On one trip, not long after he employed me, he was on a job with two patients, one of whom had to be dropped off up in the north of England, then the other in the south. As he was coming up from the south he deemed that he would reverse the offload and informed the company to change all the arrangements. There was a lot of grief about that and shortly afterwards he left us.

The first line flight I did was to Alicante. Still under supervision, I was right seat with the company examiner. In the first hour of the flight south we had an anomaly in the right engine which showed a possible fuel control unit problem. We discussed the possibility of turning back but the problem went away so we pressed on. In Alicante, we fuelled up and loaded the patient. It was my sector back, so I taxied out and held short of the runway for landing traffic.

As we sat there, the fuel control unit gave up the ghost and failed. As it did so, the fuel pump sensed a drop in pressure and went into full flow. When that happens, the engine can exceed all the red lines and then shut itself down.

It was purely instinctive. As I saw the needles racing round the gauges, my flight engineer experience kicked in and I closed the fuel shut off. The needles sped up to just below the red lines and ran back down again. So back we went. When I got to the parking area, the ramp sloped uphill and unless I built up some speed I could not follow the marshaller's car.

So, I would run at the slope on the one engine, run out of steerage, turn around in a circle and repeat the process, gaining a few yards every time. The man in the tower got agitated and gave me a telling-off for not following the marshaller. In exchange, I gave him a telling-off for not looking and not realising that I was only on one engine and could not taxi uphill in a straight line.

Having arranged for an ambulance to return the patient to the hospital, we discussed the technical problem. Clearly, we were going nowhere that day.

By the time the ambulance arrived, the sun was going down and the air became thick with mosquitoes from the old rice paddies next to the runway. As we lifted the stretcher out and into the ambulance the mossies' were all over our face and arms. I could hardly wait to put the stretcher down and brush them off.

We found a local engineer to fix it for us the next day. As it involved disturbing engine controls and replacing the fuel control unit and pump it needed a duplicate inspection. I got dispensation to sign off the second inspection and after getting the patient back out of hospital, we went on our way.

My handling of the engine failure, fortunately occurring just before take-off instead of during it, was instinct driven by thousands of hours as an F/E. Subsequently, when aircraft problems happened to me in my time as a commercial pilot, I tended to draw on my previous experience as a maintenance and flight engineer.

When the company had a problem with an aircraft but yet it was still just about fit to fly, I was generally given that aircraft to operate. In so doing the risk was more controlled by having an engineer's view on the problem rather than a pilot who did not have that background to draw upon. Usually, I would ask what the plan for rectification was going to be before accepting the aircraft. I expected, and usually got, a plan that entailed nursing the problem to get the ambulance task done with an immediate engineering fix arranged for the next day.

The firm's owners had soon earmarked me as a captain, which was a bit of a surprise as I had little experience of European operations and really wanted to get my feet under the table for six months to learn something about it before taking the left seat. So, finding myself promoted quite quickly and as I thought, above my capabilities, came as a surprise. The first few months building up my route and area knowledge was a steep learning curve but also hugely exciting.

The operating region was the whole of Europe. Tracing a line clockwise starting with Ireland the region boundary went up to Norway, across Scandinavia, through the Baltic to St Petersburg, across western Russia and the Balkans to the eastern end of the Mediterranean along the North African coast and down into the Canaries.

There were regular routes which tended to be seasonal. The Canaries was normal in the winter, as were the ski resorts in Europe. In the summer the customers were mainly found in Spain.

This type of operation was based on airways flying, which is under the control of ATC, but we often departed or arrived at an airfield outside of controlled airspace. This meant taking off and remaining below controlled airspace, then obtaining clearance from ATC to climb up and fly the route we had filed in the flight plan.

Arriving at a controlled airfield we flew the formal published approach just like anyone else, but going back into uncontrolled airports, we would be cleared down under our own procedures. Essentially, in that condition, we would have to break out of cloud at a safe height and fly to land using our own judgement whilst getting in contact with the airfield before doing so. It all made for very interesting flying and with so many destinations in Europe to go to, there was never any sense of being bored with it all, as may happen to a scheduled operator.

I had no idea what the customer base was like but it soon became apparent that package holidays are sold with travel insurance and those without it faced a huge bill if they needed repatriation by air ambulance without cover. We carried patients from their hospital to one in the UK. The insurance companies paid for immediate treatment and stabilisation, then as soon as practical we picked them up and delivered them into the NHS. The medics were tailored for the job. A broken skier may only need a nurse. Those with much more serious problems would get an anaesthetist and an Intensive Care trained nurse.

One of the medics was an ex-army nurse and as a part of his service he had cared for the ageing Nazi war criminal Rudolph Hess in Spandau Prison. Naturally I wanted to know what that had been like and the nurse told me how he looked after him and would kiss Hess on the forehead each night when he put him to bed. That seemed a bit bizarre, so I asked why. He explained that it was because he had grown fond of him.

Hess apparently hanged himself on a length of electrical cord when the Americans took their turn at guarding the prison.

On a rush job, we could be on the way with medics within an hour and half but the usual thing was that we were informed the previous evening and departed in the morning. For many years we had the contract with the Channel Islands Health Service and would be off at short notice to bring a patient into a specialist hospital in the UK.

Generally speaking, the King Air was reasonably serviceable. There were the odd occasions of the gear handle light remaining red when the gear was locked up and more rarely still, when it was down. Those problems were normally corrected by changing the gear position micro switches. Also, the engine fire warning system would get triggered by reflected sunlight getting inside the cowling past the gap where the exhaust stuck out. The fire warning sensors were light sensitive. We learned to turn through 30 degrees and if it went out to ignore it. Later, baffles were fitted to shield the sensors from sunlight which seemed to fix the problem.

Once, I had a flap failure in Seville when passing through to refuel and could not extend the flaps for take-off. Fortunately, we only had medics on board at the time. The company asked me to carry on without flaps but that was asking for trouble so I declined.

There followed a very agreeable unplanned night stop in Seville, somewhere that I have taken holidays several times since. In contact with our maintenance organisation, we decided that local assistance would be required and a Spanish engineer was found who replaced the flap motor so that by the next day we were back in service.

The landing gear went up in the bays but a red light persisted in the undercarriage lever. We cycled it, still the same. A big red light visible to the passengers was not going to go down at all well and we couldn't be sure it was only an indication problem.

I called the company and we agreed to postpone the ambulance flight and take the thing to maintenance. Working with Plymouth Military air traffic control, they offered us an inspection by a BAE Systems Hawk Jet that happened to be coming back in from the ranges out in the Channel. It sounded fun, so we put the gear down, got three green lights anyway, but went with the idea of the inspection. Unsure if I should totally trust the autopilot, I asked my mate to fly the aircraft.

Prompted by Plymouth Mil, I saw a black dot at 11 miles out to sea. Inside a minute or two he slid up close alongside our starboard wing tip and a white gloved hand gave us a wave. The Hawk looked sleek and sexy in its black paint scheme. I took the controls for a bit so my mate could see our visitor.

'Comms' were made with Plymouth Mil as the Hawk was on a military frequency. They asked permission for the inspection to which I agreed and it was relayed to our inspector. The Hawk slid

behind out of view and formated beneath us. Moments later he was back on the wing tip and gave us a thumbs up. Plymouth told us all was good and I thanked them for the service. Our visitor snapped into a right bank and sped off home.

We also took part in transplant flights when several aircraft might be waiting for organs to be harvested and would then dash off in different directions to the transplant location. Northern Ireland seemed to provide a lot of organs and Newcastle seemed a regular transplant centre. I only did three or four but a high proportion ended in failure to match the recipient which must have put a lot of people through great disappointment.

One night I got a job to go to RAF Brize Norton to wait for an organ to fly up to Newcastle. It is normal to do these at night because that's when the operating theatres are free. We landed at Brize and went into waiting mode. The transplant centre could not give me much idea when we were going to get the heart we were expecting so it was a case of waiting it out.

As the evening wore on the Movements Officer told me that we could not depart between midnight and two in the morning because all the staff would be busy handling the arrival of the Saudi Royal Family. In fact, they did not need to help us because all I had to do was start up and call the tower. However, the idiot on duty told me that I had to have fire cover to start and he had no-one to spare. Nowhere else does this but that's the Air Force way. I remonstrated and pointed out the shelf life of the organ would be used up and it may not be fit for transplant. No dice. The fool wanted to be seen to be in charge and the facts were unimportant. As it happened we did not receive the heart to go with till early the next morning but I was ready to call the station commander to ask him if he wanted this story in the *Daily Mail*.

The equipment we carried was all portable so that it could be used to and from the hospitals as well as in the aircraft. The stretcher was the kind of thing road ambulances would use and we would lift it into the aircraft with whatever help we could muster. When we got a 300lb patient to load and unload we called on the airport fire service to help if needed. They never minded helping, though the ambulance crews would sometimes be less than helpful, quoting health and safety.

Health and Safety got in the way. We were forced to carry a powered stretcher loading device which cost us in fuel which we could not carry because of its weight. It took time to put together and disassemble and was full of sharp edges and bits to trap your fingers in. We still had to lift stretchers onto it and off again when we boarded the aircraft so it was of little value. Inside, we still had to position the stretcher without help as we always did, bent double inside the cabin because of the low ceiling. How we hated this infernal contraption – if no-one was looking we did not use it.

Eventually we had two stretchers in tandem for simple transfers not involving complex cases. That put our available internal space under intense pressure and I was not too happy about the emergency exits being obstructed. Also, we had an incubator for premature and unwell babies which weighed about 250lbs with nothing in it and kept us fit carrying it in and out of the aircraft.

Many patients were elderly and ventilated. One of my first jobs was to go and see the medics to establish how much oxygen we needed to carry. Having a ventilated patient on a high oxygen flow for the eight or so hours we had them for could result in a lot of cylinders. All that added up to payload, which reduced our fuel.

In turn, that had an effect on how far I could travel without a fuel stop. Usually Operations would sort it out so our planned sectors were possible. To the Canaries, I would refuel in Seville and on the way back, as far up Portugal as I could reach. Anywhere in Turkey usually meant a stop in Budapest. We got to know the best places to stop and could often refuel, get the weather down-route, take a pee, pay the bill and be off again in 25 minutes.

Often, the patient could not be carried in any other pressure environment than at sea level. Usually, this was because of entrapped post-operative gases which would be harmful if allowed to expand internally within the patient. Usually, we knew about that in advance but sometimes the medics would ring us from the hospital with an hour's warning. That would cause some rapid replanning for another fuel stop. The maximum flight level to maintain a pressurised sea level cabin would be about 16000 feet at which the fuel consumption would often be too high to get back in one or two legs. That usually meant an extended duty time and an enforced night stop at the dropping off point.

Being Air Ambulance, we could plan to operate another two hours on top of the normal duty limits. Naturally, after an extended duty we had to take the same amount of time off. However, if we had ended up in somewhere other than base, we were expected to take minimum rest and position the aircraft back to base first thing in the morning so that another crew could take it out on another job. We were as sharp as doughnuts doing that early flight back. We then had to take all the time owed to us before we could fly again.

Air ambulance work was not the only trips we flew. One aircraft belonged to a commercial company and we would take their executives to meetings with other parts of the organisation in Europe. This was easy, we did not have to lift these people on and off with a stretcher and the only equipment we needed was a box of food and drink. The suits walked on and we would take them to their meetings at various destinations. Normally it was a day trip and we had lunch and read the papers till they were ready to come back again.

One trip to Berlin involved a night stop and we went on the tourist trail to Checkpoint Charlie, the ruins of the Reichstag and the Brandenburg Gate. I also saw the memorial to the Russian dead at the Tiergarten. It is surmounted by a Russian soldier in a greatcoat holding a machine gun and simply exudes power. General Bernard Montgomery apparently once said that only a fool advances on Moscow.

Turkey always had some kind of drama in store for me. Landing at Antalya for a night stop, we were taken by a young handling agent to the police post for a passport check to let us into the country. The post was manned by a very aggressive police sergeant who was accompanied by a bunch of officers who looked as if they had not started shaving yet and were clearly in awe of him.

Sergeant Nasty thumbed through my passport pages and struck gold. He saw a stamp for entry into the Greek part of Cyprus and immediately went off on one about how I could not go to Cyprus and how bad that was.

I was tired and have been known to be irritable after four o'clock in the afternoon on a flying duty so I gave him as good as I got. In the middle of this shouting match I realised his English was not great and he was not getting my point so I asked the handling agent lad to interpret. However, he was clearly shaken by all this and wanted nothing to do with it. Eventually, while peace did not exactly break out, our passports were stamped so hard it nearly went right through onto the back cover and with all bad grace we entered Turkey.

Coming up from the Canaries, we often needed to refuel at Porto in Portugal. This would not be the first choice because it took too long but if we were up against strong headwinds, it had to do. On one such refuel stop I got a lot of grief from an immigration official who said we had to clear customs because as we were British we were not in the

Schengen Agreement. My argument was that I was staying airside and just buying fuel but his idea was that everyone would have to come off the aircraft and clear in and out again before flying up to the UK. There began a somewhat heated discussion on my part about the patient on the stretcher having to be brought into the terminal.

Eventually Mr Schengen capitulated and we went on our way. I don't know whether that episode had anything to do with it what followed, but as I taxied out, as cleared, for a hold point before entering the runway, I looked at the taxi chart and saw that there would be a hold short line so I planned on stopping there when I saw it. Trouble was the airport was undergoing alterations and the stop bar was no longer there. As I neared the runway, we saw an Airbus landing. In my lack of concentration, I had very nearly taxied into his path. Many circumstances can factor together to cause an accident and I believe that I had allowed this episode in the airport to get to me.

I had a job to take a patient from Exeter to Kiev with a refuel stop at Leipzig. Once more, these airports were unknown to me, so as usual we boned up on the special procedures we might encounter and off we went. As it was a long day, there was no possibility of getting back home that night so the company booked us into a dull hotel next to the airport. Despite Ukraine having gained independence from the USSR in 1997, in March 2003, it was still a very Soviet-based society.

Arriving at the hotel, we methodically went through the check-in process. The hotel was spartan and each step of the process involved going to an unsmiling clerk behind a glass window. Firstly, I presented our booking paperwork and our passports were copied. With a new piece of paper in my hand I was directed to the next booth where I paid cash in advance for the rooms and breakfast. The next booth checked my papers and made us tick a box for what time we wanted breakfast and what our order would be. The menu was limited but seemed to comprise mainly meatballs, pasta, bread and that good old breakfast favourite, Borscht, a beetroot soup. We ticked the boxes and accepted a ticket for breakfast in the morning.

Now we hoped to get a room key. Think again. Another unsmiling official examined my papers and gave me a chit for a room key. Uncertain what to do with the chit I looked for another booth but instead was pointed towards a lift, I found a sullen woman sitting behind an empty desk, with, behind her, a key rack. Presenting our room chits respectfully, we were silently given our keys. The room was pretty basic and slightly damp with signs of wear. Welcome to Kiev.

147

Waiting in Chania, Crete, one morning gassed up and waiting for the medics with the patient, I got a call from the company to say the patient had passed away overnight and they had another job for us. We were to fly to Nevsehir in Turkey by 1400 Local when it closed. So, I asked them to put a flight plan in the system and we would prepare our own route log. The company said no, it was too busy, we had to do it.

Time was marching on, I now had about four hours to file and get there. We collected the Airway Charts and worked out a flight plan, filed it, wrote our log and called for a start. By now, I could just about get there in time, if not there would be an expensive diversion to Ankara. ATC said no, I had not paid for parking. I pulled the receipt out of my bag and argued it was paid and that we were on an urgent flight. They insisted I had to go back to the airport office and pay, so now I was losing my cool and I belted back into the office.

Mr Fat Controller gave me another bill for 12 drachma and said we had stayed an extra hour so I must pay more. He took his time writing me a receipt and I fumed and looked at my watch. Receipt in hand I sprinted back out and we got started up and departed. Crossing from Greek airspace into Turkish meant the usual rigmarole of working two frequencies at once to get into the next sector because the two parties would not talk to each other.

At the waypoint for Turkish airspace I checked the flight time left to run. We were going to be too late to get into Nevsehir, so all the delays and lack of help from everyone had defeated us. I mentally prepared for a diversion to Ankara and accepted that we would have to fend for ourselves for another night stop. What a cock-up. My mate called up the Turkish controller who cleared us direct from our present position to Nevsehir, saving us a longwinded airways routing north then east. We entered that into the GPS and rolled onto the new heading to the northeast. I looked at the new ETA. Deep joy, we would land by 1350.

On arrival, the handling and fuelling were a shambles. No credit cards would be accepted, so I had to make a cash withdrawal from a bank 'hole in the wall' in town on the company credit card and again on my own bank card since the company card was capped at less than the bill. That was after we had been driven to a hotel about 40 miles away by a taxi driver who did not know where it was.

It took hours to get away in the morning, further delayed by the airport bank being closed while they got someone in from the town to open it up to enable us to pay the money into the airport account. By now I couldn't care less how long it took and tried my best to remain calm. Eventually we got away and flew to Vienna to refuel and then onward to Manchester. A job like that was a real challenge but when it was all done and dusted, the crew could take some pride in what we had achieved against all odds.

We were cruising at 26,000 feet coming up from a fuel stop in Budapest. We had an old chap who insisted on wearing his three-piece suit and tie to travel with us. No hospital pyjamas for him. Suddenly, there was rapid movement behind me and the doctor demanding we land immediately. The old chap had stopped breathing. I called Brussels and requested immediate descent. As I called, I realised getting into Brussels National was going to be complicated. I chose Liège.

The controller came back with "Stand By". Not good enough, I demanded immediate descent and vectors towards Liège. We got what we wanted. The first officer dug out the Liege charts. I went down like a brick. We asked for a paramedic ambulance to attend Liège for our arrival. Fifteen minutes later I landed and fast taxied off to the parking area. We saw the blue ambulance lights flashing at our parking position right by the gates to the airfield.

Good reaction. Well done the Belgians.

The old chap was resuscitated by the medics on the way down to land but the medics booked him into Liege Hospital for a day or two in observation and we pressed on back to base with his wife. Later on, another crew went back out and brought him home.

Another time we loaded a chap and his wife from an airfield in Germany and he arrested just as we were about to start up. The ambulance had departed so I called the tower and requested another one post haste. Nothing arrived so I kept pushing ATC for some information on the ambulance we had requested but they had done what they could so we had to wait for what seemed an eternity. It took another 15 minutes for an ambulance to turn up and the medics were pumping his chest all that time but to no avail.

In the end, the medics took the body back to where he had come from and we flew the widow home.

Yet another one died in the aircraft on the way back from Spain but after a conversation with the doctor we agreed that the deceased would not be pronounced dead until we got into UK airspace. It was very moving to see the newly created widow holding her late husband's hand for some hours until we landed. She was very composed and was able to handle the relatives who were waiting for her who had become very distraught when the news was broken to them. What a brave woman.

It sometimes happened that we would set out in the morning with a reserved hospital bed but in the 12 or more hours it took to recover the person to the UK, the bed would have been taken. The NHS would never have spare capacity like that and it would always be a risk. Often there was nothing else to do but place the person in A & E until the hospital could find a ward for them.

I was given a job to go to Rome to pick up a couple of Irish priests, one of whom was on his last legs and wanted to go back to Ireland to see the gates to heaven open for him there. The medics went off to the Vatican for the two Fathers and after fuelling up and getting things ready for the return leg I had a look at the names of the passengers, as I always did so I could greet them personally when they arrived.

Later the "ambo" turned up escorted by the handling agent and we busied ourselves loading Father John on his stretcher. Before that I had spied the other priest who was escort to Father John and said "Hello Desmond" to introduce myself and let him know how long the flight would be. Poor Desmond clearly wasn't used to such familiarity and visibly stiffened at my impertinence. A posting to the Vatican clearly brings with it some protocol and respect. I had just blown it.

There was the odd occasion when we went out for a body because the family did not want it carried back as cargo in the hold of a passenger jet. One such trip took us out to pick up a body in a coffin but when it arrived with the undertakers, it was a huge sealed casket that would not fit in the door due to the narrow fuselage.

With assistance from the undertakers, we tried all ways to get the thing in, including turning it on edge. Still it would not go in. I was about to call it a day and ask them to take it back to place it in something smaller when they came up with a new plan. Putting the casket back in their vehicle, they took the lid off and laid the body on the floor of the van. Then each item, casket, body, and finally lid was rushed into the aircraft and reassembled. Without the lid, the casket just about went through the doorway. They worked fast because holiday jets were taxiing past and the charade was getting a bit of attention. We had the handling agent's vehicles drawn up round the scene like a wagon train besieged by Indians. All that successfully served to hide our movements but just when I thought we had it made, I realised that they had left the coffin lid lying on the ground outside the ring of vehicles and it stood out as only a coffin lid could.

When all was secure I went to the terminal and invited the escorts travelling with the coffin to board the aircraft.

Fortunately it was dark when we reached our destination and the undertakers at the other end were very co-operative. I had called ahead to the company and requested the handling agent take the escorts away as soon as we landed. The undertakers then reversed the process we had gone through at the beginning. Later the company bought a normal sized coffin for future body repatriations. Though I never did one myself, the new smaller coffin must have solved a few problems.

I had some flights that took me through the Balkans and, on one occasion, I recall landing in Bratislava for a refuel to find border guards coming to check the aircraft. This was no problem what-so-ever. The two guards were very attractive girls wearing the customary huge Russian style peaked hat, tight tunics, short skirts and long boots. To top it all they packed a side arm on their belt. Check me out any day.

Another job was to bring back a NATO cook from Sarajevo who urgently needed abdominal surgery. We were refused permission to land in Sarajevo so we had to go into Split and wait for the patient to be brought down to us. Even in Split, on the edge of the conflict zone, buildings were badly bullet scarred.

Venice's Marco Polo airport was another interesting destination. On a turn-round we pilots usually set up for a departure then sat around waiting for the ambulance to arrive. We could often hear the siren in the distance. Being parked near the water taxi landing stage of the airport, I could hear a siren but could not see where it was coming from. Then a water ambulance came in sight, cutting a swathe through the other boats on the inner lagoon with its blue light on. The airport ambulance picked up the patient from the boat, then the patient was with us in a few minutes.

Invariably we would get priority over other aircraft and many times I have received a taxi clearance that took me past the queue of aircraft waiting to take off. It was very considerate of Air Traffic Control and where I could, if it did not cut into the transmissions taking place on the frequency, I would break in with a quick "thanks guys" which was meant for everyone, ATC and the big jet pilots uncomplainingly letting us go first.

After I had built up some experience on type I flew the King Air alone when it was not a public transport flight. That included flying the aircraft owner somewhere or taking it to the maintenance base. The downside of taking or collecting it from maintenance was the tedious rail journey if it was destined to be there for a week.

In 1998 new rules in aviation required companies to run a quality system which included auditing the maintenance contractors. I have always grabbed these opportunities with both hands so I put my hand up to go on an auditor course. Now my ferry flights to maintenance increased because I could take it or collect it and spend a day doing an audit at the same time.

Also, we had the need to train pilots and some staff in Crew Resource Management, Aviation Security and Dangerous Goods. The first requirement was that the trainer had to have undertaken an instructor's course. That let me in as BA had put me through that. As I had been taught those subjects I got approval to instruct in all of them. That opportunity was to serve me well. Later, when self-employed, I earned a reasonable living as a DC10 flight engineer flight simulator instructor, quality manager and ground instructor. At one point I worked for six companies and had more work than I could cope with. I have always been amazed at the reticence shown by people to take on new things. As I had invested in myself, it paid back handsomely later on.

The company had some low time pilots and sometimes for a short while, retired airline people who fancied going back to basics. They did not normally last long. The job was a first or a last one. A few of the young guys went on to fly other bigger things. A couple of them are now EasyJet captains while another now flies a small "pocket rocket" air taxi jet, often carrying members of the Royal Family or government ministers. This guy started out in life as a plumber and still spends his free time restoring houses when not flying his jet. Talented man.

Not all the pilots fitted in. The company tended to have it in for someone all the time and we as a community kept our ear to ground to see who was garnering all the adverse attention. Several people were laid off unnecessarily while others who did not have any skills to speak of seemed to lead charmed lives. If your card was marked, you had to be careful.

One morning an aircraft took off and there was a bang from an engine as it threw some compressor blades out the back end. The airfield fire crew heard it and rushed out expecting to mount up and chase the aircraft to the crash site. No distress call was made and the aircraft climbed away. Eventually a call was made to our company operations asking advice for some unusual indications which, put in a nutshell, were showing an overheating engine putting out low power.

The company advised that it might be a fuel control unit problem and suggested they route to maintenance. That diagnosis was flawed. It follows with an engine problem that one could shut it down, run it at idle and monitor it, or keep it at whatever power you could get out of it. This latter choice was taken by the crew.

Amazingly, the aircraft flew past six airfields suitable for a diversion with high power set on the damaged engine. Passing the sixth, the engine gave up more compressor blades and shut itself down. There was smoke in the cockpit. Still they plugged on with the one remaining engine to reach the airfield of choice some distance away while ignoring the safe airfield just behind them. When the dust had settled the events were reviewed. The first officer was fired for not advising the captain about what he should have done, despite the flawed advice on company radio. The captain carried on in service. If your card is marked..............

On a flight with the company examiner I was flying left seat and we had a scheduled fuel stop in Bilbao, northern Spain. As we know, that area is pretty mountainous. Coming up from the south, I could see a huge thunderstorm on the radar next to the mountains and situated right on the approach track to the airport. Thunderstorms are notorious for downdrafts, which would be a bad thing on the side of a mountain. So, I remarked on it and was a bit amazed that the man in the other seat said it would be OK to fly through it. There was no great wind on the surface at Bilbao and an approach from the opposite direction to the other end of the runway would not be a problem, so I reserved judgement and gave it a try. Turning onto the approach track, we flew straight into intense hail and turbulence.

That was enough for me so I said I was turning north away from the high ground and climbed out into the clear. Once more I was taken aback by the attitude which did not see why I had rejected the approach. I got the controller to vector us for an approach at the other end of the runway and that went off without a problem.

After landing I suggested we give the controller a pilot report about the thunderstorm we had encountered so that ATC could advise other traffic about it. The man in the right seat wanted to know why I wanted to do that. All in all, a funny old day and one that bothered me.

Eventually the company decided to opt for single pilot operations for commercial flights. As the type was certified for this, it was quite legal. The CAA were consulted and their answer was that provided the procedures were documented in the Operations Manual, it would be approved. As I was by this time over 60 and legally had to fly with another rated pilot who had to be less than 60, I now had a limitation which meant my usefulness was not as good as in the previous crewing system where we flew with both pilots rated on type. Working to the new single pilot system did limit the length of the duty day so in cases of long duty periods we had to field two rated pilots again.

The aircraft was to be operated with another unrated pilot on board for tasks such as assisting refuelling, getting patients on board and working the radios. So we had a meeting with the management and requested that the "pilot assistants" as they were to be called, would at least have a twin rating and a basic instrument flight qualification. That was agreed.

What we got were a couple of low hour's pilots who had neither a twin rating or instrument capability and whose radio work was questionable. This threw a huge workload on the pilot in command since there was no procedure to delegate flying duties to the newly appointed helper in the right seat and the pilot had to monitor everything that was done by the assistant. For window dressing, the tyro pilot assistant was decorated with shoulder tabs they had never earned, thereby denigrating the pilots who were properly qualified. There were better qualified people available but that did not matter.

By this time my dodgy personal life style had produced another failed marriage. Divorce and near financial ruin followed. The object of my attention was a part time flight nurse in the air ambulance company, whose main job was in the intensive care ward at the local hospital. We are still together 12 years later as I write, I am glad to say.

We did some flying together on holiday in my AA5 and enjoy the occasional day out for lunch. At no time has she ever shown any inclination to fly the thing. I reason to her that if I ever get incapacitated, she could at least learn how to get it back down and save both our lives. Her answer is that she would rather die with me.

Touching.

In regard to sea crossings she will not contemplate surviving a ditching and would rather die at sea than have people see her with her hair wet. In the cruise she reads the *Daily Mail* and I can`t see where I`m going. I am a saint.

Recently, we were fuelled up, belted up and ready to start up to fly off for a family lunch when her earring fell off down the side of the seat and became trapped in the seat rail. Time was pressing and I had phoned ahead to announce our arrival. A quick prod about with my pen did not dislodge the offending earring so I decided we would look again when we got there. This did not go down very well and much of the cruise was executed in a stony silence. At length, the temptation was too much and my co-pilot contorted into a ring divining position which now threatened to restrict control movement. I rebuked, she huffed. Finally, with the engine shut down at our lunch stop, we extracted the jewellery and equilibrium was restored to the ear lobes. Happy days.

As the single pilot system had been adopted within the company by 2004, I expected less employment, I looked for other work. A commuter airline at Gatwick was interviewing for first officers so I applied for it.

On the appointed day, I turned up and sat in the corridor awaiting my turn. At length, I was shown into the interview room. It was quite a small room and within it were squashed two huge desks with barely enough space for two chairs on one side for the interviewers and, two desk widths apart, one chair jammed against the opposite wall for me. I stopped and sized up the possibility of moving the furniture to reduce the distance between us, convinced that this must be some form of initiative test. Short of carrying a desk out into the corridor, there was no solution, so I squeezed into the other chair.

The interview went OK, but the chief pilot got completely mixed up about the rules pertaining to someone over 60 years old and said that I would not be able to work with them and that the interview had been a complete waste of time. This charming man then terminated the whole affair leaving me with an urgent need to quote the regulation to him.

As soon as I arrived home I confirmed my assertion that he was not correct and rang to speak to him. He was not available but I did speak to the personnel manager who was also present at the interview who confirmed I was right about the age limit and my assertion that I could still operate with them for several more years. However, the chief pilot did not want to accept my information and would not agree to re-open my interview. Maybe he wanted younger people but I on reflection, I don`t think we would have got along very well so perhaps it was for the best. Maybe I failed the overcrowded room initiative test, who knows? Anyway, thanks, pal.

I also saw an opening as a self-employed instructor. There was a vacancy for an instructor on the DC10 simulator on which I had previously been employed, back in my BA days. As I had been off the DC10 as a flight engineer instructor/examiner for more than five years, I had to requalify by taking the type examination again. Two weeks later, in March 2004, I sat and passed the exam and got employed as a consultant simulator instructor.

The simulator clients at that time were mainly an Asian airline and the Royal Netherlands Air Force. The RNAF had Mc Donnell Douglas KC10 tankers but the simulator was close enough to their aircraft configuration for us to do conversions and recurrent checks, while the RNAF took care of the differences. Their prime purpose was to air refuel their General Dynamics F-16 fighters while also being able to carry military personnel and equipment. They took care of the specialised training for air refuelling on line flights. The cultural difference between the Asian outfit and the Dutch Air Force was wide. The former were very likeable people but did not always exhibit great flying qualities while the Dutch guys flew and operated very well.

The Asian airline had a few people to whom Crew Resource Management and good discipline was not their strong point. For one crew, it resulted in a botched approach and runway excursion. Total confusion reigned as the training captain took control from a junior co-pilot on line training.

The approach was a mess. Far too late the flight engineer called out the unstable approach but the captain continued in his landing. The co-pilot made some half-hearted attempts to correct the captain but the seniority gradient was just too steep for him. The aircraft touched down with one main landing gear off the side of the runway and it set off across the airfield with bits coming off as it went. When it came to a halt there was fortunately no fire and in the evacuation which followed, there were only some minor injuries. Luck was on their side. We instructors were appalled by the accident. I was frankly glad when we stopped signing them off on the simulator.

I worked with both customers and enjoyed the conversions and recurrent training and testing for a period of about eight years until the RNAF commissioned their own simulator in Amsterdam and the simulator in the UK was closed down in September 2012. The Asian airline were treated badly when the simulator was decommissioned. They were given only two weeks' notice to quit which left their training programme in tatters.

The F-16 nosed under our tail boom and held station. The boom operator 'flew' the refuelling probe into the receptacle behind the F-16 cockpit. The boom plugged in and within a couple of minutes the F-16 took on board the jet fuel. The pilot throttled back and disconnected. The wing camera saw him slide out to take up station on the wingtip. The next F-16 slid in from the other wing tip and tucked under us. The camera on the refuel position recorded his elevators pumping up and down. This guy was nervous. Conditions were not perfect. The best refuel box was at the mid 20 Flight Levels and the whole formation was in light cloud. He got his uplift and another one slid in for a feed.

The Royal Netherlands Air Force had honoured us, their simulator instructors, with a fantastic air refuel sortie to show us what we had never been able to experience in the years we had worked with them on the simulator. The plan was that we were to get ourselves to Biggin Hill to fly over to RNAF Eindhoven in a Dutch Fokker 50 to then board a KC10 on a refuel exercise over the North Sea. The weather in the North Sea was pretty poor and the peacetime limits on sea swell precluded the F-16s operating there in case anyone had to 'bang out' and survive in those conditions.

That was all changed when the F50 was not available, so the RNAF flew the KC10 into Brize Norton. We duly assembled at Brize and boarded the KC10 to go out to a refuelling area in northern Germany. It was great to see the guys working in their natural environment and also to see the refuel operations up close.

Following the exercise, we landed at Eindhoven and enjoyed a meal and drinks in the mess that evening. The next day we went to Amsterdam to take a look at the new KC10 simulator and fly it ourselves. By this time the F50 was back in service and was able to take us back to Brize. It was a fabulous gesture by the RNAF and 334 Squadron in particular. It was a great time working with those professionals and it is recalled with affection.

During this time from 2004 to 2012, as a simulator instructor, I also used my other qualifications to take on CRM, Dangerous Goods and Security training for small airlines and air taxi operators. Also, my auditing qualifications came in useful and I took on the job of auditing for a couple of operators and became the quality manager for an air taxi company.

The air taxi company was a challenge. There were many silly problems that were preventable. Their priority was to fly charters but mine was to ensure it was done to the regulations. During an audit of pilot training records, I came across some training certificates which had my signature on but which I knew from my diary could not be correct.

On closer inspection, the certificates were poor reproductions with the dates altered. Taking those certificates to the Chief Executive, I put them in front of him and sat down to await his explanation. There followed a brief conversation in which he asked if I going to report him to the CAA and I said that if he did it again, I was going to walk. Actually, the whole thing was really amusing but I only allowed myself to enjoy it when I was far enough from his office so he continued to take it seriously.

As the air ambulance company did not need me very much for line flights, I concentrated on building my portfolio outside in the wider industry.

After an interval of several months off flying I was requested to assist by operating as co-pilot to a captain so that we could extend the duty day and get a patient back from Bergamo to Doncaster. The trip got set up so that we needed to refuel on the way back because to do it in one sector was not possible, so on that basis we set out for the day.

Coming up from Bergamo to Ostend, our intended refuel stop, we had plenty of fuel but not quite enough to make Doncaster. Neither did we have the weather for the next leg so going beyond Ostend was not an option at that point. I was doing fuel checks en-route and we still did not have enough fuel to fly on to Doncaster, but as we descended into Ostend working the approach radar, we were given some short cuts. My last fuel check showed a small surplus which could conceivably get us onward. We still needed two things: another flight plan in the system and weather for both Doncaster and an alternate. As we were only five minutes or so from landing at Ostend, we went ahead and landed. The alternative was too complicated and may well have delayed us at low level, burning lots of fuel before we were given a clearance to proceed, so the choice we made seemed to me a safe one.

Once on the ground with the engines off, there was no cabin heat for the patient so we needed a brisk turnaround as it was pretty cold. We got the weather for the next leg, paid the landing fee but there was still no fuel truck. A small top-up for comfort was all we needed but when I chased up the handling agent they told me that there was only one refuel truck, that it was refuelling a Russian cargo aircraft and it would be at least another 45 minutes. We discussed it. We had the minimum fuel, though more would be nice, but to delay would be bad for the patient in the cold aircraft. On that basis, we fired up and departed and delivered the patient safely to Doncaster.

A couple of days later the company asked why we landed at Ostend without refuelling and yet still departed for Doncaster. Both of us attended a meeting in the office while our decisions were torn to shreds. The upshot later delivered to me was that I had failed the captain of the flight, my Crew Resource Management was no good and I was not required for any more flying. Furthermore, I was not to continue to deliver Crew Resource Management Training as I had demonstrated that I was not fit to do it any longer.

However, in the judgement of the company, and no doubt for their convenience, I would be allowed to continue to audit the flight operations and maintenance and deliver Dangerous Goods and Security Training. Oh good I thought, not all bad then. Those who have also been similarly offended will recognise the pattern. I did not realise my card was marked, or why, but it clearly was. It was a simple decision. I returned their manuals and told them to stuff it.

The captain that I flew with on that flight was exonerated from whatever they assumed we had done wrong. Coincidentally, he was the pilot who had the engine failure and decided to keep it running until it blew more compressor blades and gave them smoke in the cockpit. Golden balls.

Despite the challenges encountered by many of us while flying the air ambulance, it was an enjoyable and rewarding experience. A local pub enjoys our custom every couple of months to get us ex-ambulance pilots together again and shoot the breeze about old times. There were many good times with some great people and I'm glad I did it.

CHAPTER FOURTEEN

Instructor at Large

By February 2006, when I quit the ambulance company, I had, as I've said before, built up a considerable client base for quality auditing, simulator instruction and ground training of Crew Resource Management, Dangerous Goods and Aviation Security. To win those qualifications I had assumed grandfather rights, but as time went on, I was required to attend a full course on DG and AVSEC.

The Dangerous Goods course was pretty intense and I managed to scrape through but in doing so, gained a lot more knowledge. It certainly meant that I understood the subject far better and was able to pass that knowledge on more effectively than if I had not been asked to attend the course. The governing body for DG in UK Aviation was the Civil Aviation Authority.

While I agreed absolutely that doing the course would be a good thing, any criticism of the authority's management of the subject was met with resistance. Rather than accept any comments on how carriage of DG could be improved, the authority replied in an email to me, informing me about the fines and court settlements for non-compliance. Work with us please, Mr CAA (DG).

I was also required to attend an Aviation Security Instructors course. This comprised three days at MI5 in Thames House and a further two days at the Army Defence College at Shrivenham where we were taught to recognise parts of explosive devices and weapons. They arranged to set off some small amounts of Semtex and rounds from different calibre weapons to demonstrate the effects. We also fired some weapons such as the AK47 on the range. That was all jolly good fun and it certainly gave you the feeling of being included in AVSEC matters. The information gathered was of course, limited to the attendees and only to be passed on in AVSEC training. However, we did not have clearance to be briefed on the more specific counter terrorism activities.

I had a number of ground instruction contracts to deliver training to pilots and just as importantly to operations staff of companies who would accept charters. For the courses, I advocated having those operations guys along with the pilots, because these people were clearly the first line of defence in preventing problems getting on board the aircraft. Usually after I put the case to include them, clients would add those people to the course even though it was not required by the authority. Making it easy for them, I did not charge any extra unless they exceeded ten attendees. My charges were never extreme. Comparing my fees with the bigger training companies, I always undercut them. That way, I had a steady supply of work.

I had a steady amount of work with a cargo airline at Stansted and did the CRM, DG and AVSEC training for them.

During the AVSEC training I always gave it over to the guys to tell me about their experiences in the subject. One rather taciturn captain told me that he had been on his way through the crew security channel and been treated rather off-handedly by the security people. The security man told him to open his flight bag for inspection and as this pilot was feeling a bit grumpy he did so but with what was apparently rather bad grace. The security man then got a bit cheeky with him saying, "Oh, we're in a bad mood today then are we, Captain?" The captain replied that his bag was open for inspection but his mood was not. I wish I could think of things like that at the right moment.

Another time I had some Russian crews to train and putting across to them some of the more democratic points of Crew Resource Management was a bit of a challenge. A lot of CRM is about teamwork. I was concerned about one of the Russian pilots who would not take any part in the discussions and when we took a break, went off by himself, not even taking a fag break with his own guys. That prompted me to give feedback about it to the chief pilot but I never did understand what the individual's problem was.

CHAPTER FIFTEEN

IATA Auditor

At the meeting, the maintenance auditor outlined the deficiencies and illegal defects on the Boeing 737. This was Tuesday and I was due to fly in it auditing the flight crew on Thursday. We were in the middle of Africa looking at an operator who leased an aircraft from another equally dodgy African state.

Enough. I informed the meeting that I refused to fly in it. There was uproar. They would have it fixed by Thursday. No way Jose, not possible. Not my problem. It did not get fixed and passengers were still being flown in it. Totally illegal. What had I got myself into?

By April 2005, I was auditing for the International Air Travel Association and employed on a consultancy basis by an IATA Approved Audit Organisation. A couple of months before, there had been an advertisement placed in an aviation industry periodical asking for suitably qualified auditors to apply. Arriving at the offices of this august quality audit company I met the main man. He was standing ankle deep in paper, hole punching waste, puffing a fag and putting manuals together. Did I have the qualifications? Yes, no problem. A course to qualify me in this new discipline swiftly followed and there began another career move.

The audit system I embarked on was the International Air Travel Association Operational Safety Audit, commonly known as IOSA. There were seven agencies in the world and this audit is mandatory for all IATA member airlines. Other non-members do it for prestige. The audit is every two years and takes 25 man-days which cover in the region of 960 standards and recommended practices based on international standards.

The standards were written by committees who might well have been credited with designing the wildebeest. Several objectives were built into one or two sentences with conditional phrases and choices to select from to enrichen the experience. If the text could not handle everything the standard wanted to cover, a table would be attached to it with anything up to 30 points, any of which could result in a finding if not documented and implemented. No wonder Johnny Foreigner often had problems with it, English not being his first language. So, of course, did we, and interpretation remains one of the most difficult parts of the whole programme.

National regulators do not like it. It interferes with their control of airlines, but if all the world's regulators had been doing safety related audits instead of regulatory ones, then people involved in the IOSA program would not have a job. I have been to some countries where the regulatory authority was a single government minister with a typist who issued meaningless Air Operator Certificates, took the fee and left the airline to its own devices.

By contrast, there are very good regulators in Europe, North America and elsewhere. Most of the rest of the world represented our greatest risk area and was where we made the biggest difference to air safety. IATA compiles accident and incident statistics which show the best and worst regions of the world. Africa and parts of the Far East come out badly. It is a compliment to the programme that these high-risk areas have shown a big improvement. Of course, there is still a long way to go.

The real embarrassment to the industry as a whole is that some of the world's finest still have preventable accidents. To eradicate some of these accidents it will take a change of mindset in design and training to operate modern aircraft. Looking back to the eighties when I flew with some of the better UK airlines, it was evident even then that pilot skills were degrading due to over-reliance on automation.

Beyond that are huge challenges involving culture, a problem with no geographical boundaries.

What has improved safety immeasurably is that the older types have been consigned to the scrap yards; in particular, the older Russian-built Tupolevs and Ilyushins have been withdrawn from service at IATA`s behest. At airfields in the old Soviet states and other pre-*Glasnost* parts of the world there are quiet corners of airfields with dusty, neglected older Russian aircraft with flat tyres. Most of the old Western types had been broken for parts. Even now, there is a thriving industry in 'parting out' old airliners. I heard of one Airbus twinjet that had only seen six years' service but it had done so many hours, it was not commercially viable to put it through a costly maintenance programme to bring it back to work.

As there were three IATA audit organisations in the USA, there was no audit work to be had there. There is one AO in each of Germany, France and Australia. Initially we did very well in Europe and later in the English-speaking parts of the world including many in Africa. IATA put a limit on how many times you could audit the same company so eventually, the airline would have to select another company for their next audit. As that policy affected all the other audit companies, there was a sudden demand for French speaking auditors so we got a lot of French speakers on board to cope with that demand created by the two audit rule. Also, we had Russian speakers and did a number of audits in Russian-speaking countries.

As I had an engineering and pilot background I was able to qualify in just about all of the audit programme. Also, before each audit, there was a pre-audit visit to establish the preparedness of the airline and gather the logistical information needed to plan the full audit. I got a lot of those, usually by myself for several days because I could cover the whole thing. I enjoyed it, being my own boss for a while and able to assist an airline instead of being "the inspector". I was also qualified to observe, as part of the audit, the flight operations in the cockpit and in the simulator. That gave me an insight into the operation of numerous types and was interesting work.

As I say, it was customary to conduct a pre-audit visit before the main job and I was tasked with going to an airline in Orenburg, Russia. I had a Ukrainian colleague with me to help out where the language might be a problem. Being winter, the outside temperature was -25 degrees centigrade and trudging back to the hotel from a restaurant there was a light shower of ice crystals which made the snow shine like diamonds in the street lighting.

My room was far too hot. The Soviet system used massive heat pipes ducting through all the buildings. I tried to turn it down but it seemed to be jammed on full heat. To counter the stifling heat, I opened the window above the radiator pipes and went to bed.

Some hours later, I awoke to a hissing sound and a smell of something hot and wet. I launched myself out of bed and plunged my feet into several inches of hot water. At the same time, just as I was pulling my strides on, there was a furious hammering on the door and shouting in

Russian. I opened the door and the hotel receptionist burst in accompanied by an engineer with a box of tools who set upon the leak. A replacement room was allocated and I was ushered off down the corridor.

In the morning, I witnessed the reception area with soaking wet walls and a leaking ceiling. My room had been directly above it. On reflection, I believe having +25 degrees inside the room and an open window admitting air at -25 degrees had presented the plumbing with a thermal shock of such magnitude that it had cracked the hot water pipe. Fortunately, I checked out before anyone figured that I had been the cause of it all.

There was a grunt outside the tent wall and I could dimly make out a moon shadow of something huge on the other side of the canvas. Should I get up and run for it, or keep quiet and hope it went away? I kept quiet. The huge outline trundled past the tent wall, puffing and grunting as it went. Four big feet thumped along. I was now wide awake. It was a hippo on its way back to the river and they can cut up a bit rough if they think you are in the way. For them the river is safety. Good choice. I stayed put and listened to my pulse until I heard no more movement.

A colleague and I had just finished an audit in Dar es Salaam and we had flown out for a short safari to a bush camp in Tanzania. The tented camp was on a high river bank of the Rufiji River, below which hippo lay in the water all day grunting, gurgling, yawning and fanning their turds in the river with their tails. At night they leave the safety of the river and go inland to forage. Our native guide explained that they crap along the path to the foraging area and find their way back before dawn by smelling their own droppings. Clever. My visitor had got a bit lost on the way back and found himself in the lines of tents. Fortunately, he worked it out without blundering into mine.

The camp was in the Selous game park. Convenient from Dar es Salaam, but not an easy place to see wildlife. It has suffered from poaching and a part of it was reserved for hunting. Animals know no boundaries but once alerted to hunting and the sound of vehicles they make themselves scarce.

We also had several audits in Nairobi and that gave me the opportunity to stay in another tented camp just outside the Masai Mara game park. Game parks are not cheap and I usually blew whatever I had earned that week on a long weekend in the bush but it was worth it. The flight home paid for by the host airline was adjusted back a few days so that was no problem.

After a good day out on safari, I was sitting by the camp fire with some other guests having after dinner drinks and the time came to go back to my tent. At night, the Askaris would see you to your tent armed with no more than a torch and a spear. They were good Bushmen and could deal with any problem.

Just as I set off with my guide, he stopped dead and whispered "Simba Bwana". I did as he did and froze. In the faint light of near total darkness, a light brown shadow crossed the path in front of us. He was a young male lion who had lost touch with his females. Foremost in his mind was finding them, not us and he ambled silently away in the direction of my tent, disappearing beyond into the night. We gave him a couple of minutes and then the other Askaris checked where that the infatuated young Simba had gone.

All became quiet and the guys took me to my tent and zipped me inside. What a feeling to be next to nature and so close. The next night I heard him calling his ladies and it was magical lying in my bed with a lion roaring a few hundred yards away.

On one trip out to the bush, I flew back into Nairobi's Wilson Airport in a Cessna Caravan. The pilot was a Kenyan African and as the seat up front was vacant I asked if he would mind if I sat up front with him, promising not to touch anything. He was fine about that and we taxied out to the strip and clattered our way into the air. I noticed that as soon as we got off the strip, he put his seat fully down.

Looking at a few buzzards floating around and looking at some pretty awful scars on his face, I put two and two together. Broaching the subject as diplomatically as I could, I asked if there was there a problem with birds and he told me that was how he had got the scars. It turned out that he was co-pilot in a De Havilland Twin Otter some years before and a buzzard crashed through the windscreen with the result that the broken plastic had cut him up really badly. He said that other aircraft were no problem because you could hear them on the radio but the biggest risk was bird strikes.

Getting back into Wilson at five o'clock in the afternoon was incredibly busy with my pilot having to slow up near to the stall to fit in behind the other traffic on finals. He made a really good job of it so I paid him complements on the standard of his flying.

My first audit for IOSA was in the Netherlands and the plan was to share cars, leave home about 0300 hours and drive to Stansted for the early flight. This would get us there about 0800 local time and we would work till 1700. That was not a plan I accepted. I booked a hotel at my own expense and drove to Stansted the previous evening, joining the other guys at the airport after a reasonable night's sleep. The audit kicked off and we worked through the day. By 1800 we were in the hotel bar at Eindhoven drinking with the managers of the airline.

Drinks were flowing and the ethos of the audit appeared to be disappearing as a very tired group of early risen auditors made prats of themselves. Not an auspicious start to a new career.

Whilst many of the major airlines could put up a really good show at the IOSA audit, some were so arrogant that they would not accept any criticism. I recall one major who thought their Safety Management System met all the criteria. I disagreed. Consequently, the lead auditor, our project manager and my lowly self were given a lecturing on the subject. They stood and we sat and were spoken down to. I still disagreed and they had to accept the decision. Fortunately, the lead auditor and the project manager accepted my viewpoint and backed me up so we had solidarity. Thank you for that, guys.

Another major airline was aiming for zero findings and we had a problem in Aviation Security. They provided me with about ten subject matter experts who tripped out the document references and examples of implementation like robots. However, when they realized something had got missed they lost all composure. I suggested another manual and within it lay the documented process that they had not found. I wonder what sort of pressure people are put under. It was almost as if jobs were on the line if they had even one problem. That is not an enlightened way to run a safety dependent operation.

One airline in Africa did rather badly and had about 100 findings against them. It became so complicated that two of us were sent out to them for several days to work through the evidence for closure of their findings. We slogged through it and at the end of the third day I reached the last finding which I was dealing with and provided the suggestions to close it. Our work concluded, I told them that we were done. At that point, the manager who I had been working with put his face in his hands and burst into tears. Poor guy, he had been under a lot of pressure.

In another, I was assigned to help clean up a list of findings against an airline. I duly arrived and was taken to a tourist hotel which felt like a huge prison with an atrium in the centre. The hotel ran as an all-inclusive with full board. Drinks at the bar were free but, unfortunately,

167

undrinkable so I struggled to find anything palatable. The clientele was mainly Russian with some East Germans. Heavily tattooed, beer bellied men in vests swaggered around with dyed blondes. The occasional less brash family with children looked shell shocked. Food was unimaginative and warmed up.

I got stuck in with the airline department managers and worked on solutions to their findings. It was not easy. To amend the content of a manual appeared to be quite beyond their capabilities. I put forward actions to take and it creaked into life. Whether or not those changes would ever be fully distributed and implemented would be anyone's guess. The quality manager was a young, abrasive kind of guy who had a personal vendetta against the flight department.

It is custom and practice to go through a series of progressive steps to close a "Finding". The responder would start with the root cause, or in other words, what's wrong so you know what to fix. This chap wrote in each finding that the root cause was that the chief pilot did not do what he had told him to do. Not a way to get people onside. I edited all this vitriolic stuff out so that IATA would accept the process of closure, but I did have to get a bit inventive to bring it to a close. Hopefully I will never go there again.

I did an audit in Johannesburg and needed to go out of town to Lanseria Airport which was an interesting general aviation facility. The female quality manager drove me out there and then had to leave for a meeting back in Jo`burg. I got a lift back into town later to find that she had encountered a line of rocks placed on the road and in running over one of them had burst a tyre. Fortunately, a car full of white South Africans had been behind her and they took care of the wheel change and made sure that the attempted road stop and robbery did not take place.

Another woman in the airline was the ground handling manager. She had to try and control robbery from passenger luggage apparently being committed by a number of Nigerian employees who had managed to secure positions in the handling company. She dealt with it by investigation and firing certain employees. In response, she endured phone calls at home which said that they knew she had a daughter and they knew where she went to school. That was one brave woman.

When I answer the question what do I do for a living, I avoid the old cliché "As little as possible" and say that I am an airline auditor. People immediately think that means a financial audit so I have modified my response to Airline Safety Auditor, which is more near to the truth.

IATA's audit is based on safety practices and management. This has a different objective to a regulator's audit of the regulations. The audit has over 960 of what are called "standards", most of which have more than one part and can be accompanied by tables with over thirty sub points. It is a monster to prepare for, with the airline having to document procedures for each standard in a controlled manual and be able to show records of implementation.

The auditor typically identifies the standard by number and asks for evidence. There are three main requirements for the auditor. He has to see the correct documentation, interview the right person and sample records of implementation. I found it pretty hard going at first, but nearly eleven years later I seem to be running on experience. That is not to say it is a breeze because it is a very hard week.

As each audit organisation has a different way of approaching an audit there is always a problem of consistency. Within an audit company there can be variations in interpretation due to individual feelings but where one compares audit companies, there are often differences in strengths of adherence to the standards. This can result in an airline being audited in succession by two different audit companies and getting a marked variation in results. It is always difficult to explain the reason for that to an aggrieved airline manager.

The ideal airline size for a successful audit was one that had only one type of aircraft and a fleet size of about six. The company would have enough staff to handle the audit preparation, working in close proximity to each other and with no different aircraft types so it was not a challenge to administer. The worst were often those running on a shoestring, with several older aircraft types and in a third world environment. Despite that, we were often surprised how well some airlines did perform. The most common denominator for a success was a good project leader and a supportive chief executive who saw more in the exercise than a tick in the box.

I have also formed the opinion that senior male managers, especially pilots and those airlines who exist in ego driven male dominated societies were not the best people to document procedures and organise an airline to prepare an audit of this magnitude. Invariably, women excelled at this kind of work and this in no way is to decry their position in the airline, or their gender. They were just generally better at it than the men. If the male could be seen to be in charge, he was happy. If he assigned the task to the women, then they were usually more superior at this task then he was. Unfortunately, he might take the credit, where it really was not his to enjoy.

The older generation of managers also found it hard going. Below them were young up and coming university graduates who were internet savvy. It was not hard to spot the next accountable manager, chief pilot, head of training, operations director or engineering director amongst the younger managers. The industry needs their talents and will benefit from them in the future.

The new thrust in aviation management was Safety Management Systems to which other evidence-based risk controls would be attached. It was and still is rushing down the tracks too fast for some organisations. We barely understood the meaning of these new ideas before we were auditing it.

In some cases, airlines got accredited with an SMS system and yet I felt we were being too generous. The truth will emerge when their next audit confirms or contests the decision previously made. All parties are now gaining understanding how to provide procedures and implementation for SMS and the bar will hopefully have been raised in the future audits.

The audit company I worked for now became involved in another level of auditing. This time it was run by the Flight Safety Foundation and administered from Melbourne, Australia. This audit programme was to address the smaller airlines operating in remote locations, often for the mining and oil industries.

To start it off they offered a course in Cape Town and the boss kindly paid for two of us to go with him to get qualified. This we accomplished in a few days. The course was presented by a formidable Australian woman, who herself was a Lead Auditor. She told us a story of how she had taken her team of Aussie auditors somewhere or other and they had got into trouble with the local plod and been locked up. I can imagine the scene when she went to get her auditors from the lock-up and what she would have said to them.

She also taught us how to debrief an audit to the auditee by the method she called "The shit sandwich". In the debrief, it may go something like this: "Well I`d like to thank you for being so open with us and all the hard work you put into the audit. However … (Then the problems would be spelt out) and followed by assurances … we have every confidence in your ability to close these findings in the very near future". (And then you get out sharpish before they have a chance to think about it.)

The course completed, we had a day off to look around and I went to the old Cape Town Garrison museum to see the military history and went up to Table Mountain.

I had seen the mountain earlier and the cloud was streaming over the lip of the mountain, evaporating as it was driven downhill. That was a memorable sight. On the day I went up to the top, the cloud had dispersed so I had a fantastic view of the whole peninsular. The government district of Cape Town had the most impressive buildings and with statues of Queen Victoria and Jan Smuts, a famous Afrikaner general, in every free space.

Later, the boss and I started on this new audit programme by going to Yellowknife in Canada and visiting another two towns to cover the small airlines based there. The equipment they had was fascinating. In winter they operated some aircraft on skis and in summer on floats. One company had a Lockheed 382, the civil version of the C130, which operated on frozen lakes. This aircraft could weigh close to 100 tons and could land where the ice was measured and in excess of one metre thick.

A problem that emerged was that although the operators met the Transport Canada standards, the audit required items of equipment to be fitted to smaller aircraft and it became obvious that they simply could not afford the investment. It must have been a tough place in winter. The ice road across the Great Slave Lake had just been closed, so it was a big detour round it with the melt waters roaring down the Mackenzie River and the ice floes crashing into each other. Some of the local Indians didn't seem to have much more in life than getting drunk. I saw several lying in the snow having a rest before the next drink. No-one seemed too bothered by them.

Travelling to audits abroad was sometimes a really unpleasant experience. Usually anything over four hours' flight time was done in business class, though some were not and a team would travel in steerage. It became a very uneven playing field where some audit organisations were able to arrange discount fares with associate airlines and others could not compete with them. It became a bone of contention and some auditors would not accept the job if the travel conditions did not meet their expectations. I was one of them but other people accepted it because they could not afford to pass over the job offer.

Fortunately, most long-range jobs involved business class. The variations were marked. Going to Cuba in an ancient Tupolev sitting in a business class seat that resembled a 1950s leather armchair was a surreal experience. The chicken main course was so overcooked that it had the appearance of a ship's hawser. Going to Dubai in the business deck of an Airbus A380 and chatting to other passengers in the bar was a new high. I could have lived in it for a weekend, it was that good.

Some of the world's airports have huge variations in standards. Queuing in a boarding room in Nairobi with no windows or air conditioning for an hour before getting out bathed in sweat to walk across the tarmac was no pleasure. Compare that with Heathrow's Terminal 5 or Abu Dhabi's business lounge and it's another world.

I had a consultancy assignment in central Africa. It took a flight through Nairobi, then a connecting flight to the destination. The airline needed a lot of work and two of us went either together or singly to try and get all the ducks in a row so that the airline was ready for the IOSA audit. We spent some months going to and fro prompting the airline to document procedures and put them into practice.

On our return, some of the jobs we had set out to be done had been accomplished but a lot were still waiting. Eventually, it reached the point where I recommended the airline undertake the audit and although there were a number of findings, the airline managed to close the findings and gained the IOSA registration.

In April 2010, Iceland's Eyjafjallajokull volcano exploded into the headlines. At the time, I was doing a pre-audit visit to a Bulgarian airline in Sofia and was due to leave on the Wednesday. As northern European airspace was now being affected by the volcano, I naturally recall it as Ash Wednesday.

My flight with the host airline to London was cancelled, so I arranged to catch their flight on the next day to Paris. By the next morning Paris was also cancelled. I discussed the position with the airline and we took into account me staying in the hotel as their guest for an indeterminate period of time or going back overland. They said it was up to me but they did have a flight to Vienna and could get me on it, so I decided to go.

We arrived into Vienna to find some aircraft had diverted from landing there as there were reports of ash in the vicinity. I saw nothing apart from a slight haze which was nothing out of the ordinary. Of course, we now have better risk analysis and reporting, but then everyone urged caution so operators cancelled flights. Later I found out the very aircraft the UK Met Office would have used to investigate the problem was having a new paint job and was unavailable to assist in proving if it was safe or otherwise to fly. Shortly after I got into Vienna, they closed the airspace there.

I arrived in the early evening and along with hundreds of other travellers, caught a bus to the Hauptbahnhof to jump on a train to Paris for the Eurostar service to take me on to London. How naïve of me to think I could. With all the other stranded passengers, I queued for three hours to buy a ticket.

All tickets to Paris were sold out so I enquired how far could I get in that direction. The only option was a train leaving at midnight to Frankfurt which was a local service stopping at every station. Armed with the first of several train tickets I wandered off for a bite to eat and a glass of wine.

Bored beyond belief I got on the train early and settled down for a long night. My mobile phone was OK and I had kept in contact with home where my partner told me that her internet enquiry to Eurostar had told her that all tickets were sold out for the next three days.

Plan B was brought into effect. Despite not having a map of Europe to hand, I could pretty much draw on my knowledge from the air ambulance days and construct a mental map of where I needed to go next. Plan B was Ostend for the Dover ferry.

Shortly before midnight, while sitting in the train waiting for it to go, I was accosted by a large eastern European type who tried to take my rail ticket, which happened to be in front of me on the table. I was tired and irritable and so I told him to "F**k off!" That seemed to the trick but I did not sleep through the whole night in case the bugger came back.

Eventually, at about six thirty in the morning, I got out at Frankfurt and queued up for one and a half hours to buy a ticket to Cologne, nothing being available for Paris even if I had still wanted to go there. However, things were looking up and the queues were getting shorter. With the sun came rising energy and a faster train.

At Cologne I got a ticket for Ostend but needed to change at Aachen and Liège. There were no queues now.

As the day wore on I was feeling pretty tired and thought Ostend would be far enough with an arrival estimated at six in the evening. I badly needed some rest and refuelling with food and wine so I got home to book me a hotel for the night near the ferry. The station is a mere hundred yards from the ferry office at Ostend and opposite that was the hotel. With some relief and anticipation of a good plan being executed I walked over to the ferry office to orientate myself before heading to the hotel. The office was closed and a new notice was taped onto the door. The notice said that the ferry company would not accept foot passengers. Bugger.

I crossed the road and checked into the hotel. The lady at the check-in listened to my story about the ferry not accepting foot passengers and related how all the old bikes in town had been bought up by stranded travellers so they could get on the ferry with wheels. We discussed how I might get to Boulogne the next day to have another crack at boarding a ferry. Apparently, there was no direct line so I would have to go back inland to connect with another train route. Still, there was a bed for the night and restaurants outside for the much-needed food and wine uplift.

I picked up a room key and was about to leave reception when an English voice behind me asked if I was stuck and did I want a lift onto the ferry in the morning? What good fortune. To cement our relationship and this kind offer, I bought the gentleman dinner and topped us both up with wine. Later I charged the company for that extravagance in lieu of a ferry ticket.

In the morning, we first had to drive to Brussels to pick up his daughter who was also stuck without a flight and then after landing in Dover my saviour dropped me off at the railway station. I then had a train journey to London, changing at Ebbsfleet, then a tube train to Heathrow, changing at Heathrow again to get to my original departure terminal.

Walking through the terminal, it was deserted. The business parking shuttle bus whisked me off to my car and an hour and a half later I drew up outside my house. It had taken two and half days from Sofia. One flight, one bus ride, one ferry and eight rail journeys completed the odyssey. Nice to be home.

Security is a big thing in aviation. Some airport security systems are pointless. Screening staff who talk to each other and ignore the hand baggage X-Ray picture are not uncommon. Measures to protect passengers from the perceived risks are not understood by the travelling public and when I listen to fellow passengers complaining about hold-ups and the seemingly silly things which are confiscated by security staff it tends to confirm that we do not do enough to get Joe Public onside.

As an aircrew security instructor I always observed the screening process with interest. Generally I could see things being done well, though many places needed a lot of improvement.

I recall back in my airline days that we had a saying: if Kate Adie was in first class, we should consider whether the destination was safe to go to, because carrying war correspondents was a clue that all was not well. These days it would be Orla Guerin or Jeremy Bowen.

Travelling to audit an airline some years ago I routed through Belgrade. In the check-in area was a special desk for the deposit of weapons. There the traveller could, on arrival for his flight, check his gun in for safekeeping and pick it up again on his return.

If I was in an area of the world with a reputation for unrest, it was not unusual to see a sign set up at check-in illustrating what the traveller may not take on board. We are all used to these – they show an article with a red cross through it, which indicates forbidden items. A picture of a handgun, grenade or knife with a red cross through it gets me feeling a little nervous.

The other way passengers are informed of dangerous goods which may not be carried is to have a poster on the wall showing the international Dangerous Goods signs for inflammable liquids, corrosives etc. I sometimes wonder if anyone has ever done a survey to see if the travelling public could decipher these mystic messages.

Recently I was asked to go to audit an airline in Bangkok. Though this was much further than I wanted to travel, I allowed myself to be persuaded to accept it. Because some desk-bound person decided it would save a little money, we were routed through Frankfurt and in economy class.

It was a slog to Bangkok's Suvarnabhumi Airport, but things did not end there because we had a 45 minute taxi ride to the old airport of Don Muang where the airline was based. In all, that was a ball breaking nineteen hours door to door.

As I had never had any serious tourist time in Bangkok during my preceding glancing blows with the city, I stayed on an extra day to visit the Temples and Wats on the Chao Phraya river bank. I did the sightseeing in the morning, then had a beer and Thai meal in the old Thai Navy sailing club. Having a little more time in hand, I took a water taxi tour of the Klongs, the back rivers and canals of the city. I wish I hadn't, as huge sewage pipes plopped untreated sewage into the water at regular intervals.

Next, I let myself be assigned to Krasnoyarsk in Siberia, which was a long way via Moscow with a few hours on the ground before the next flight. The audit went OK. Then on the Friday afternoon, despite being rather exhausted, we were put into a bus and given a tour of the city which was pretty droll; the highlight of the trip was seeing President Putin's summer place within a monastery on the river bank.

Oman beckoned again when I was asked to go to Muscat and deliver a five-day course for airline internal auditors so that they would be able to understand and audit to IATA's standards. I looked at the material, which only appeared to be sufficient for three days, and it seemed as if I would have to drag it out – which would have been awful for all concerned.

I need not have worried; the translation was complicated and I had two stalwarts who always wanted to ask a question. In the end, I made a class joke of it to see who would get their question in first.

On a purely personal level and nothing to with aviation what-so-ever, my daughter retired from the US Army after about 22 years' service. Her last posting had been to Fort Myer, which is home to a number of Pentagon military staff and also to the US Army Old Guard. The latter undertakes all of the ceremonial duties in nearby Arlington Cemetery, as well as other ceremonials tasks, including providing an escort to the President. My daughter arranged for me to get onto the post to witness the retirement parade.

The Old Guard dates back to 1784 and was founded in colonial times. They are formally known as the 3rd US Infantry Regiment. Part of the Guard is a recreation of a 16th Century fife and drum band which plays and marches to the old high stepping marching fashion in uniforms and wigs of the day. Not only is the modern Old Guard immaculate in its drill, but the fife and drum band is absolutely spell binding. Their commander gave them orders in a contemporary style sounding not unlike as if he had just stepped off the Mayflower. "Shoulder Firelocks" being given in a singsong cadence. My daughter's last 'Generals Aide` employer, Lieutenant General Bob Lennox, attended, even though he had now retired.

Each retiree was presented with a Stars and Stripes flag in a triangular display box as a memento of their service.

CHAPTER SIXTEEN

Libyan Lessons

A ripple of gunfire rattled out in the night air. The local feral youth belted their BMWs over the flyover outside the hotel and performed 'doughnuts' in the road. Other drivers honked their horns angrily. There were no police. There was no government. Welcome to Libya.

The hotel had been changed at the last minute. We were now faced with an 18 kilometre ride from the airport to the hotel which was on the Corniche in downtown Tripoli. The poor attempt at intelligence gathering before we arrived had indicated an embassy source as saying that there was only a "slight risk" of kidnap on the airport road. Well, that's OK, then.

Before going to Libya in July 2014, I had requested a risk analysis and suggested some security measures were put in place. The company did what was possible, which was next to nothing. The airline had no resources to offer us any security and the embassy simply referred us to the Foreign Office website, which merely said of Tripoli that only essential travel should be undertaken. The website made reference to several Swedish people having been killed a few months before and other bad news about keeping to daylight travel and avoiding crowds. The only thing that did get done that might have helped us in an emergency was that the embassy were supplied with our details, hotel and expected movements.

Not entirely satisfied, I joined the rest of the audit team and took the flight to Libya. The problem was that visas took a long time to fix and to back out at that late stage with little more than a hunch that things were not safe would have been pretty disruptive.

On arrival, I was surprised to see a British Airways Airbus A319 parked up, doors closed and steps removed. I learned later it had gone unserviceable and the entire crew had been flown out immediately to Istanbul.

Tripoli airport was a shambles. There was no visible security and an unattended police pick-up truck parked outside the terminal gave me no confidence. We piled into a small family-sized vehicle and were driven to the hotel. The car had smoked windows and no external markings. That much was good. At the hotel, we found a screening machine and an archway scanner in the foyer. We dutifully passed our bags through the machine. The operator gawped at us infidels and forgot to look at his laptop pictures of our bags. We walked through the archway which burst into a cacophony of warning sounds as it detected our mobile phones and loose change. There was no reaction to that, so we just kept going.

The office block opposite the hotel belonged to the Libyan Ministry of Customs and Finance. It was deserted. The streets were almost empty of people and the few persons to be seen were all men. There were cars parked up and left, covered in dust and seemingly abandoned.

The week that followed was uneasy. I learned that our hotel change was due to the first hotel we had been booked into now hosting all the local chiefs to sort out who was going to run which ministry as Libya struggled to form another government. That bothered me because that was unlikely to go peacefully as they were likely to vie with one another for the biggest slice of the cake.

To add to my nervousness, not long before we had arrived the serving Prime Minister had been kidnapped from a supposedly secure apartment block. I noticed life-size posters at road junctions of aspiring politicians who wanted a part of the government. The next morning the faces had been cut out of the posters.

The airline office was in downtown near the hotel and there we would meet with managers to conduct the audit. The heavily bearded security man at the front desk on the ground floor of the office was reading aloud from the Holy Koran and could not be bothered to acknowledge us. He had his feet up on the desk in front of him, which in the Arab world is taken as an insult. As soon as some of the managers I worked with had played their part in the proceedings, many of them vanished. My enquiry about where the senior managers were, whom I had expected to see, was answered by telling me that they were in Benghazi. I asked why they were there as I knew both the airport and airspace around Benghazi was closed. There was no clear answer.

Some flights were cancelled because the loads were too low and they also said that they could not get the crew to come in. By that time, I was making the daily journey to the airport. If they would not go there what was I doing?

I had an airport pass to go airside for my part of the audit which was a page torn from a notebook with a passport sized photograph of yours truly and some Arabic writing to go with it. The security at the entrance comprised a group of locals sitting having a chat some distance from the bag scanner. They were not interested in my airport pass and simply waved me through.

The airport had been going through an improvement programme and there were signs of the beginning of a new terminal building. The contractors had left the country because it was judged too unsafe to continue, so it had been abandoned. The same could be seen of partly finished tower blocks on the road from the hotel to the airport. Some of those apartment blocks had bullet spatters round the window openings which faced out onto the main road. It was eerily quiet.

While we were there, two military attaches from our embassy visited our hotel to eat. It was reported that they were armed when travelling around Libya. Some of the hotel staff were from the Philippines and told us if they went to the souk to buy some fresh food there were gunmen waiting outside to take the food and any money off them. This was clearly not a healthy place.

We completed the audit and managed to catch an earlier flight back home, glad to see the back of the place. A week after we returned two rival militias fought for control of the airport with rockets and small arms. According to websites about 80% of aircraft there were damaged or destroyed and the control tower was also hit. What did they gain when what they had fought over was destroyed?

Shortly afterwards the fuel installation by the airport was set on fire. The US Embassy staff left and they closed the embassy. The British Embassy tried the same but got shot up on the road to Tunisia. Luckily no-one was injured in the attempted car-jacking. The remaining UK embassy staff arranged an evacuation involving the Royal Navy before pulling out themselves. An attempt was made to set up a commercial ferry to leave from the port but that fell through.

Later on I had an invitation to go to Karachi for a short audit. Checking on the Foreign Office website gave me another rundown on how the baddies like to take hostages.

These days, I am trying to limit the long-range jobs, as I have developed emphysema and sitting in an aluminum tube with lots of other passengers for protracted periods of time usually results in me getting a chest infection. Age comes into it, but smoking like a chimney for 25 years has not helped.

CHAPTER SEVENTEEN

Dawn Over Kabul

The Boeing 737 flew steadily on at 29,000 feet towards Kabul. The sun had not yet risen and moonlight faintly illuminated the mountainous landscape below.

We slipped beneath a military aircraft holding 2,000 feet above us in a racetrack pattern. I could see his recognition lights were on and the aircraft's movement was repeated on our Terminal Collision Avoidance System indicator as a yellow diamond shape moving in relation each other's aircraft position. Below us, many thousands of feet below our assigned altitude, a host of white diamond shapes tracked like bees round a hive. They were also military, possibly helicopters or unmanned aerial vehicles being remotely piloted and flying in support of ground forces.

The two pilots in front of me made no special comment about this – they saw this military activity on a regular basis. Somewhere below, south-west of Kabul near Ghazni, bad people were getting a lot of unwanted attention.

When we were clear of the activity below us, the American controller came back on the radio and cleared us down to 16,000 feet to begin an instrument approach into Kabul Airport. The handling pilot selected the autopilot to descend to the assigned level. As we descended, the sun came up to meet us, casting deep shadows over the mountain valleys.

It all looked so breathtaking and peaceful, but peace was still not a friend of Afghanistan.

The flight observation that I conducted was part of an audit for an airline that operated into Kabul, though, because of the security situation, it based itself in Dubai.

I naturally had reservations about this assignment because of the debacle that had blighted the audit in Tripoli. Security was forefront in my mind, though I reasoned that the time spent on the ground in Kabul was only going to be about an hour. Also, the airline did have a good risk analysis process, which gave me some confidence in the fact that if they considered it safe to fly at that time, with the intelligence they had access to, then I would be OK.

The other reason that convinced me to go was that I am a medal collector. I have medals from participants of all the previous three Afghan wars the British fought – in 1842, 1878, and 1919. Being able to relate to the ground in which those wars were fought over would be a great experience.

Earlier at the crack of sparrows, I had met the crew at their pre-flight briefing and introduced myself. Most crew would not experience a flight check like this in their entire career, so I set out to assure them that I am only there to observe and not to interfere. On the way to Kabul, I would be on the jump seat behind the pilots and on the return, in the cabin observing the cabin crew procedures and checking the safety equipment.

The two pilots were relaxed and professional. Regarding the cabin crew, it looked like the airline had chosen its best lookers, but who was I to complain.

During the inbound flight, I checked the aircraft's manuals and papers and then monitored the flight until landing. After ATC had cleared us down to 16,000 feet, the pilots located the approach fix, stepped down to 14,000, then from 20 miles out flew the instrument approach to land at the airport which has an altitude of nearly 6,000 feet above sea level.

As we taxied in I noticed a blast wall constructed around most of the perimeter and what I assumed to be Afghan Army vehicles patrolling inside the perimeter. While we were on the ground, pairs of Black Hawk helicopters took off at intervals and disappeared into the mountains, possibly going back to do business around Ghaznee.

The airfield is roughly midway between the town and a mountain which rises to the north-east. On the lower slopes of that mountain had been the early landing strip used most famously by the RAF in 1929 when they evacuated all the foreign embassies staff using Vickers Victoria biplanes. Looking hard at the hillside I could just make out part of the perimeter wall of the old military area that the landing strip had been built inside.

Thanking the flight crew, I looked around the cabin and then took a seat as the passengers boarded. There were very few female passengers and the men were dressed mainly in the typical Pashtun Shalwar Kameez with the ubiquitous round Pakul hat. I wondered if any of them had ever fought for the Taliban on their days off? They all appeared to be what we have come to refer to as being of `fighting age`.

Cleared for take-off, we climbed out towards the north-west, all the while being vectored by ATC in a giant box until we had reached about 16,000 feet from which we then turned on course for Kandahar and onwards through Iranian airspace back to Dubai. As we climbed out over Kabul I could see the snow-capped Tora Bora Mountains to the north-east, these from where Osama Bin-Laden had given the US forces the slip to escape into Pakistan.

I had made sure that I was on the right side of the cabin so that I could see the route through the valleys taken by General Roberts, who, having assembled a field force in Kabul, relieved Kandahar which was under siege in 1880. I have the campaign medals awarded to a Gurkha Havildar (Sergeant) of the 2nd Goorkha Regiment who marched the 320 miles with Roberts and fought alongside the 92nd Highland Regiment.

As we flew south-west towards Kandahar, I could see the green expense of the Helmand River valley which has, in recent years, cost much in blood and sweat. In the distance, out in the desert, there was what I took to be Camp Bastion, the military base.

Crossing Kandahar, we continued on and made our landing back in Dubai. Thanking the crew for their hospitality, I went back to the hotel to catch up on some sleep.

In due course I discovered that the Taliban had taken control of the city of Ghaznee, where all the air activity had been, and at that time, the Afghan Army had pushed them back out. Since the Afghans had no air force to speak of, the airborne military activity we had seen was still being provided by coalition forces.

When I look back on a career which I never imagined having, it is with some incredulity that I realise I was lucky enough to have been in the right place, at the right time, on so many occasions.

What if I had been inducted into agriculture as Plan A had been? I think it would have been good for me, though undoubtedly I would not have seen so much of life and the world. My mechanical aptitude would probably have taken me into farm machinery maintenance and the streak of independence I found in later life might have had me running a business in self-employment. I will never know.

Plan B has worked out pretty well on the whole. The sixties were the air force, and the seventies aircraft engineering with a couple of redundancies along the way. By the eighties, I was moving along quite nicely, then came the flying obsession which continues to this day.

Into the nineties, I prepared for opportunities to fly commercially, then with a spade-full of luck, actually did it. By the noughties I was back on the ground as an instructor and auditor which took me happily into the twenty- tens. I never made a fortune, divorces saw to that and so did spending larges sums of cash on aeroplanes, but money never mattered that much as long as I had an aircraft to fly and a glass of Rioja to follow.

A total of 14,800 hours as a flight engineer, and nearly 7,000 hours as a pilot of one thing or another, have furnished me with a great career. There are times when travelling back in an airline cabin after an audit somewhere, I look out of the window, day or night, and if it is not too cloudy, I can recognise the area we are passing over. As I listen to the airflow and engine noise, I recall flying into that airport I can see off the wing for a patient, or the hassle I had on the ground trying to fix a hydraulic leak on the CL44. Good times.

All those experiences are difficult to sum up. If I said everything is possible for all men, that would be a lie. But, if you want something enough you will overcome a hell of a lot along the way to achieve it – and even if you do not get the prize at the end, the journey will still be life enhancing. My advice is, therefore, is go for it.

So, when does retirement come? I have tried to identify it as being when I can no longer make sense of anything, or cannot stand the idea of doing another year of it. To that I can add when I'm no longer fit enough.

Fortunately, I still enjoy working and it puts wine on the table. I have seen some people keep on going well past their sell by date, sometimes struggling to continue with a burdensome ego driving them on. Mindful of that, I try to self-examine my performance and listen keenly for any negative feedback.

I only hope I can recognise when it's time to quit. In the meantime, so far, so good, as the man said passing the 13th floor.

Appendix

TYPES SERVICED, OPERATED AND FLOWN

MILITARY TYPES SERVICED
Avro Shackleton   Blackburn Beverley
English Electric Lightning
Scottish Aviation Single Pioneer   Scottish Aviation Twin Pioneer

CIVIL TYPES SERVICED
Boeing 707   Bristol Britannia
Canadair CL44   Conroy CL44 Guppy
Douglas DC8   Lockheed Constellation
Vickers Vanguard

TYPES OPERATED AS A FLIGHT ENGINEER
Boeing 707   Canadair CL44
Conroy CL44 Guppy   Douglas DC10

TYPES FLOWN AS A COMMERCIAL PILOT
Beechcraft B90   Beechcraft B200

TYPES, TWIN ENGINE, FLOWN AS PRIVATE PILOT
Beechcraft 18   Beechcraft Be 55 Baron
Beechcraft Be 76 Duchess   Cessna 310-260
Piper PA 23 Apache   Piper PA 23 Aztec
Piper PA 30 Twin Comanche   Piper PA 34 Seneca
Piper PA 44 Seminole

TYPES, SINGLE ENGINE, FLOWN AS PRIVATE PILOT

Aeronca Chief	American Champion Decathlon 180
Antonov AN-2	Bellanca Viking 300
Beechcraft 23	Boeing Stearman
Cessna 120	Cessna 140
Cessna 150	Cessna 152
Cessna 162	Cessna 172
Cessna 177	Cessna 182
Cessna 210	Christen Eagle II
De Havilland Chipmunk	De Havilland Tiger Moth
Diamond Katana DV20	Fuji 200
Grumman AA5A	Jodel Mascaret D150
Maule MX7	Mooney M20

Mudry CP100

North American Aviation Harvard AT6

Percival Piston Provost P56

Piper J3 Cub	Piper PA15 Vagabond
Piper PA23 Arrow	Piper PA28 Warrior
Piper PA28 Archer	Piper PA32 Cherokee
Piper PA38 Tomahawk	Robin 100
Robin DR400	Rockwell Commander
Ryan Navion L17	Socata TB20 Trinidad
Socata Rallye ST100	Vultee BT13